הסטוריה
The ArtScroll History Series®

This gift is presented by the
KOL YAAKOV TORAH CENTER
as a token of
our affection and appreciation
on the occasion of our
Founders Dinner
•
GUEST OF HONOR
Rabbi Yaakov Kaminetsky shlita
HONOREES
Ed Croman
James Lavin
Tom & Shari Steinberg
Zvi Tress

These volumes have graciously been donated by a friend of Kol Yaakov Torah Center to enhance the meaningfulness of this occasion.

HEROINE

by
Joseph Friedenson / David Kranzler

Foreword by Dr. Julius Kuhl

OF RESCUE

The incredible story of Recha Sternbuch
who saved thousands
from the Holocaust

Published by

Mesorah Publications, ltd

FIRST EDITION
First Impression … February, 1984

Published and Distributed by
MESORAH PUBLICATIONS, Ltd.
Brooklyn, New York 11223

Distributed in Israel by
MESORAH MAFITZIM / J. GROSSMAN
Rechov Bayit Vegan 90/5
Jerusalem, Israel

Distributed in Europe by
J. LEHMANN HEBREW BOOKSELLERS
20 Cambridge Terrace
Gateshead
Tyne and Wear
England NE8 1RP

ARTSCROLL HISTORY SERIES®
HEROINE OF RESCUE
© Copyright 1984 by MESORAH PUBLICATIONS, Ltd.
1969 Coney Island Avenue / Brooklyn, N.Y. 11223 / (212) 339-1700

ALL RIGHTS RESERVED.
No part of this book may be reproduced
in any form without **written** permission from the copyright holder,
except by a reviewer who wishes to quote brief passages in connection with a review
written for inclusion in magazines or newspapers.

THE RIGHTS OF THE COPYRIGHT HOLDER WILL BE STRICTLY ENFORCED.

ISBN
0-89906-460-4 (hard cover)
0-89906-461-2 (paperback)

Typography by CompuScribe at ArtScroll Studios, Ltd.
1969 Coney Island Avenue / Brooklyn, N.Y. 11223 / (212) 339-1700
Printed in the United States of America

Table of Contents

Foreword vii

Author's Introduction xii

1 The Bar Mitzvah Rescue — One of a Thousand Incidents The Three Escapees / The Border was Heavily Guarded / Saving a Life: Greater than Shabbos 19

2 Roots of Heroism An Open House for Great and Humble / Chassidic Family in Switzerland / Model of Hospitality / "You Were in Your Own House" 23

3 First Struggles for Rescuing Jews — The Mayer-Sternbuch Confrontations The Vienna Connections / Caring for the Influx of Refugees / The Swiss Attitude / Sternbuch and Mayer: The Dramatic Difference 29

4 Imprisonment and Trial — The Ordeal of Recha Sternbuch "I Refuse to Inform on Third Parties" / Charges Dismissed 37

5 HIJEFS — The Sternbuch Rescue Organization Birth of HIJEFS / Expanded Activities / Not Just Shanghai / Food to Nazi-held Poland / The HIJEFS Network / Work without Salary, Labor without Respite / Postwar Activities / HIJEFS Attachés 44

6 Ambassador Lados and Nuncio Bernardini — Two "Righteous Among the Nations" Ambassador Alexander Lados / Legalizing the Rescue / Saving the Belzer Rebbe / ... and the King of Lodz / Vital Communication Link / Philippe Bernardini / The First Encounter: "You Don't Even Know Me!" / Modest Beginnings / From Criminal to Persona Grata / Rebuke in Rome / Postwar Assistance / Free the Children for Judaism 57

7 Shanghai — A Torah Outpost Saved With the Help of the Sternbuchs When the Borders Closed / Scholars in an Alien Land / Activating HIJEFS for Shanghai / Vaad Hatzalah: on Order from Vilna / Coded Messages through the Poles to Shanghai / More than Money Dealings / Dividends of the Partnership 77

8 Two Cables from Europe — Two Cries for Help and Their Difference Riegner and the Wise Response / Not a Moment's Hesitation / Reading the Differences / The Domb Source / "Uncle Gerush" at Work in Warsaw / No Rest for the Concerned / The U.S. Reaction / Isolating the "Hysterical" Orthodox / "What Will You Answer?" / November 24: The Twelve Week Silence is Broken / The Meeting vs. the Press Release / The Public Condemnation / A New Public Awareness and its Consequences 86

9 Latin American Passports — Another Avenue of Escape The Steel Trap / The Paraguayan Ploy / Dead End at Drancy / Knock on Every Door / Too Late for Too Many 100

10 Extraordinary Schemes — A Plea to Bomb Auschwitz and a Ransomed Train The Auschwitz Protocols / Change for the Worse in Hungary / Bringing the Message to the Allied Powers / Undiplomatic Desperation / Two Bridges from Life / The Kastner Train / Blood for Money, Money for Blood / Train of Uncertain Destination / Jew on Ice 106

11 The Kuhl-Sternbuch Mission — to France and Belgium Saving the Survivors / Dangers and Disappointments / The Positive Aspects: "They Know We're Here!" / Establishing Equality / Finding the Children / Polish Homecoming 116

12 Triumph and Disappointment in Rescue — The Musy Mission Eight Months of Frustration / Considering the Unthinkable / Himmler: Eager to Negotiate / Who Will Put Up the Ransom / Himmler's First Move / Good Press for the Nazis / Swiss Fears: Flooded with Jews? / Short-lived Optimism / The Insurmountable Obstacles / The Third Trip: Doomed from the Outset / Last Attempts at Saving Survivors / Negotiation under Fire 124

13 **Last Minute Rescue Efforts — Eisenhower's Warning and Red Cross Shipments** *Desperate Cable to New York / The Eisenhower Warning / Saving the Starving Inmates / Moving the Red Cross / Trucks of the Lifeline* — 139

14 **After the Liberation — Reviving the Survivors** *A Galaxy of Problems / Myriad Tasks, Few Shoulders / International Task Force* — 146

15 **Recha Sternbuch in D.P. Camps in Germany** *Unsatisfying Assurances / On-Site Visits — A Hazardous Task / Courage for the Despondent / Practical Accomplishments / Creating Channels for Help* — 153

16 **Recha Sternbuch and the Jewish Exodus from Poland** *Polish Hospitality: Hatred and Resentment / Exit Impossible / Avoiding the "Bricha" Route / "Returnees" to Poland from Russia / Headquarters in Lodz / The Orenstein Report / Escape from Reichenbach / The Zakopane Caper* — 160

17 **Help for the Transition Centers — Czechoslovakia, Austria and Italy** *"How Can We Help You?" / Short-lived Rehabilitation / The Prague Testimony / The Stetin Cross-over / Her Net Spread to Austria / Free ... and Stranded / Little Packages of Great Hope / Radical Increase in D.P. Population / Meeting D.P. Deficiencies / Stranded in Italy* — 174

18 **Roumania and Hungary — Rehabilitation and Emigration** *Roumanian Barriers / Aid Now, Ask Later / Breakthrough / Special Delivery Problems / Escape from Soviet Control / Increasing Needs, Diminishing Funds / Roumania Emigration / Recha Sternbuch "Not Wanted" / Hungarian Lapse* — 186

19 **Recha Sternbuch's Work in Western Europe — Saving the Jewish Children** *Preparing France as a Haven / The Initial Twenty in Aix-Les-Bains / Meeting at the Border / "They Are Not Your Children" / Breaking the Resistance / The Miracle of Aix-Les-Bains / More to Follow / More than Children / Concern Across the Border / Lasting Imprint* — 196

20 **Survived, But Not Spared: Switzerland, Belgium and Holland** *Switzerland: A Battleground for Souls / "Sternbuch Agitated, Moves Heaven and Earth" / The Belgian Struggles / The Precarious Dutch Terrain* — 207

21 **Sweden: Unravaged but on the Sternbuch Map** *Physical Haven, Spiritual Swampland / "Send Us All the Names" / "Help All the Children!" / Inspiration Stays in the Camps / Long Reaching Impact* — 212

22 **Recha Sternbuch and Her Individual Beneficiaries** *"Save the Bobover Rebbe" / "The Only Address We Knew" / "Where is Buna Blacher?" / The Polish Vigil / Messenger to the Missing* — 219

23 **"K'vod HaTorah" — Special Deference to Scholars** *R' Mordechai Pogramansky and the Sternbuchs / Smuggled to the West / Spiritual Guide in Aix-Les-Bains / Rabbi Dr. Yechiel Weinberg / "Send Papers, Avoid Repatriation to Russia" / Move to Montreux / Torah Leaders at the Sternbuch Home / Recha and Beth Jacob: a Member in Spirit / Personal Footnote* — 226

24 **The Sternbuchs and the Sekulener Rebbe — Partners in Postwar Rescue** *Father of Orphans / The Sternbuchs' Contact with the Rebbe / Battling Aliyat Hanoar / Salvaging a Mission / Contacts, But No Documents / Arrest and Appeal / With the "Family" in Antwerp* — 237

25 **A Holocaust Survivor Tells His Story — With Recha Sternbuch in Germany, Poland, Czechoslovakia, France, and Switzerland** *Landsberg: She Dispelled Our Despair / Lodz: She Brought Us Hope — and Visas / On the Way to Prague: A New Locomotive / Aix-Les-Bains Shmurah Matzos for Recha Sternbuch / Davos: Recuperation from Ailment* — 245

Epilogue: Recha Sternbuch — As I Knew Her
Charismatic ... and Silent / On a Quiet, Cold Winter Night ... / Once Again Recha Had Her Children / "Dear Recha, Please Forgive Me ..." — 250

Appendix — 257

Index — 312

✌️ Foreword

Some people never begin a task unless they are convinced that they can succeed in bringing it to completion. Such uncertainty is one of the most frequent excuses for inaction. This is probably one of the most tragic factors in the recent black chapter in Jewish history, the Holocaust.

Now that close to forty years have passed since that terrible destruction, a number of studies have been launched to assess blame for the meagre efforts expended in saving Jews. Aside from accusing the actual murderers and their eager allies, historians are uncovering a vast array of sins of omission that, in their own way, were almost as horrendous as the brutal crimes of commission.

Many arguments have been advanced by the Allied Powers in defense of their apathetic inactivity — mainly that the major thrust of their efforts had to be directed toward their first priority, winning the war. These pious arguments are now being destroyed by clear documentary evidence and photographs showing how easily bombers could have been diverted only a few miles from industrial plants in German-occupied territory (which the Allies bombed consistently) to demolish the death camps. More damning evidence is surfacing, which describes how Allied governments actually hampered efforts to save Jewish lives or simply turned their backs on many such opportunities.

Jewish guilt in this area is of an entirely different nature. In their helplessness, even those Jews who were aware of the annihilation of European Jewry did not believe that they could succeed more than minimally. This defeatism, however, which kept them from even trying, constitutes the greatest crime. By contrast, those who proved the Jewish establishment wrong, albeit in a limited degree, were few and far between. Because of this, I prefer the course of reporting rather than condemning, and to permit the facts to speak for themselves. These pages will deal with the activities of a single valorous woman, Recha Sternbuch, who could not stand by idly, and therefore succeeded with the help of her husband, Yitzchok Sternbuch, in accomplishing far more than huge organizations. I refer not only to the number of people whom she helped, which was very considerable, but also to her self-sacrifice and the neglect of her family life — to which I was a witness — for the sake of the *Klal*. But to her that was a negligible concern when taken in the context of the tremendous losses our people were suffering.

In my last meeting with Recha Sternbuch in Bnei Brak, shortly before she passed away in 1971, she complained movingly to me that she had done so little during the period of the Holocaust, while there was so much to be achieved (despite all her efforts she belittled her activity). Unlike others, she lived by the credo set forth in *Pirkei Avos:* It is not for you to finish the task, but you must have the courage and sense of duty to begin it. It is to our eternal shame that Recha Sternbuch was alone.

I owe it to her — and I made that promise to myself when I saw her last — to bring her story to the attention of historians who could document it and make it public knowledge. This book is not merely an impressive and important historical record that has been ignored up to now. Recha Sternbuch's story is an inspiration and a challenge. It is one of those few brave chapters in history that shows how much can be accomplished by a lone human being who cares — and dares. I am deeply grateful, therefore, to the writers and editors who did justice to this task, and to Mesorah Publications for providing this rich wine with the fine cask it deserves. May the horror that catapulted her into action never be repeated, but if it is, ח״ו, may Recha Sternbuch's story be a model for others.

Julius Kuhl

I Adar 5744 / February 1984

~§ A Note About Switzerland

One cannot generalize about the people of any particular nation, for no nation is composed exclusively of good or bad people. At times, some men and women rise to the challenge and transcend difficult circumstances, becoming exemplary in their actions, while others fall to the depths of depravity. It is in times of test and crisis that a person's true qualities are to be judged. Swiss men and women were no exception. Many rose to the occasion during the darkest days of the Holocaust to come to the aid of Jews in a most humane manner. I, personally, was the beneficiary of the generosity of certain Swiss people when I received a scholarship as a foreign student in order to attend the University of Bern. I cite this one act as indicative of the capacity for good that this nation possesses.

J.K.

∽§ Mah Enosh?: What Is Man?

In the Bible, the question "Mah enosh," meaning what is man, appears twice — in Psalms 8:5 and in Job 7:17. Secular philosophers like Kant dealt with the quality of what is a *Mensch*, and even Mark Twain wrote a book called "What is a Man?"

The question deserves to be reviewed seriously — not as overblown rhetoric — but as a challenge meant to be answered by each of us. Each of us is called, but few respond. At the dawn of man, Adam was called and so was Cain; their replies defined the future of the history of man: one was evasive and then blamed someone else, while the other "was not his brother's keeper." It was not until God called to Abraham that a mortal responded with "*Hineni!*" — I am here, always at Your disposal. Moses, too, when summoned by God to redeem His people from slavery, answered: "*Hineni!*"

These are paradigms or models for man, that appear throughout history, in literature as well as life. While it seems that those who respond to the call are more often found in literature than in history, we have examples of those who, even if only for a brief period of time, changed the course of human events and altered the definition of Man by echoing the patriarchs' *Hineni*.

Though they may have been active and effective only for a relatively short while, they became reference points for all generations and for people all over. Because they demonstrated what man is capable of becoming, it is incumbent on those who know of their deeds to make their contributions public; otherwise we give credence by default to those who proclaim hopelessness as the norm and deem everyone to have been silent and paralyzed by lack of choice.

Much has been written about the period of the Holocaust — even by me — explaining why, because of their meagre power and limited resources, Jews could not exert themselves sufficiently to save their brethren from destruction. I have stated in the past, that 1943 was not 1983, when we have six million Jews living in America, where there are 30 Jewish members of the House of Representatives and nine Jewish senators, so parallels between the two are superficial and false. Similarly, all those who seek reasons not to respond to whatever call, who fumble for an excuse for inaction no matter what the crisis, who plead political impotence, these people will always find ample justification for their failure. They do not need my assistance.

It is the one who *does* choose to act that interests me. This is a book about such a rare individual. Ever since I came into my wife's family, I have heard about Recha Sternbuch as the paradigm of *Hineni*. Her selfless and effective work in the face of impossible odds to save thousands during the Holocaust must be told. I congratulate my father-in-law, Dr. Julius Kuhl, for making it his responsibility to inform the world that there were people worthy of the name "Enosh," who derived from their sincere religious belief a sense of duty and sacrifice, and were ready to undertake what others thought was impossible — or did not think of at all. We are all as enriched by her life as we were impoverished by that period.

Israel Singer

✑ Authors' Introduction

While thinkers, historians, and commissions grapple with the searing question of why so little notice was taken and even less done to save the Six Million, we have chosen to focus on one woman who, with her husband, risked position, freedom, and even her life to save her brethren. In those tragic years, she raised herself above her generation by trying to save Jews. This is the story of Recha Sternbuch, a heroic Jewish wife and mother who single-handedly and single-mindedly developed and carried out many rescue projects that actually succeeded in saving the physical lives of thousands and later rescued, directly and indirectly, the spiritual lives of untold thousands more.

Recha Sternbuch is remembered with awe and admiration by thousands who knew her and owe their lives to her — but she is still unknown to the millions who should be carrying her name to eternity as a badge of honor for her people and the human race. All that she accomplished — first alone and then with the help of others — sounds fantastic and stretches the human imagination. Nonetheless, this story is true, based on thorough research, and corroborated by thousands of documents, and the personal testimony of many witnesses still alive.

All over the world there are Jews who eagerly testify that they owe their lives to the self-sacrificing efforts of Recha Sternbuch. And there are tens of thousands of Jews who willingly admit that their spiritual rehabilitation after the traumatic war years, was due only to the remarkable efforts of the Sternbuchs. Quietly working alone from 1938-1942, Recha Sternbuch helped several thousand German and Austrian Jews enter Switzerland illegally, after spending dangerous days and nights at the Austrian and French-Swiss borders. Although a handful of Swiss humanitarians helped, she had to work against the mainstream of Swiss officialdom and public opinion. And she had to fight the opposition of the Jewish leaders who feared that an enormous financial burden and heightened anti-Semitism would come in the wake of a flood of refugees. Even a jail term did not deter this singleminded heroine.

In 1942, her rescue activities broadened. Among other things, she helped provide aid to Polish Yeshiva students stranded in Shanghai, sent food packages to Jews in Nazi-occupied lands, and provided Jews with the protection of Latin American papers. With the help of a key collaborator Dr. Julius Kuhl, who held an important position at the Polish Embassy in Switzerland, she enlisted the Polish Ambassador and the Papal Nuncio, to assist in both positive rescue schemes and in preventing the deportation of Jewish refugees.

With their help she alarmed the world with the first news of deportation and mass murder in Poland, and later transmitted the unheeded cry to bomb Auschwitz. Among her greatest yet least known accomplishments was her negotiation with Himmler, via a former Swiss president, to free surviving Jews from concentration and death camps.

The world owes a debt to Dr. Julius Kuhl for not allowing Recha Sternbuch's courage and dedication to be forgotten. Painfully aware that mankind produces few Recha Sternbuchs, he took upon himself the task of enlisting people to research, write, and publish her story. And he insisted that it be done with fidelity to her absolute and uncompromising insistence on the truth. That any human being's unembroidered life story can be so inspiring is a lesson for every time, and Dr. Kuhl has earned history's gratitude for bringing it to society's attention.

This book is based on painstaking research among the many thousands of documents in the Sternbuch papers; the papers of Dr. Julius Kuhl, Rabbi Abraham Kalmanowitz, Vaad Hatzalah, Michael G. Tress, the Agudath Israel Archives and the vast collection of the National Archives. In addition about sixty taped interviews were conducted with close collaborators and people rescued by the Sternbuchs. Much of the documentation unearthed in the course of researching this book will appear in scholarly journals and other volumes.

We are grateful to many, many people who assisted immeasurably in the research and interpretation upon which this work is based. A full list may be found at the end of this book. We would be remiss, however, if we failed to acknowledge the work of those who edited and refined the manuscript and integrated much of the massive documentation: ABBY MENDELSON of Pittsburgh lent his considerable literary talents to the task of writing and streamlining the manuscript. MARK FRIEDMAN and RABBI NISSON WOLPIN of New York provided valuable editing and RABBI A. CH. FEUER of Miami Beach offered a host of important suggestions. SHEAH BRANDER, the graphics genius of Mesorah Publications, has demonstrated his skills in scores of books. To all previous encomiums, we say amen.

This book could not have been written if Recha Sternbuch had been alive. She would not have permitted it. Imbued with traditional Jewish modesty, she would have recoiled at the very thought that her activities were extraordinary, or that her achievements were exceptional and praiseworthy. As long as she lived, she would not tolerate any publicity or praise. In all the years of her manifold activities in the service of Jewish people, only once, when she had to raise funds for rescue, did she allow her name to be published — and even then, simply as the "secretary" of HIJEFS, the organization she founded and led. At no time did she permit anyone to write about her work and achievements.

But now that she is no longer with us, there are many who feel deeply that she and her work should not be forgotten, who want her unique role in our history to be known and cherished. In the spirit of this obligation, we assembled the story of her hallowed life — a life dedicated to G-d, Torah and *Klal Yisroel* — to be eternally perpetuated, to correct the record of alleged inactivity, and to set an example to be emulated.

Joseph Friedenson / David Kranzler

I Adar 5744 / February 1984

About the Authors

JOSEPH FRIEDENSON has edited *Dos Yiddishe Vort*, the world's leading Orthodox Yiddish magazine since 1953. Born in pre-War Lodz, Poland, he received his grounding in community involvement and journalistic research from his father, Eliezer Gershon Friedenson, who was a leader of both Agudath Israel and the Beth Jacob educational network, and was editor of the prestigious Beth Jacob magazine. Ordained at the famed Lublin Yeshivah and a survivor of Auschwitz-Birkenau and five other camps, Friedenson became a major expert and chronicler of the history of Agudath Israel and Polish Jewry, most prominently in various Hebrew and Yiddish magazines and as a major contributor to the *Eileh Ezkerah*, an eight-volume biographical encyclopedia of rabbinic victims of the Holocaust.

DR. DAVID KRANZLER, a professor at the City University of New York, is a well-known historian with a specialty in modern Jewish history and the Holocaust. He is the author of *Japanese, Nazis and Jews: The Jewish Refugee Community of Shanghai 1938-1945*, the definitive study of an unusual chapter in East Asian and Holocaust history; *My Jewish Roots, A Guide to Jewish Genealogy and Family History; Solomon Schonfeld: An Extraordinary Orthodox Rescue Hero of the Holocaust;* and the forthcoming *Thy Brother's Blood: Orthodox Jewish Rescue Personality Portraits*. He is also a contributor to the Goldberg Commission Report on the Holocaust and American Jewry, as the author of chapters on the role of the Orthodox and the Jewish Labor Committee.

HEROINE OF RESCUE

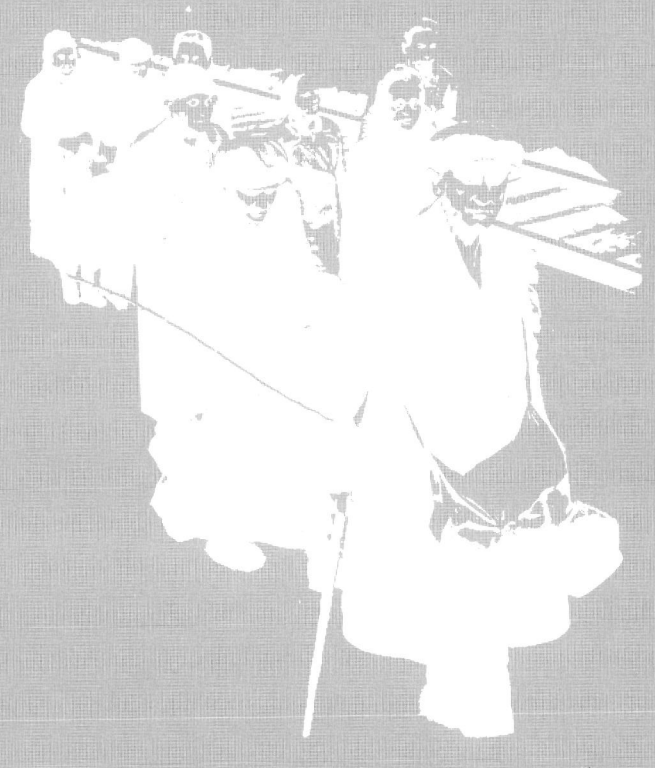

CHAPTER ONE
The Bar Mitzvah Rescue
— One of a Thousand Incidents

DURING THE DARK DAYS of 1942, when, day after day, thousands of European Jews were being consumed by the flames of Hitler's crematoria, there were some young Jewish men and women, still flushed with optimism and hope, who tried to escape death. Very few succeeded, but try they did.

The Three Escapees

Among those who struggled with the Angel of Death were three young men who had been together from childhood. They had a fourth companion who seldom left them: terror.

In 1938, the Nazi *Anschluss* (i.e., annexation) of Austria forced them to flee their native Vienna for the "safety" of Belgium. But a mere two years later, when the Germans marched into Western Europe, the men were captured — by the British — who imprisoned them in an internment camp as "enemy aliens," even though they were Jews. Shortly thereafter, Belgium fell to the Nazis. The three young men escaped to the southeastern French city of Lyons. Soon France too, fell, and Lyons — although not occupied by the Nazis — came under the control of the collaborationist Vichy French government. Near desperation, the young men sought refuge in the only safe haven in Nazi-dominated Europe: Switzerland.

The Border was Heavily Guarded

THE FRANCO-SWISS BORDER was heavily guarded on both sides. Crossing it was fraught with great danger for anyone — especially for Jews trying to escape Nazi-controlled territories by entering Switzerland illegally. Nevertheless, crammed into a small box in the back of their landlord's truck, the three refugees struck out for freedom under the cover of an iron shipment. Although the truck was stopped a number of times, it was not searched, and the three arrived safely at the Franco-Swiss border. Their travails, however, were not over. They emerged from their hiding place and began the next step of their escape: finding a way to get into Switzerland. It was difficult to find reliable guides to take them across the treacherous, frozen border. It took many hours under the most brutal conditions, but they finally succeeded in eluding both the Nazi-French and Swiss border guards, and they arrived in Switzerland.

Still too close to the border to feel secure, the men pushed further, walking all day and night Thursday. By nightfall they were exhausted and sought refuge — but where? When they finally spotted a house with lights burning, they weighed the risk and took it. Again, they were lucky: the owner was a sympathetic Swiss city policeman. "You came to the right house," he told the grateful men. "I will not say anything."

The next morning, the policeman helped them elude the guards patrolling a nearby bridge. The men boarded a train for Montreux, home of the Etz Chaim yeshivah, perhaps the last remaining Talmudic academy on the European Continent. The men arrived in Montreux on Shabbos morning, hoping that this would be their final destination. They thought they were only minutes from safety, but it was not to be.

Despite the popular myth that Switzerland was a neutral democracy offering safety to refugees from the Nazis, this was not the case where Jews were concerned. The Swiss did not consider Jews to be "political" refugees from Nazi persecution so they closed the borders to them, even though this meant certain death. With very few exceptions, the Swiss border police turned back Jewish refugees. Consequently, these three Jews, although deep in Swiss territory, were not yet safe.

Why did the three young men choose Montreux? For two reasons. During World War II, Montreux was famous for its Etz

Chaim yeshivah — which made it an attractive haven to the three former yeshiva students. Also, it was the home of Yitzchok Sternbuch and his wife, Recha, two tireless rescuers of European Jews. So renowned were the Sternbuchs for their rescue efforts, that their telephone number was written in railroad stations for refugees to use — at anytime.

The morning that the three men arrived in Montreux was a special one for the Sternbuch family — the Bar Mitzvah of their only son Avrohom. Among the highlights of the Shabbos agenda was a dinner in the Torah atmosphere, to which Recha Sternbuch was accustomed, for she was the daughter of the famed Rabbi Mordechai Rottenberg, of Antwerp. The Sternbuchs were anticipating a memorable Shabbos. However, like the three disheveled refugees approaching the city, they had no idea of what was in store for them.

As the dean of the yeshivah, Rabbi Eliyahu Botchko, Recha Sternbuch's brother-in-law, began the Shabbos prayers at Etz Chaim, the three strangers hailed a cab to take them to the yeshivah. Although such travel is forbidden on Shabbos, the fugitives correctly reasoned that their lives were in danger until they found a safe haven. Again, everything seemed to be going their way — but unknown to them, the cab-driver went directly from the yeshivah to the police to inform on his passengers. Within minutes, Swiss police swept down on the yeshivah without warning. They arrested the young men and spirited them away.

IT WAS SHABBOS, when all work is strictly prohibited; it was their son's Bar Mitzvah day; but the Torah puts the highest priority on **Saving a Life: Greater than Shabbos** saving a life, so the Sternbuchs immediately went into action. Yitzchok Sternbuch went to police headquarters while his wife began making telephone calls, frantically seeking to protect the three strangers from deportation to France.

At first, both Sternbuchs experienced little but frustration. The police played a cruel game, giving conflicting destination points for the detainees. Police officials told Yitzchok that the three had been taken to Lausanne, so he contacted friends in Lausanne to try to rescue the young men. In truth, the men had been taken to a military base in Martiny, on the border. When it became obvious that the officials were lying, Recha Sternbuch sought the telephone number of the police chief who might reveal their true whereabouts. She called an observant Jew, ringing for twenty minutes. When he finally answered the phone, she convinced him to find the number she needed so desperately. She called the chief and begged him not to send the refugees back into occupied France. She promised the chief that she would find a way to legalize their stay in Switzerland.

Her "way" came in the person of their family friend and associate in rescue work, Dr. Julius Kuhl, an Orthodox Jew in Bern who was the Assistant for Jewish Affairs to the Polish Ambassador Alexander Lados. As the Sternbuchs had done before him, Dr. Kuhl moved without hesitation. He called the police authorities and told them to set the young men free — they would be guaranteed Polish protection. Not wishing to let the matter rest without a backup, Dr. Kuhl also called Papal Nuncio Monsignor Philippe Bernardini: if Ambassador Lados objected to the way they had dealt with the Swiss police, Dr. Kuhl reasoned, Nuncio Bernardini could intercede on behalf of the Jewish prisoners. Then he called back Recha Sternbuch: they had been successful. The young men were set free.

When Recha Sternbuch and her husband were finished with their rescue mission, the Bar Mitzvah of their son was over. But they had no qualms about having missed the event. For the Sternbuchs, the great event of the day was the fact that they were able to have saved the three endangered Jewish souls. This was so poignantly expressed by their nephew, Dr. Shaul Weingort, when he told the Bar Mitzvah boy Avrohom, "You have received the most precious Bar Mitzvah gift a Jewish boy could get in these days — the lives of three Jews!"

A remarkable story? Certainly! Yet for Recha Sternbuch it was just one of thousands of instances in which she put the needs of her fellow Jews above her own needs and those of her family. In fact, she did much more. In the dark years of the Nazi era, and in the years thereafter, there were many times that she exposed herself to countless dangers, and even put her life in jeopardy. Quite often Recha Sternbuch risked imprisonment for her activities. None of these risks frightened her because she was undaunted in her resolve to save other unknown Jews from the countless dangers that threatened them.

CHAPTER TWO
Roots of Heroism

TO UNDERSTAND the astounding work of Recha Sternbuch and her husband Yitzchok during the Holocaust years and immediately afterward, it is important to delve into their family background. Their *Ahavas Yisrael* and *Ahavas Chesed* — their selflessness and perseverance in helping fellow Jews — were part of a family tradition, which was tenaciously devoted to the perpetuation of traditional Judaism, and to serve the wide range of needs of the local Jewish community, as well as *Klal Yisrael* as a whole.

Recha was born in 1905, the fifth of Rabbi Mordechai Rottenberg's nine children. Originally from Cracow, Galicia, the Rottenbergs had settled in Antwerp, Belgium, when the father assumed the position of Chief Rabbi of the Orthodox community — a post he held until taken by the Nazis to the Vittel internment camp. (Ironically, near the end of the war, his daughter managed to negotiate his release. Rabbi Rottenberg, however, refused to be freed without all the other Vittel inmates. However, his wish was not fulfilled, and he and his wife died in Auschwitz.)

A member of its *Moetzes Gedolei Hatorah* (the Council of Torah Sages) Rabbi Rottenberg achieved world renown as a leader of Agudath Israel, the international Orthodox Jewish movement founded in Katowice, Poland in 1912, by such great Torah authorities as Rabbi Chaim Soloveitchik of Brisk; Rabbi Israel

Rabbi Mordechai and Mrs. Dvora Rottenberg, parents of Recha Sternbuch

Meir Kagan of Radin (better known as the Chofetz Chaim); the great Chassidic leaders Rabbi Avrohom Mordechai Alter of Ger and Rabbi Israel Friedman of Chortkow; Rabbi Chaim Ozer Grodzensky of Vilna; Rabbi Shlomo Breuer of Frankfurt and others. A man of great Torah erudition and *tzidkus* (piety), Rabbi Rottenberg accepted a call to Antwerp to save the Orthodox Jewish community from the infiltration of subtle reforms that had already started to make some inroads. With unswerving dedication, he performed this task superbly. In the heart of Western Europe he succeeded in maintaining an Orthodox Jewish community of the highest standards. No wonder he instilled in his children a deep love for all aspects of Torah life: learning, joy of *kiyum hamitzvos* (*mitzvah* performance), *chesed* (loving-kindness) and especially *hachnosas orchim* (hospitality). All his sons learned in the great Yeshivos of Telshe, Mir and Brisk and developed into recognized Torah scholars. Of his three surviving sons, one, Rabbi Chaim Yaakov Rottenberg, the Rabbi of the Kehilas Hachareidim in Paris, is a well-known rabbinic authority in Europe. The other two, Dr. Menachem Rottenberg, a retired physician now in Jerusalem, and Mr. Josef Rottenberg, an industrialist in Antwerp, are also well-known for their Talmudic scholarship and piety.

THE ROTTENBERG HOME was an open house with an endless stream of guests, both famous and humble, who came in search of sage advice or simply a warm meal.

An Open House for Great and Humble

As for Recha Sternbuch, Antwerp had no suitable girls' school for higher Jewish education at that time. As an extremely bright girl with an avid interest in learning Torah, however, she attained sufficient knowledge and practice at home to enable her to lead a *Bnos* girls' group of Agudath Israel. In fact, she became so conversant in Torah matters that she had regular scholarly exchanges with rabbis and scholars.

While her primary emphasis was on the spiritual and intellectual levels, with little interest in the mundane or luxurious, Recha Sternbuch did have an esthetic appreciation for fine table linens and silverware — though she never hesitated to give them away to the needy. Occasionally, especially after the war, when the pressures of saving Jews subsided somewhat, Recha Sternbuch would even indulge in the occasional purchase of an exquisite antique.

She rarely wore jewelry and never any cosmetics; she dressed simply but well, whether appearing before government officials or at home. Adhering to the traditional Jewish practice of a married woman keeping her hair covered at all times, she managed to make her ubiquitous turban part of a stylish outfit, which never raised an eyebrow amongst the highest diplomatic or government circles. Indeed, she never failed to inspire respect, even when appearing before avowed anti-Semites. Recha Sternbuch was always conscious that she spoke not merely as a Jewess but as an Orthodox one, to people both sympathetic and antagonistic.

THE SAME YEAR that Recha Rottenberg was born, Yitzchok Sternbuch's Russian Chassidic father, Naftali, relocated from Roumania with his wife and seven children in Switzerland. Most of the

Chassidic Family in Switzerland

small Swiss Jewish community — even with refugees it had swelled to a mere 19,000 by 1939 — traced its roots to Germany and mirrored the cool, reserved, hard-working, frugal, rational, and punctilious character of the original homeland. They were in many ways the very antithesis of the East European Jews — pejoratively referred to as *Ostjuden* — whose attitudes, dress, religious customs, cultural traits and more emotional nature made them stand out among the Swiss in general and the Swiss Jews in particular. The arrival of Chassidic families like the Sternbuchs made the host community uneasy, to say the least. Naftali Sternbuch, a scion of devoted Chortkower Chassidim in Czernowitz, Bukovina, did not allow himself to be culturally engulfed by the new surroundings. Tenaciously he carried on, even in Switzerland, his Eastern-European lifestyle and tried to bring up his children, whom he sent to study in Eastern European yeshivos, in his spirit. Indeed, he founded the first Swiss Chassidic *shtiebel* (prayer house) in Basel. At the outset, he was met with suspicion and animosity, but he soon succeeded in winning the hearts of many of his Orthodox neighbors. His Chassidic warmth, his devotion and commitment to community affairs, his extreme honesty as well as his many other personal values were impressive. Eventually, Naftali Sternbuch and his family succeeded in exerting a positive influence on the entire Swiss Orthodox Jewish community.

AS WAS THE CASE with the Rottenbergs in Belgium, the Sternbuch house in Basel and later in St. Gallen — in contrast to the majority of Swiss Jewish homes — was constantly graced with guests and distinguished visitors. Among the famous scholars to benefit from the Sternbuch hospitality were the renowned Polish-Lithuanian Gaon, Rabbi Chaim Ozer Grodzensky of Vilna and the Chief Rabbi of Palestine, Rabbi Abraham Isaac Kook. The latter came to Switzerland for a two-day visit in 1914 and, when the War broke out, stayed on as a guest of the Sternbuchs for two years. They provided him with an apartment and took care of all his material needs. Rabbi Grodzensky, while in St. Gallen, participated in the dedication of the first *mikvah* (ritual bath) in that tiny Jewish community.

Model of Hospitality

But not only the great and famous enjoyed the hospitality of the house of Naftali Sternbuch and his wife. Their home became a model of hospitality. Many poor travelers from Eastern Europe, refugees from Soviet Russia and other lands of oppression and poverty, always found a welcome haven in the Sternbuch house.

Their backgrounds melding as well as their personalities, Recha Rottenberg married Yitzchok Sternbuch. The home they set

Naftali and Devorah Sternbuch, parents of Yitzchok Sternbuch

up — first in St. Gallen and later in Montreux — was permeated with the spirit of the homes they were brought up in. Young Recha Sternbuch quickly became known for her kindness and consideration. For example, in those years many older houses did not have running hot water — but were heated with gas, which was rationed. Regardless of her personal laundry needs, Recha Sternbuch always made certain that water was available for her older or poorer neighbors so that they would never have to ask for any ... If a new mother needed help with her baby — a "hospital" was nearby — Recha's home was always open ... and busy with all sorts of charitable activities.

It was especially after 1938, when Jewish refugees from Germany and Austria began to pour over the border, and countless strangers found food and lodging with them, that the young Sternbuchs' commitment to *Ahavas Yisrael*, love for fellow Jews, became the stuff of legend. It was *hachnosas orchim* on a grand scale. People came and went all day, it seemed; the tables were constantly set. The house was so crowded, in fact, that it was not uncommon for refugees to believe at first that the Sternbuch home simply *had to* be a small hotel — for no family home could be that

Chapter 2: ROOTS OF HEROISM / 27

open, crowded or busy. The Sternbuchs worked tirelessly to find a home for their transients, but success was not always possible. When no other solution could be found, the Sternbuchs simply made them part of their household.

MR. ZECHARIA REINHOLD, who entered Switzerland illegally, recalls the Sternbuch house in those days. He described what he saw:

"You Were in Your Own House"

> When I came in, there were tables surrounded with people as if at a *simcha* [festive occasion] where they ate and drank ... [It was] an open house ... people coming and going all day ... The floors of the house were covered with mattresses for the people ... There were all kinds, not all *frum* [Orthodox] ... she helped everyone ... a *Yid* [Jew] is a *Yid*.

Mr. Reinhold related further how the minority of Orthodox refugees attempted to set up a small room as a temporary synagogue, but were thwarted by the non-religious, who no doubt were afraid of arousing the gentiles with their prayers and "strange" *taleisim* [prayer shawls]. Mrs. Sternbuch entered the dispute and settled it, with the establishment of a daily *minyan* [prayer quorum]. "One *Yom Kippur*," Mr. Reinhold recalled, "we each *davened* [prayed] clad in a *kittel* [a white robe] and the amazed *goyim* [gentiles] stood by the door — they had never seen it."

Despite the fears of the non-Orthodox, the gentiles did not create any disturbance. To the contrary, when the festival of *Sukkos* came, they helped climb the trees to cut down the *s'chach* [branches to cover the *succah*].

> Whenever I needed anything, I went there [to the Sternbuchs]. When you came in, you were in your own home ... She gave us new clothing ... anything we needed. New clothing, not old things ... with dignity and respect. We didn't have to beg for anything. When our second child was born, the *bris* (circumcision) was in her house.

But all these activities were only the beginning.

CHAPTER THREE
First Struggles for Rescuing Jews — The Mayer-Sternbuch Confrontations

FOR RECHA STERNBUCH, her personal open-door policy was not enough, even though that was far in excess of what the vast majority of her fellow Jews did for the Jews in distress. Equipped with extraordinary energy, vast intelligence and *Ahavas Yisrael*, she felt that she had to do much more than merely let people wander up to her door. Instead, Recha Sternbuch was determined to actively pursue the problem. The helpless Jews of Germany and Austria were forced to leave these countries, but had nowhere to go. It was her mission to seek them out and to help them. She was driven by dedication to the Torah ideal (absorbed in her father's house) that *pikuach nefesh*, the saving of a life, overrides almost all the other dicta, and that rescuing Jews was the highest priority at all times.

Recha Sternbuch's rescue work began shortly after Hitler's annexation of Austria in March 1938. In Germany, the Nazis required five years (1933-1938) to accomplish the complete political, economical and physical strangulation of the Jewish population. Now, their techniques honed and perfected, they succeeded in devastating Austria Jewry almost in one fell swoop. The first blow was the overnight expulsion of all Jews from the well-known *sheva kehillos*, the seven communities of the Burgenland province. While these Jews were temporarily cared for by the Viennese Jewish community, particularly by the Orthodox Schiff-Schul under the guidance of Mr. Julius Steinfeld, many tried to cross into Switzerland, which at that time had open borders with Germany. At the border the refugees ran into problems when they encountered the Swiss policy of *refoulement* [literally, "repelling"], which resulted in the return of all non-political refugees to Nazi hands.

The Vienna Connections

RECHA STERNBUCH HAD a contact in Vienna who reached individuals and gave them instructions on which routes to take. She had arranged for a series of associates — sympathetic individuals, farmers, truckers, taxi drivers and policemen — who would bring the refugees across certain designated places along the border into St. Gallen. The refugees were hidden in fully camouflaged vehicles. They were usually brought to her house where they were given a chance to relax in a friendly atmosphere, a change of clothing, and an opportunity to seek further help. Once in St. Gallen, the problem was one of legalization, which was often solved with the help of the local Police Chief, Paul Gruninger.

As conditions worsened in Germany, further efforts were made in Switzerland to repel the ever-growing number of Jewish refugees. The Swiss, and more specifically Dr. Heinrich Rothmund, chief of the *Fremdenpolizei*, the Alien Police, began to urge the German government to mark Jewish passports with a large, red "J" to make the Jew easily identifiable to the Swiss border officials. It was not easy to convince the Germans to add the humiliating badge of a "J" on the Jews' passports. First of all, they were interested at that time in making Germany *Judenrein*, free of Jews. In addition, the Germans feared retaliation. They feared that other countries might place special markings on the passports of its own German citizens. Moreover, Germany demanded reciprocity, whereby Switzerland would mark the passports of its Jews in Germany, a situation the image-conscious Swiss would not tolerate. In September, Rothmund went to Berlin to try to devise a "safe" method of locking out the "unassimilable Jews". At that time 2,300 destitute Austrian Jews had already entered Switzerland. These Swiss-initiated negotiations, concluded in

October, 1938, resulted in the fateful inclusion of a red "J" on the passports of all German and Austrian Jews, branding them as outlaws in the eyes of the world. In keeping with Rothmund's fear of publicity, no word of these Berlin negotiations was either reported by the press nor uttered at any public meeting.

Recha Sternbuch frequently took along false Swiss visas with her to Austria or Germany, to provide Jews with an opportunity to enter Switzerland. Once she took as many as sixteen visas, whose bearers all succeeded in crossing the border. In time she also rescued dozens of Jews from Dachau with such visas. At that time, the Germans were eager for their country to be rid of the Jews, and they even released Dachau inmates with end-visas [i.e., visas which indicated final destinations.]

The majority of the Jewish refugees that Recha Sternbuch rescued merely used Switzerland as a transit station on their way to other countries. Four hundred were provided with Chinese visas, with which they traveled through Italy to Palestine via the illegal *Aliyah Bet.* Others were provided with visas to various other countries which she obtained from consulates in France and Italy. Recha spent several months in Italy during 1938-39 in search of such visas.

Caring for the Influx of Refugees

THIS SUDDEN INCREASE of Jewish refugees in Switzerland posed an immediate problem of feeding and housing on the *Schweizerischer Israelitischer Gemeindebund* (Federation of Swiss Jewish communities), known by its initials SIG. At that time the SIG was headed by Mr. Saly Mayer, a retired lace manufacturer. Beyond the immediate problem of support, there arose a deeper long-range dilemma for the Swiss Jews (especially its leadership) the solution of which was to have serious repercussions for the rescue of Jews during the Holocaust (even when the full dimensions of Hitler's mass murders were fully revealed). In essence, the problem was one of determining what was ultimately good for the Swiss Jewish community, and what was to become its order of priorities.

Early in its history the Swiss Jewish community, about 19,000 in a population of four million, had endured a prolonged period of anti-Semitism and expulsions the effects of which were not fully erased even after full equality was granted in the latter part of the nineteenth century. Democratic Switzerland, despite its tradition of asylum for the persecuted and a pluralist trilingual society, remained essentially insulated and xenophobic. The Swiss despised foreigners or "aliens" in general and East Europeans in particular. Jews, as foreigners *par excellence*, were considered the worst aliens of all, nor were they accorded the dignified status of political prisoners.

The Swiss Attitude

IN ADDITION TO THIS hostile climate, the existing geopolitical "facts" go far to explain the Swiss policy toward refugees as well as the Jewish reflection of that policy. At the same time these "facts" highlight the conflict between Mrs. Sternbuch and her Jewish opposition. As a small, landlocked, mountainous country with little in the way of agriculture or food production of its own, Switzerland was almost entirely surrounded by Nazi Germany, Austria and Fascist Italy, and after 1942, by Nazi-occupied France as well. Naturally, its highly vaunted precision machinery and other manufactured goods found a ready market in these countries in return for food and other raw material. Moreover, all sides of the conflict found it very convenient to utilize this strategically located neutral country as a center of espionage and counter-espionage.

By 1940, the Swiss feared a German invasion. Switzerland was not ready to surrender easily to the might of the apparently invincible Nazi war machine. Switzerland, with universal military conscription of adult males in peace time, was ready to fight, should such an invasion have taken place. Hitler was fully aware of this and did not find it worthwhile to pin down so many of his divisions to achieve a victory whose fruits he could essentially enjoy without conquest. Nevertheless, fear of invasion did persist and it made Switzerland accept the unenviable role of strict neutrality vis-a-vis the Nazis.

Naturally, such fears heightened the existing tension and exacerbated anti-Semitic tendencies. Under these circumstances one can better appreciate the reaction by many Swiss Jews toward entry of Jewish refugees, as epitomized by the tragic career of Saly Mayer, who played a central role in the unfolding drama of Recha Sternbuch's rescue work.

Saly Mayer, as president of SIG (among other things), was very active in the fight against anti-Semitism, especially after 1933.

Roll call of Jewish refugees captured on the Swiss-Austrian border, interned in a camp by the Swiss

Moreover, from 1938 on, when the first refugee influx of German Jews came into Switzerland, he established ties with the American Jewish Joint Distribution Committee (JDC), the giant relief agency created during World War I. This relationship became official in 1940 after a visit by Dr. Joseph Schwartz, head of the European office of the Joint, when Mayer became its unsalaried representative in Switzerland.

The relationship between Mayer and Rothmund was a good one; that is, as Rothmund told Dr. Schwartz, they essentially agreed that:

> Switzerland is among the very few countries in Europe which has not adopted anti-Jewish laws, and in order to maintain that record, it would be far better if the refugee population were diminished. (Bauer, *JDC*, p. 233)

Rothmund demanded of the American head of the Joint that America take in the Jewish refugees. In the meantime, Rothmund said, speaking of himself, "he was doing all he could, and so was Saly Mayer, 'the untiring optimist and philosopher and good friend.'" His policy was essentially similar to that of assimilationist Jews throughout the world: to try to avoid bringing up the Jewish question which would raise the level of anti-Semitism. Their policy was to maintain *"Minhag Swisse"* (customary Jewish policy as practiced in Switzerland): a low public profile, inner unity, and cooperation with the government.

Sternbuch and Mayer: The Dramatic Difference

ONE OF THE EARLY EPISODES involving Recha Sternbuch's rescue efforts concerned two illegal refugees who made their way across the Franco-Swiss border. The incident highlights the difference between the Sternbuch's Torah perspective and that of Saly Mayer. This incident marked the beginning of the rift between these two parties.

It began at one of the usual crossing points near Lac Leman (Lake Geneva) on the Franco-Swiss border. Two fleeing refugee brothers named Blum had been caught by the Swiss border guards who were prepared to return them across the border to France and, inevitably, to a concentration camp. Members of Recha Sternbuch's rescue network sent word that something had to be done quickly if these two were not to be deported. After weighing the options, Mrs. Sternbuch went to see Saly Mayer.

Recha Sternbuch perceived the need to do everything in her power to save her fellow Jews from tragedy and she expected Saly Mayer, who wielded great power as the representative of Swiss Jewry, to exert himself to the utmost to help save the two brothers. She therefore implored him to speak to Dr. Rothmund and to use his various government contacts to somehow find a way to permit the refugees to remain in Switzerland, even in a civilian internment camp, if necessary.

To her shock and dismay, instead of helping her, Saly Mayer censured her with a lecture on Swiss patriotism, "Frau Sternbuch, if you were a good Swiss citizen you would consider it your duty to take the two men who had crossed illegally by the collar and hand them over to the police. You know the Jewish rule of *dina demalchusa dina* — the rule of the land has *halachic* (Jewish religious law) validity."

In icy tones this Jewish woman of valor answered, "Herr Mayer, you obviously don't know me. I am a Jewish mother and I

"Swiss Anti-Jewish Refugee Measures Recalled ..." Swiss Magazine "Blick" publishes interview with Dr. Kuhl about the stern anti-refugee measure taken by the Swiss Alien Police Chief in Bern against Jewish refugees

don't know what the law says. I only know that we have to save these people. If you refuse to be of any help, I will have nothing further to do with you!"

In fact, she did not. Without the support of Saly Mayer and without fear, she continued not only to help legalize the status of those refugees, but also organized numerous initiatives to bring in more Jews from Germany and Austria.

Without the help of the official Swiss Jewish establishment, Recha Sternbuch nevertheless enjoyed many successes as the previously-quoted Mr. Zecharia Reinhold related:

> In the beginning Mrs. Sternbuch tried very hard to have us legalized. It was not easy, but she finally succeeded. They [the Swiss] wanted to send us back ... We had been locked up as criminals — we were about twenty or thirty people. It was night and we were sitting in despair. We heard someone climbing up near the window and we were frightened. A voice at the window said, 'Don't be afraid. Nobody is being sent back.' This was Eli Sternbuch [brother of Yitzchok] bringing us the good tidings. In the morning we were taken to the police

Chapter 3: FIRST STRUGGLES FOR RESCUING JEWS / 35

station, where they took our names and divided us among several villages.

Recha Sternbuch had again successfully intervened with Chief of Police Paul Gruninger, and Mr. Reinhold and company were saved. She soon helped bring the rest of the Reinhold family in as well. They were put up in a makeshift "hotel" in a village and they eventually received some support — even from the American Jewish Joint Distribution Committee, through its representative, Saly Mayer.

By the end of 1938, about 800 refugees had found their way into St. Gallen, creating a problem for Saly Mayer, who saw these refugees not only as a burden for the Swiss-Jewish community, but perhaps of greater import, an incitement for anti-Semitism. Mayer's assistant prepared an unsolicited report on these refugees, which he submitted to Dr. Rothmund, head of the Alien Police. The Sternbuchs considered it a *mesirah*, a traitorous act of informing. Using these very statistics, Dr. Rothmund began legal proceedings against Paul Gruninger, Chief of the St. Gallen police, on charges of aiding the entry of illegal aliens into Switzerland. Gruninger was removed from his office and was not reinstated for thirty years until *Yad Vashem*, the Israeli Holocaust Authority, honored him in 1968 by naming him as one of the "Righteous of the Nations." While no Swiss Jew ever attempted to have Gruninger reinstated, the Sternbuchs provided him for many years with an opportunity to earn a living.

How did Gruninger view the role of Saly Mayer in all this? He did not hesitate to state in a deposition given in 1945:

> I declare herewith that Saly Mayer, then president of the *Schweizerischer Israelitischer Gemeindebund*, did not save even one Jew. He was disappointed that so many people were constantly being brought in, and refused to have anything to do with it. Saly Mayer refused to be of assistance, he actually made the work more difficult ... Because of the [illegal] entry of refugees, I was deposed from my position as police captain and Mrs. Sternbuch was later arrested. Had the work of rescue been eased both from within and without, then it would have been possible to have rescued a minimum of 10,000-20,000 people during the peaceful [part of] 1939.

CHAPTER FOUR
Imprisonment and Trial — The Ordeal of Recha Sternbuch

RECHA STERNBUCH HAD NO USE for the niceties of civil authority when the lives of Jews were at stake. Given her complete dedication to the rescue cause, and the fearlessness with which she carried on even after the dismissal of Mr. Gruninger, there was little surprise that she ran afoul of the law. In the spring of 1939, she was arrested for complicity in what had been done many times to help save Jewish lives — acts of bribery and illegal immigration. Her methods of dealing with the accusations she faced are a dramatic lesson in Jewish valor, as the record shows.

Recha Sternbuch was charged, among other things, with the violation of the regulations of the Alien Police by helping refugees enter Switzerland, since those who possessed Austrian passports were required to have a visa for entering Switzerland. This change was introduced by government decree on March 28, 1938. Further, she was accused of illegally harboring many of these refugees in her own home, and especially of building an entire network — or (in legal terms) "collusion" — with others who helped her. In this respect, two border policemen were also among those accused of "violating their official duty," by looking the other way, at the request of the Sternbuchs, so that refugees could enter unimpeded. Their superior, Dr. Stocker, was likewise accused of complicity in this matter, because he (by his own admission) "gave directions to the two policemen." He further "advised them to sometimes close one eye and to let these people through even if the legitimacy of their passports would have caused doubts."

Dr. Stocker was also accused of aiding the two policemen in providing fraudulent papers to the refugees crossing the borders in order to "fool German border authorities." The worst part of this crime in the eyes of the authorities was the fact that "such actions would naturally discredit the Swiss, in the eyes of the Germans. [This could not be tolerated] especially in these times of international tensions, full of the possibility of war."

LAST IN THE LITANY of accusations against Recha Sternbuch and her accomplices was the charge of bribing a consul in order to obtain Cuban end-visas.

"I Refuse to Inform on Third Parties"

Of the prosecutor's charges against Recha Sternbuch, the primary one was that of collusion. It was clearly the object of the entire investigation and trial to force her to inform on her accomplices. The authorities were certain that she had a substantial network of individuals helping her, a point that was constantly reiterated in the proceedings.

On the witness stand, Recha Sternbuch said, "I hereby declare my willingness to give truthful information as far as the investigation concerns me. However, I refuse to provide any information about third parties who in any way or manner were helping me with the illegal entry of immigrants into Switzerland."

Describing some aspects of her early role in the process involved in bringing the refugees, she continued, "In August, 1938, I cared for about fifteen or twenty immigrants who had come to Switzerland and stayed in my home ... In September, 1938, I furnished the Waldau Heim in St. Gallen West, and the refugees that I had maintained up to this time in my home were moved there, where they were under the care of the refugee organizations ... I have financed these immigration transports out of my own means; when these refugees didn't have the money, I paid their debts to chauffeurs and others ... because I didn't want these people to suffer damage ..."

Then came the question by the District Attorney that cropped up many other times, "Are you ready to divulge the names of the

```
Stadt St. Gallen                          St Gallen den 5.Mai
Polizei Inspektorat                                      1941
Spezialdienst SD


Es erscheint aus der Haft vorgeführt:

Sternbuch- Rottenberg,Recha St. Leonhardstr. No.65
           Personalien bekannt

        und sagt nach Ermahnung zur Wahrheit folgendes:

  Auf Vorhalt  : Wir haben durch weitere Erhebungen und im be-
                 sondern auch durch die Sichtung des bei Ihnen
                 beschlagnahmten Materials festgestellt,dass un-
                 ser Verdacht,Sie hätten einen organisierten
                 Emigrantenschmuggel betrieben und unter zu Hilfe
                 nahme von Drittpersonen auch durchgeführt,durch-
                 aus berechtigt ist. Die bei Ihnen beschlagnahm-
                 te Korrespondenz belastet Sie ausserordentlich
                 schwer und es steht Innen nunfrei,der Wahrheit
                 entsprechend auszusagen,oder aber durch ein hart-
                 näckiges Leugnen die Untersuchungshaft zu ver-
                 längern.

Was mich persönlich betrifft,habe ich durchaus keine Bedenken

und keine Veranlassung hier nicht die Wahrheit zu sagen. Aber irgend

welche Aussagen in Bezug auf Drittpersonen ,lehne ich ganz ent-

schieden ab. Wenn man mich zwei Jahre einsperrt,werde ich Britt-

personen ,die diesen Emigranten eigentlich einen Liebesdienst

erwiesen haben, nich verraten.

  Auf Vorhalt :   Haben Sie die illegale Einreise von Emigran-
                  ten gefördert oder in irgend einer Weise dazu
                  Beihilfe geleistet?

Ich will das ohne weiteres zugeben und ich erklare hier eigent-

lich erstaunt zu sein,dass mich die Polizei nicht schon längst

geholt hat.

  Auf Vorhalt:   Auf welche Weise haben Sie diesen Emigranten
                 geholfen um den Grenzübertritt illegal be-
                 werkstelligen zu können. Es war doch sicher
                 notwendig,dass Sie von hier aus, d. h. schon
                 in St Gallen die nötigen Vorarbeiten dazu
                 geschaffen haben. Es war vor allem notwendig
                 ,dass Sie im Rheintal d raussen oder eventuell
                 auch im Ausland Ihre Gewährsleute hatten,
                 die bereit waren,Emigranten illegal über die
                 Grenze nach der Schweiz zu bringen. Denn nach un-
                 serer Auffassung werden Sie selbst diese
                 Führung kaum übernommen haben.
```

*The police indictment against Recha Sternbuch
for smuggling people into Switzerland*

chauffeurs, be they taxi drivers or the drivers of private cars?"

She very firmly responded, "It is quite impossible for me to permit myself to be used as an informer, and I think it grossly unfair to expect such a thing of me."

Chapter 4: IMPRISONMENT AND TRIAL / 39

The District Attorney questioned further, "On December 31, 1938, you had a taxi driver take you to St. Margarethen where you picked up a family. It has been reported to us that prior to the arrival of this family you contacted the police there ... We wish to learn from you the names of all your middlemen of whose services you have availed yourself in order to bring immigrants illegally and unobserved over the Swiss border ... We have some definite evidence in this respect."

Recha Sternbuch replied curtly, "I will not answer that."

In a letter written from prison to the District Attorney (circa May 10, 1939) Mrs. Sternbuch elaborated on her fierce opposition against informing on others:

> ... I always believed that when innocent persecuted people ask me for help and nobody suffers a loss through my help, that only I will be punished — I will gladly choose to be punished, because if one has seen the mental and physical exhaustion of these people when they come from the border, one would prefer, with satisfaction, to endure punishment rather than to send them back.

Recha Sternbuch continued to make a statement which in effect deserves to be a model for humanitarian thought, a statement which impressed even the hard-nosed Swiss District Attorney:

> ... I was so agitated yesterday when they sent me a lawyer. I don't want anyone to cover up my actions or to try to cast them in such a light that I would escape punishment. I want the law to clearly judge my transgression. And if I deserve punishment, I want to bear it, because I have respect for the law and I do not fear it. If I have sinned against the law, I want to suffer so as to ease my conscience. Your demand, however ... that I should denounce human beings that haven't harmed anyone, and for the most part are poor, decent workers who could not bear to suffer a punishment, be it financial or a loss of their employment for a few months, bringing extreme hardship to their wives and children, this I cannot do! ... Do you really expect me to denounce the fathers of these families and bring them misfortune? ... Impossible, Mr. District Attorney! Totally impossible! I will not permit anyone to rob me of the things that make a person's life pleasant and worthwhile.

Considering herself as patriotic a Swiss as anyone, she continued:

Because of those things, we are so happy — we thank G-d that we are citizens of Switzerland! You can't choose those very acts that you condemn in our neighboring countries [i.e., Nazi Germany] and ask me to commit them. I am not so naive as to believe that I have to explain to you the immense harshness of your request. I know that you understand it better than I do. But I have no idea why you ask it of me. Day and night, I have thought over how I could protect myself from lies and I now know that I have to refuse to divulge information even if I be kept in prison as a result.

Recha Sternbuch concluded:

I want you to know that I refuse unconditionally to give any information about third parties, and that I also refuse to respond to any further challenges of this sort.

As for her own activities, she admitted:

I let the immigrants stay in my apartment on St. Leonard Street. They were refugees who entered illegally, possessed no residence permit, and had not yet been registered ... In most cases it was a matter of keeping them for a few days ... Sometimes such a stay had to be extended ... On occasion, refugees stayed with me several weeks [even] after they had received a residence permit, until they got a proper apartment.

She did not deny awareness that "non-registration of such immigrants" residing in her house was a violation of the existing regulations.

As for the question of bribery to a Mr. J. Menzel, a non-Jew, who the officials knew helped her provide end-visas for refugees so that they could leave Switzerland — a situation backed by the authorities who wanted to help send the refugees on to another country — Recha Sternbuch responded again with her sharp Torah perspective on rescue:

He is an immigrant who was registered in Zurich, and who occasionally obtained for me visas for several countries. Conditions today are unfortunately such that many times it appears impossible, or is in fact impossible, to obtain a visa in a legal manner and for payment of the regular taxes. This is particularly so if entry to a certain country has been closed or where there are also other difficulties with the Alien Police. Many times there is no choice but to resort to the rather unpleasant means of bribing a consular official. I personally consider this completely against my convictions, but conditions actually force me to resort to this means. Mr.

> Menzel in Zurich is my middleman who helps me obtain visas through this aforementioned means. I have to compensate Mr. Menzel for his efforts, 400 lira for each passport. On occasion I handed him eighteen passports to obtain the necessary visas to Italy.

She clarified in another letter concerning this matter, that Menzel usually obtained valid Cuban visas, which had originally been obtained by people in a regular manner, but had been returned because they lacked the requisite landing fee of $1,000 in United States currency. These legitimate visas were then sold by the consuls to others, and based on such visas, Italy provided transit visas.

At one point the Swiss Government was interested in expediting alien Jewish emigration from Switzerland without too much concern for the method used. It was this atmosphere that Recha Sternbuch exploited to help many refugees relocate in a more receptive, permanent haven. In fact, her lawyer pointed out:

> ... A few weeks before Mrs. Sternbuch was arrested and kept in prison, she went to the Alien Police in Bern with sixteen refugee passports. They told her that if she had any difficulties about emigration she should refer them back to Bern.

Furthermore, her lawyer reminded the court of her role in *Aliyah Bet*:

> ... One should also point to the Palestine transport in the spring of 1939, in which Mrs. Sternbuch took active part. In this case, there were hundreds of passports that were equipped with Chinese visas, although the real goal was to land illegally on the coast of Palestine. These visas were used with the intention of fooling the countries where they passed through, because Italy, for instance, would never give a transit visa unless the final destination was indicated.

There was even further complicity in this emigration scheme by the Swiss authorities. In fact, a few days following the release of Recha Sternbuch, the investigative judge, Dr. Brummer, wrote to her that:

> As far as we are concerned, you can occupy yourself with the travel continuation of the emigrants [out of Switzerland]. But we would recommend that you first occupy yourself with the problem of emigration of the immigrants in the canton of

St. Gallen, because you have to realize that these people are not allowed to work here and therefore have no means of support.

In other words, as the lawyer pointed out, to a great extent Mrs. Sternbuch's work

> ... was in the interest of the Swiss Alien Police ... If these assumptions were not correct, or eventually became a matter of legal infraction, it's hard to assume that the office of the investigating judge would have made such a request to continue in this direction.

FINALLY, IN MAY 1942, about three years after her arrest — three years of extreme mental anguish — Recha Sternbuch's lawyer moved that the case against her be dismissed, claiming that all the accusations against her had no basis either in fact or in law. Given the Swiss officials' own varied attitudes towards the inviolability of the border, along with their general acceptance of transit methods to leave the country, the worst that could be said — or proven— was that Recha Sternbuch was guilty of an infraction of an Alien Police regulation, punishable by a small fine — but hardly deserving imprisonment. The charges of bribery also seemed spurious, if for no other reason than that consul officials themselves were charging high prices for visas all during those years. The question that remained, then, was not of her guilt — but instead, the real reasons for her arrest and imprisonment in the first place. As such, her lawyer asked what many thought, but few dared to articulate: was Recha Sternbuch set up for the arrest? and if so, by whom? "There is another question," the lawyer noted, "as to whether denunciations of other unknown persons caused this investigation. Unfortunately, in looking over the documents, one has the feeling that Mrs. Sternbuch has been made the scapegoat."

Charges Dismissed

On June 30, 1942, a Swiss judge dismissed the charges against Recha Sternbuch due to "lack of evidence." All costs were borne by the court. Finally, she had won.

In an ironic concluding twist, at the end of the trial, the prosecutor himself who for three years attempted to prove the Swiss case against Recha Sternbuch, personally presented her with one hundred Swiss francs as his contribution toward her rescue efforts.

CHAPTER FIVE
HIJEFS*
— The Sternbuch
Rescue Organization

DURING THE TEN YEARS between 1941 and 1951, several organizations received wide recognition for their accomplishments on behalf of the victims of the Holocaust. Prominent among them was HIJEFS, of Montreux, Switzerland. Jewish and non-Jewish groups involved in rescue and relief during and after the war recognized HIJEFS as one of the most important and effective of the Jewish relief organizations. This is verified by thousands upon thousands of copies of correspondence, letters, and telegrams that HIJEFS exchanged with the War Refugee Board in Washington, the International Red Cross, UNRRA and the embassies and consulates of many countries, in addition to the vast correspondence between HIJEFS and various Jewish aid organizations throughout the world. It all points to a long chain of unparalleled efforts and achievements.

Yet, few people are aware that this foremost rescue and relief organization, with its impressive global reach, dealing with so many groups and so many thousands of individuals, was actually

---

*Acronym for Hilfsverein fur Judische Fluchtlinge in Shanghai (Relief Association for Jewish Refugees in Shanghai)

run by a minute staff under the *de facto* leadership of only Recha and Yitzchok Sternbuch.

HOW DID HIJEFS come into being?

Birth of HIJEFS
By the end of 1941, Recha and Yitzchok Sternbuch were already totally immersed in various rescue and relief projects. They did not satisfy themselves with bringing people to the safety of Switzerland, but they also provided for them after their arrival. Since a large number of those whom they brought illegally to Switzerland were interned in special refugee camps, the Sternbuchs also tried to free them. Thanks to their efforts a good number of those interned were later freed by the Swiss government and received permission for temporary stay in Switzerland. For those whom they could not free, the Sternbuchs provided kosher food and all other religious requirements. They mobilized other Jewish groups and individuals to take a deeper interest in the fate of the many unfortunate refugees and their various needs.

In time, the Sternbuchs broadened the scope of their activities. Learning of the precarious living conditions of Jews under the Nazis, they started sending food packages to Jews in the ghettos of Lodz, Warsaw, Cracow and other cities where countless Jews were starving. They also encouraged other individuals and groups to do the same. Their list of recipients included many rabbis, Torah scholars and Jewish communal leaders, who had lost all sources of livelihood. Mr. Leib Justman, a relative of the Gerer Rebbe and a survivor of the Warsaw Ghetto, recalls:

> Very often I visited the daughter of the Gerer Rebbe, who used to receive such packages via Portugal and often shared them with us ... A small package of just two to three pounds, which contained a little coffee, a chocolate and a few cans of sardines, was a life sustenance for a month. A pound of coffee [for example] could be exchanged for ten loaves of bread and many kilos of potatoes.

The Sternbuchs also became very active in sending medical supplies to the Warsaw Ghetto, where a typhoid epidemic broke out at the end of 1940 and lasted through 1941. They organized a *Bikur Chaulim* organization in St. Gallen, whose relief work for the sick in Warsaw was led by Eli Sternbuch, Yitzchok's brother. Eli played an active role in the work of his brother and sister-in-law during the entire ten-year period.

THROUGHOUT 1940 AND 1941, the Sternbuchs concentrated all their efforts on the above projects, setting an example for others to take a greater interest in the precarious fate of the Jews in the countries under Nazi domination. But in December of 1941, another great need arose. Japan attacked Pearl Harbor, leading to the Japanese-American

Expanded Activities

Before HIJEFS was founded the Sternbuchs worked with the Red Cross under the name of Bikur Chaulim in order to help Jews in Poland. But this organization did not cease its operations even after the establishment of HIJEFS. Under the leadership of Mr. Eli Sternbuch, Bikur Chaulim continued aiding the Jewish sick and victims of epidemics in the Jewish Ghettos of Poland. In this letter the International Red Cross expresses some willingness to help Bikur Chaulim fight the typhoid epidemic in the Warsaw Ghetto.

war. With this expansion of the theatre of war, hundreds of rabbis and Torah scholars — some with families — who had escaped from Vilna to Shanghai which was in Japanese-occupied China in 1940, were suddenly cut off from their source of sustenance.

Until then, these members of the Polish-Lithuanian *yeshivos* were receiving regular support from the Joint Distribution Committee and the Vaad Hatzalah in the United States. Suddenly, all connections between America and Japan were severed, and Shanghai became isolated as enemy territory. The leaders of the *yeshivos*, facing the threat of virtual starvation, turned for help to the only neutral country with a substantial Jewish population: Switzerland. They sent desperate appeals for help to prominent rabbis and orthodox community leaders in Switzerland, pleading that only they and their compatriots could help them in their desperate situation.

The first ones to respond to these pleas were Recha and Yitzchok Sternbuch.

Until then, the Sternbuchs had financed all of their rescue activities from their own pocket — even though it involved substantial sums of money. To sustain more than a thousand people over a longer period of time, however, required larger funds, which they personally could not provide. So they created a special organization for this purpose, enlisting a number of rabbis and businessmen who were ready to cooperate in this venture. But time was of the essence, and they could not wait until the entire committee took shape. So, just a few days after they received the appeal from Shanghai, the following notice appeared in the synagogues of Switzerland:

> "If someone saves one Jewish life, it is as if he saved the entire world." 400 young men and many rabbinic families from Mir, Telshe, and Lublin etc. are detained in Shangai en route to America, and are studying Torah. Their last telegram reads: "Save us from starvation!" No Jewish heart should, or could, be closed to this call. Please save our hungry brothers in Shanghai! Every contribution for this purpose, during the reading of the Torah, contributes to saving a most noble Jewish human life.
>
> Signed:
> Relief Association for Jewish Refugees in Shanghai.
> Secretary:
> Recha Sternbuch, Montreux.

This was the first official proclamation of the new organization with the name *Hilfsverein fur Judische Fluchtlinge in Shanghai*, or HIJEFS.

אשרי משכיל אל דל ביום רעה ימלטהו ה'

Die jüdische Not hat eine nie gekannte Höhe erreicht. Immer dringlicher, immer zahlreicher werden die an uns gestellten Aufgaben.
Von allen Seiten erreichen uns erschütternde Hilferufe führender jüdischer Persönlichkeiten aus den besetzten Gebieten:

Rettet die letzten Reste des europäischen Judentums!

Wir haben heute keine andere Wahl mehr:
Entweder entschliessen wir uns, neben den grossen Verpflichtungen die auf uns lasten, zu einer wirklich grosszügigen Hilfsaktion unter spürbaren persönlichen Opfern oder die letzten Trümmer des Judentums in den Okkupationsländern sind rettungslos dem Untergang geweiht.

Entweder opfern wir unser Geld oder unsere Brüder.

Die Antwort darauf kann nur eindeutig lauten.
Keiner wird sich einer solch geradezu geschichtlich werdenden Aufgabe entziehen wollen. Niemand darf in dieser historischen, vielleicht letzten Stunde der Hilfsmöglichkeit versagen! Jedermann, ob reich ob arm, hat die natürliche Pflicht über den Rahmen seiner Möglichkeit zu helfen!

Unsere Vereinigung hat keine geringere Aufgabe, als die Hilfeleistung an die bis zur Verzweiflung bedrängten Brüder in Ost und West.
Wir erwarten von jedem, der uns noch nicht angehört, seinen sofortigen Beitritt!
Wir erlauben uns, eine kleine Aufmerksamkeit zu Chanukah beizufügen, mit der Bitte, beim Zünden der Chanukahlichter

des Flüchtlingselends im Ausland zu gedenken.

Schweiz. Hilfsverein für jüdische Flüchtlinge im Ausland
HIJEFS

Der Arbeitsausschuss:

Zürich: W. Rosengarten
Basel: H. Orzel
Genf: Maitre Müller
Luzern: Rabb. Dr. Grünwald
St. Gallen: N. Sternbuch
Lugano: B. Schreiber

Der Vorstand:

A. W. Rosenzweig, Zürich
Josef Rosenbaum, Zürich
L. Rubinfeld, Lugano
M. Bofleg, Montreux
J. Erlanger, Luzern
Maitre M. Müller, Genf
R. Sternbuch, Montreux

HEIL DEM DER DES ARMEN NOT ERFASST,
AM TAGE DER BEDRÄNGNIS WIRD G'TT IHM BEISTEHEN (Ps. 41,2)

One of HIJEFS's calls appealing for public support of the yeshivos and Torah scholars in Shanghai

The first notice was signed by one person — Recha Sternbuch, secretary. While subsequent notices were signed by a full committee of prominent Swiss Orthodox Jewish leaders, in reality, the soul and body, as well as the guiding force of HIJEFS, was Recha Sternbuch. Nonetheless, the name "Recha Sternbuch" never again appeared in public documents and rarely even on private communication.

AT ITS INCEPTION, HIJEFS did concern itself primarily with raising and sending aid to the refugees in Shanghai. Through various means of collecting donations, Recha Sternbuch succeeded in arousing public interest, popularizing the name of HIJEFS, and mobilizing larger funds, enabling her to supply substantial aid for the refugees in Shanghai. This aid virtually saved the lives of almost one thousand people.

Not Just Shanghai

Subsequently, Recha and Yitzchok Sternbuch were somewhat relieved from this burden by working out an agreement with the Vaad Hatzalah in the United States, whereby the latter would send aid to Shanghai via the Polish consulate in Bern. (See the chapters "Righteous Among the Nations" and "Shanghai.") Although the Sternbuchs did not completely give up fund raising in Switzerland for the *yeshivos* and scholars in Shanghai, their main duty from then on was to make certain that the funds that came from America were promptly transmitted to the scholars in Shanghai, a vital task which they performed superbly.

Even though their share of the Shanghai burden was lightened, HIJEFS did not cease its operations. As the Sternbuchs widened their relief and rescue operations for the Jews in Europe, the existence of a recognized organization for their activities became increasingly important. As long as the Sternbuchs were carrying on their work secretly, an official organization was not only unnecessary but could also be harmful. The organization was also unnecessary when the Sternbuchs — in addition to helping Jews enter Switzerland — tried to influence other aid groups in Switzerland to enlarge their relief efforts. However, when they witnessed the slow pace of some aid groups and the gross negligence of others, they decided to expand their own activities, and a formal organization became a necessity to lend them more prominence and assure wider recognition.

Thus HIJEFS, originally caring only for refugees in Shanghai, became the *Schweizerischer Hilfsverein fur Judische Fluchtlinge* in Ausland — a Relief Association for Jewish Refugees in Foreign Lands. In a short time, its programs expanded to include all possible rescue and aid projects during the next eight years, effectively converting two good-hearted individuals into an international organization. From then on, Recha and Yitzchok Sternbuch while dealing with the various agencies and individuals who could contribute to the rescue and aid for Jews appeared as representatives of a Jewish organization. As such they could open many doors that were previously closed, and they were able to appreciably expand their efforts. Yet, to everyone acquainted with the facts, it was no secret that behind the name HIJEFS and its impressive steering committee stood only Recha and Yitzchok Sternbuch.

THROUGH HIJEFS, the Sternbuchs expanded the distribution of food packages, clothing and medication to many Jews in Germany, Poland, Czechoslovakia, and other countries under German occupation where Jews were suffering starvation. HIJEFS collected addresses of Jews in those countries, some of them hiding among gentiles, and supplied them with packages of food and clothing. As we know today, these packages arrived in the ghettos of Warsaw, Lodz, Theresienstadt and elsewhere. Their packages were even reaching Birkenau (a division of the Auschwitz concentration camp) until the middle of 1943, when Auschwitz became an extermination camp. HIJEFS was instrumental in arranging the transport of food parcels to Nazi-occupied Europe from Tangiers via Spain, a project headed by the devoted rescue worker, Mrs. Renee Reichman.

Food to Nazi-held Poland

From the HIJEFS documents we learn that it steadily supplied aid to JUS (Judische Unterstutzungsstelle), the Jewish self-help organization in Poland with headquarters in Cracow. JUS was the only official Jewish aid organization that functioned with the permission of the German authorities and had the right to be in contact with Jewish relief organizations in foreign (neutral) lands as well as with the International Red Cross. According to letters dated July and August 1944, JUS received aid from HIJEFS almost until the end of the war. HIJEFS was also instrumental in influencing other Jewish groups in Switzerland to help JUS.

> | JÜDISCHE UNTERSTÜTZUNGSSTELLE | CENTRALA POMOCY DLA ŻYDÓW |
> | FÜR DAS GENERALGOUVERNEMENT **JUS** | W GENERALN. GUBERNATORSTWIE |
>
> Nr. ...44-Wt/GH.
>   Krakau, den 21 Juli 1944.
> Titl.
> Schweizerischer Hilfsverein
> für jüd. Flüchtl... HIJEFS
> M o n t r e u x, Les ...ondalles.
>
> Betrifft: Tätigkeitsbericht Nr. V.
>
> Wir schätzen Sie im Besitze unseres Schreibens
> vom 6.ds.M. Nr.880/44 und gestatten uns, in der
> Anlage unseren Tätigkeitsbericht Nr. V. für die
> Monate April-Juni l.J. Ihnen zu übermitteln.
>
> In Ergänzung des Berichtes wäre noch mitzuteilen,
> dass wir in der ersten Hälfte VI.M. 7 Kisten To-
> matenkontrakt im Bruttogewicht von 385 kg, 60
> Säcke a 100 kg weisse Bohnen aus der Schweiz und
> ein Waggon mit ca.15.000 kg Nährsuppe aus der
> Slowakei - ebenfalls über die Veranlassung des
> Internationalen Roten Kreuzes in Genf - erhalten
> haben. Ueberdies sind aus Portugal weitere 2940
> 1/2-kg-Päckchen angelangt.
>
> Ihren weiteren Mitteilungen entgegensehend be-
> grüssen wir Sie
>   mit vorzüglicher Hochachtung.
>
>   Dr. W...hert /
> Einschreiben.
> Anlage.

Jewish self-help organization JUS in Cracow acknowledging receipt of a large food shipment from HIJEFS

The HIJEFS Network

ALTHOUGH HIJEFS'S MAIN CONCERN was to save Jews from the Nazis to help them survive under their domination, the Sternbuchs, through HIJEFS, also often concerned themselves with problems in Switzerland, especially wherever they noticed official neglect in providing proper care for refugees. On their initiative, for instance, a large number of Jewish refugee children were placed in a special Orthodox children's home.

Other rescue activities of HIJEFS during the war years included:
- Constant clandestine contact with Jewish community leaders and rescue activists in Slovakia, Roumania, Hungary, and Turkey, concerning all sorts of rescue projects for Jews in danger of Nazi persecution.
- Clandestine contact with Poland; monitoring the untold persecutions and annihilation of the Jews in Eastern Europe and alarming the free world about it, especially the Jewish leadership in the United States.
- Saving Jews by providing many of those in Poland, France, Belgium, and elsewhere with fictitious documents from South American countries and attempting to ensure their acceptance by the proper authorities.
- Various rescue operations in the last month before the downfall of Germany, through which thousands of Jews were saved at the last minute. Included in these is the famous Musy mission to Himmler, which was carried out under the name of the Union of Orthodox Rabbis of the U.S. and Canada, an organization that carried more moral and political weight in the eyes of the Germans than the others. This particular effort resulted directly in the liberation of 1200 inmates from Theresienstadt to Switzerland, which indirectly led to the release of many others from concentration camps.
- Maintaining contact with the International Red Cross and various neutral governments concerning saving Jews or helping them out of danger and distress.

(These operations are described in greater detail in the chapters that follow.)

In 1944, when the War Refugee Board was established by the U.S. government, HIJEFS officially became the Swiss representative of the Vaad Hatzalah of America. This enabled the Sternbuchs to officially receive funds from the U.S. and to establish a closer contact with the representative of the U.S. embassy in Switzerland, through which it launched many rescue projects. In the course of time the Sternbuchs pursued their activities under the name of HIJEFS or Vaad Hatzalah, as well as that of the Union of Orthodox Rabbis of the United States and

Canada — depending upon which was best suited for the mission at hand.

THESE MANIFOLD ACTIVITIES of HIJEFS were pursued by the Sternbuchs with the greatest dedication and perseverance, day and night, without interruption. It became the main "business" activity of Recha and Yitzchok Sternbuch. In the first year the office of HIJEFS was in their dining room. Not only did they not receive any remuneration for their work, but they actually continued to contribute much of their own personal and business funds to funding HIJEFS, while they neglected their family business. For instance, the Sternbuchs were never reimbursed for the telephone and travel expenses they incurred for their HIJEFS activities, which ran into thousands of dollars. It was well known in Switzerland that during the war years and afterwards, the Sternbuchs never took even a single vacation and never stopped directing the activities of HIJEFS. Rescuing and helping the Jewish Nazi victims physically and spiritually was a holy cause for the Sternbuchs.

Work without Salary, Labor without Respite

SINCE HIJEFS MAINTAINED constant contact (both officially and illegally) with almost every European Jewish community during the war years, it was also the first to know the problems and needs of these communities which were comprised of Holocaust survivors when the war was over. It is no wonder, then, that every Orthodox Jewish organization interested in helping the Jewish survivors had to turn to HIJEFS in Montreux. It was, in fact, the only address through which they could initiate some contact with the surviving Jews. In the first year following the war, almost the entire aid of the Vaad Hatzalah in the United States to the Jews in Poland, Germany, Czechoslovakia, Italy, Hungary and Roumania, was conducted through HIJEFS. All emissaries from the Vaad Hatzalah and Agudath Israel who came to Europe had to visit the headquarters of HIJEFS for their orientation to receive the information necessary to coordinate their work. Later, the American Vaad Hatzalah established its own offices in France and Germany. Many activities there and in all the other European countries were performed by

Postwar Activities

HIJEFS until the end of 1950, when the majority of Jewish survivors had left for America or Israel.

HIJEFS remained under the leadership of the Sternbuchs for another five years after the conclusion of the war. The same selfless dedication that the Sternbuchs had devoted to the rescue of Jews during the war, they later devoted through HIJEFS to the physical needs and spiritual rehabilitation of the survivors, as will be detailed in the chapters on their legendary postwar activities.

MANY OF HIJEFS'S ACCOMPLISHMENTS can also be credited to three other mainstays of its rescue work: the secretary of HIJEFS, Mr. Herman Landau, his co-worker Mr. Chaskel Rand and its "foreign secretary" from 1944 till 1946, Dr. Reuben Hecht.

HIJEFS Attachés

At the end of 1942, Mr. Herman Landau arrived in Switzerland from Belgium. He had entered Switzerland illegally and was interned by the Swiss authorities. Through the intervention of the Sternbuchs and the help of Monsignor Bernardini and Polish Ambassador Lados (see chapter 6), he was later freed, and joined the Sternbuchs as secretary of HIJEFS. Already recognized as an Orthodox activist in his earlier years in Germany, Mr. Landau served as secretary of HIJEFS until 1951. With his considerable ability and his unquestioned loyalty, Mr. Landau accomplished much for HIJEFS. Since the Sternbuchs were sometimes occupied with their private business ventures in Zurich, Mr. Landau and Mr. Rand were in charge of the HIJEFS office in Montreux. There they maintained steady contact with the United States, England and *Eretz Yisrael*, as well as with all European countries, to dispatch aid to many parts of Europe. Mr. Landau also organized various aid projects for the Jews in several European countries. He often personally visited these countries, despite the difficulties such trips entailed.

Mr. Chaskel Rand came from Vienna to Switzerland in 1938. At the inception of HIJEFS Mr. Rand helped Mrs. Sternbuch carry out various rescue projects like the sending of food packages to the refugees at the Swiss internment camps and also abroad; collecting money for HIJEFS projects in Switzerland etc. Later Mr. Rand assisted Mr. Landau in HIJEFS activities with great dedication.

Another key figure in HIJEFS was Dr. Reuben Hecht, who joined the Sternbuch operations at the beginning of 1944. Hecht, a

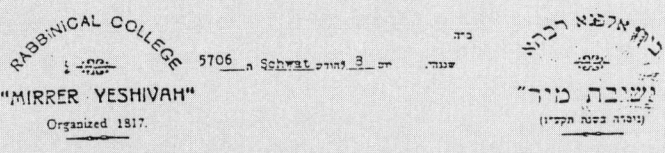

A letter from the famous Mirrer Rosh Hayeshiva Rabbi Chaim Shmulevitz in Shanghai, expressing thanks to HIJEFS for their steady support during the war

staunch Revisionist Zionist, came from a totally assimilated background. In fact, his father, far removed from his Jewish heritage, had disowned Reuben because of his work with the Revisionists in rescuing Jews from Nazi-occupied Europe and sending them on for illegal immigration to Palestine. Hecht was the only non-Orthodox member of the Sternbuch team and worked harmoniously with the Sternbuchs in some of HIJEFS's greatest achievements.

Dr. Hecht originally came to the Sternbuchs at the suggestion of the legendary Sam Woods, the U.S. commercial attaché in Zurich. Hecht had transmitted information from Dr. Kuhl and the Polish embassy to Woods, who had a direct channel to the U.S. Secretary of State Cordell Hull. Many of Hecht's reports on the treatment of Jews and on German military plans came from his father, Jacob Hecht, who owned a huge shipping and grain storage company in Basel, with branches throughout Europe. For example,

Jacob Hecht discovered information on the location of the center for the Nazi production of the dreaded U-1 flying bombs in Peenamunde, Germany. On the basis of Hecht's reports, which Woods forwarded to Hull, the Allies later bombed these sites. It was Sam Woods who told Reuben Hecht to join with the Sternbuchs, "since they were the only ones doing something."

Dr. Hecht became a sort of "foreign secretary" of HIJEFS as well as its director of public relations. He had excellent connections with government circles in Switzerland and with many of the foreign missions in Bern. He was very active in the Musy action (see chapter on the Musy rescue mission) and was especially successful in creating a close contact between HIJEFS and the International Red Cross (IRC). In the last months of the war, he succeeded in persuading the leaders of the IRC (who until then cooperated only reluctantly with Jewish relief organizations) to transport food to Bergen-Belsen, Theresienstadt, Landsberg and other concentration camps. He also succeeded in retrieving some important information from these camps. The contact with the IRC was also extremely important after the liberation, as the Red Cross agreed to carry HIJEFS transports of food, clothing, and religious articles to the liberated Jews, and even to intervene with the Allied military authorities for speedier passage.

After the war, Reuben Hecht continued to play an important role, traveling to Czechoslovakia and Roumania in 1945 to gather information on the Jews in those countries. He was very active in Recha Sternbuch's work in France, obtaining visas for Jews from Poland, rescuing children from non-Jewish homes, and helping to establish homes and hostels for the children.

In addition, Mr. Landau, Mr. Rand and Dr. Hecht were joined by a number of distinguished activists in Switzerland who gave of their time to help the Sternbuchs in their activities. Mr. Angelo Donati, a wealthy Italian Jew (a brother-in-law of the future French prime minister Pierre Mendes-France) was also very helpful to HIJEFS through his many connections with influential circles. Others who rendered significant help were Mr. Hugo Donnenbaum, Dr. Shaul Weingort (son-in-law of Rabbi Botchko of Montreux), Mr. Joseph Rosenbaum, Mr. Leibish Rubinfeld, Mr. Wolf Erlanger, Mr. Jacob Erlanger, Mr. Pines and his son and Mr. S.S. Guggenheim, the head of all Swiss aid institutions for refugees.

CHAPTER SIX

Ambassador Lados and Nuncio Bernardini — Two "Righteous Among the Nations"

THE STERNBUCHS' RESCUE WORK could not have been carried out on such a large scale without the help of a number of people whom Recha Sternbuch impressed and won for her cause. Somehow, her zeal, her determination and noble bearing made two gentiles stand out as *chassidei umos haolam,* "righteous among the nations," an appelation reserved for those gentiles who show special kindness towards the Jewish people. They were the Polish ambassador to Switzerland, Alexander Lados, and the Papal Nuncio in Bern, Monsignor Philippe Bernardini.

MANY DOCUMENTS of those frightful years offer eloquent testimony to the enormous role that Ambassador Lados played in the activities of Recha and Yitzchok Sternbuch. In addition, Mr. Lados — and often some of his assistants — also made it possible for the Polish embassy in Bern to develop into a major center for the rescue of European Jews. In a 1944 letter to Mr. Jacob Rosenheim, the president of the Agudath Israel World Organization, the Sternbuchs wrote that "without the help of

Ambassador Alexander Lados

Polish Ambassador Alexander Lados; in rear is Mr. Stanislaw Nachlik

Ambassador Lados, hardly a solitary soul would have been rescued."

In most cases Mr. Lados's help came through the mediation of his Jewish assistant, Dr. Julius Kuhl, through whom the Sternbuchs had originally made contact with Lados. Dr. Kuhl was born in Sanok, Poland, to a prominent Chassidic family. He studied in Switzerland where his doctoral thesis concerning Polish-Swiss trade relations qualified him for a coveted position at the Polish embassy in Bern. Despite his Jewishness, his excellent performance won him a promotion, and he developed a close friendship with the ambassador.

IT WAS NATURAL that when the Sternbuchs were in need of help from the Polish consulate, they should turn to its Jewish official.

Legalizing the Rescue The first problem which the Sternbuchs brought before the Polish consulate was the desperate need for passports for many Jews

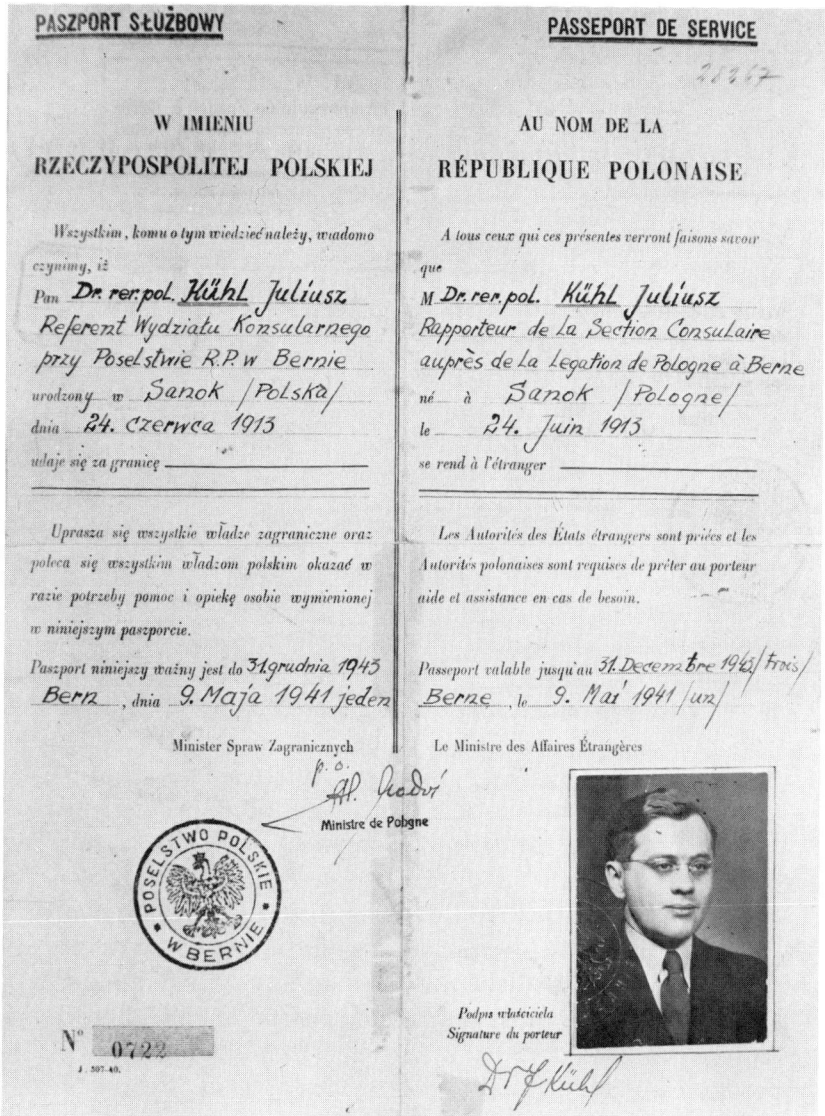

Dr. Kuhl's diplomatic service passport that enabled him to visit the internment camps in Switzerland, and later to visit the concentration camps that were liberated by the advancing allied armies

whom they wished to rescue. There were also many Jews who already had been brought to Switzerland secretly, and were in need of legal papers. Many did not have any legal documents, nor any kind of citizenship papers, as these were lost in their hurried escape. Others had legal papers that had expired. In Austria as in Germany (and soon after the outbreak of the war, in France and Belgium), there were many Jews who originally came from Poland, and for various reasons never renewed their passports. Suddenly, as with one stroke, their very survival hinged on those passports, for without a passport they were in constant danger of expulsion from Switzerland. Similarly, obtaining a visa to flee across the ocean was impossible without a passport. Other Polish consuls were not inclined to issue passports to people, especially Jews, without ample evidence of their valid Polish citizenship. In Bern, however, with the backing of Mr. Lados, many hundreds of passports were issued by Dr. Kuhl to people of just such standing, including many Jews sent to him by the Sternbuchs. With passports in their possession, many Jews who hitherto were forced to wander from place to place in Europe, received visas to countries in North America, South America, Africa, or Palestine. Some Jews, on the other hand, managed to legitimize their continued stay in Switzerland. It is now clear that were it not for the "blank check" approval given by Mr. Lados to Dr. Kuhl to freely issue those passports, many of those Jews would not have been rescued.

Saving the Belzer Rebbe

ONE PARTICULAR CASE is memorable. The world-renowned *tzaddik*, the late Belzer Rebbe, Rabbi Aaron Rokeach, of blessed memory, was miraculously rescued at the end of 1942 from Nazi-occupied Poland and brought to Hungary. This was a deliverance from sure death, for it is now known that the Nazis had launched an intensive search for him. But even upon his arrival in Hungary, the Rebbe's rescue was not complete, since he was there illegally. Although the British government had granted him a visa to Palestine, he could not use it without a passport. The solution came from the Polish embassy where Dr. Kuhl, with Mr. Lados's approval, issued a passport to the Belzer Rebbe. Because of the abnormal postal conditions Dr. Kuhl issued two passports. One was forwarded to a Belzer chassid in Zurich, Mr. Shmayahu Binder, and the other was sent to Budapest via a diplomatic courier

The Belzer Rebbe *Mr. Shmayahu Binder*

with the help of the Papal Nuncio. The Belzer Rebbe was thus enabled to continue on to Palestine where he was greeted with tremendous joy and relief.

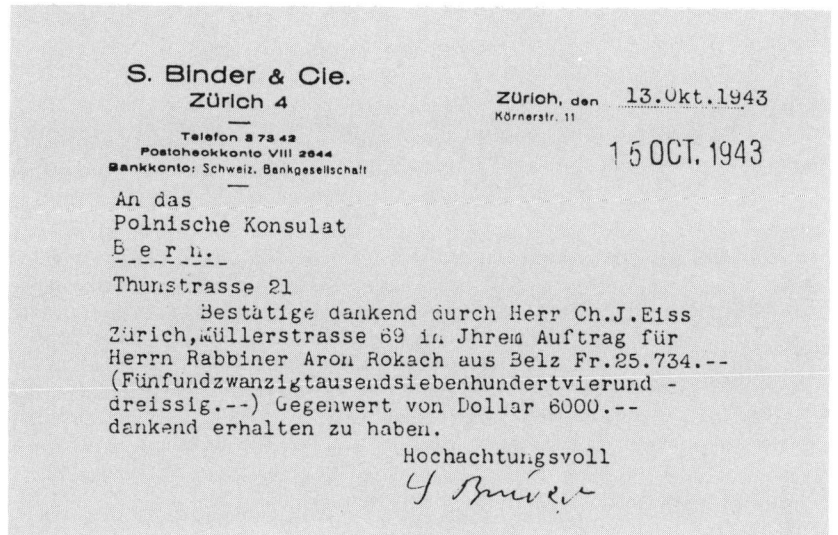

Letter from Mr. Shmayahu Binder, who was instrumental in rescuing the Belzer Rebbe from Poland, thanking the Polish Consulate for funds he received from the United States through the Polish legation. The rescue mission was financed through these funds.

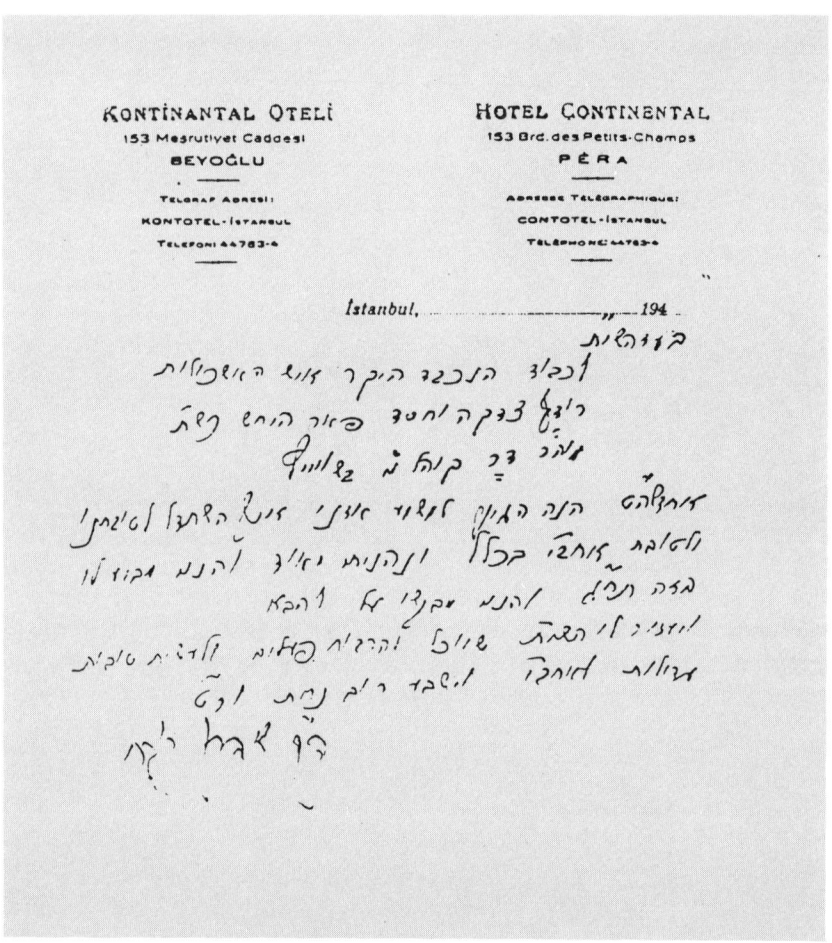

Letter from the Belzer Rebbe, Rabbi Aaron Rokeach, written on his arrival in Istanbul, thanking Dr. Julius Kuhl of the Polish Consulate for the help extended to him through the Polish Consulate. Dr. Kuhl observed that this correspondence reflects the awesome greatness of the Belzer Rebbe. By rights the Rebbe should have been shattered: his family was slaughtered before his own eyes; thousands upon thousands of his followers were cremated in the death camps; the cries of the millions of suffering Jews tore at his heart. Moreover, when the Rebbe wrote the letter he was still in danger, for he was in Istanbul, Turkey and he had not yet reached safety in Eretz Yisrael. Still, he was not too preoccupied with his personal problems to send thanks and encouragement to a young man who played a very minor role in his rescue. Small wonder that when this holy man watched his son being shot, he transcended his personal loss and saw his martyred son's bravery as an act of Kiddush Hashem (sanctification of the Divine Name). At that horrifying moment, the Rebbe recited a blessing of gratitude — Shehecheyanu — thanking G-d for letting him live to witness the horrifying event. He forsook his personal trauma and grief to thank G-d for the opportunity to offer a korban, a sacrifice before his Creator!

ANOTHER ILLUSTRATION of what the passport meant to many Jews who were stranded in Switzerland was provided by Dr. Kuhl himself, when he recalled issuing a Polish passport to one of the wealthiest Jews of Poland, Mr. Asher Kohn, who escaped from Poland to Switzerland at the last moment:

... and the King of Lodz

> Asher (also known as Oskar) Kohn was one of the most prominent Jewish industrialists in Poland. In his native Lodz, where he had his factories, he was king, living in a big mansion. But in Switzerland, he was a stranger, without even a permit to stay for a prolonged period. On top of all his tribulations he did not have a valid passport, because the Polish government had confiscated it just prior to World War II. The government wanted him to sell his factories to a Polish concern, but it did not want him to take the money abroad, so the government officials confiscated his passport. I do not know how Mr. Kohn managed to come to Switzerland on the last plane from Poland without a passport, but there he was — stateless, depressed, and dejected. Knowing his past, it was heartbreaking to witness his humiliation. So I was extremely happy to be able to provide him with a passport thus saving him from his homeless situation. Through the Polish consulate in Madrid I even arranged several transit visas so he could travel on to Mexico.

The cases of the Belzer Rebbe and Mr. Kohn are merely cited as illustrations. We could also mention here the famous Zionist leader Dr. Jacob Klatskin, and many other well-known personalities, especially those recommended to Dr. Kuhl by the head of the Swiss office of the Jewish Agency for Palestine, Dr. Samuel Scheps. However, the Consulate dealt not only with prominent people, but also with thousands of other Jews whom they provided with passports. Many of these were issued, of course, at the request of the Sternbuchs. As important as the passports were, another emergency service provided by Ambassador Lados overshadowed them: the practical assistance to the thousands of Polish Jews in seventy separate Swiss internment camps. Their condition, while certainly better than that of their fellow Jews in the concentration camps, was far from comfortable. Often completely without funds or any other means of support, the refugee Jews were ignored by all sides — Swiss and Polish alike. Ambassador Lados, however, succeeded in persuading the London-based Polish government-in-exile that these Jews were no different than all other Poles who received a monthly government-issue displaced-person allocation of up to 130 francs. Appointing Dr. Kuhl as his overseer, Ambassador Lados mandated that a Jewish representative be appointed at each camp to insure that all deserving persons received the assistance due to them. This aid totalled several million dollars during the War.

Mr. Lados also displayed profound sympathy for the special needs of religious Jews in the Swiss detention camps, as documented in the Sternbuch letter to Mr. Jacob Rosenheim. At the outset, the Swiss administrative officers frowned upon any activity of a religious nature. They refused to be bothered with sectarian requirements even though the Sternbuchs personally offered to make all necessary accommodations. After several meetings, Ambassador Lados, prompted by Dr. Kuhl and bolstered by the Sternbuchs' pleas, succeeded in softening the Swiss position. As a result, religious Jews were provided with kosher meals and other basic religious necessities.

In Switzerland there were also a number of camps of Polish army units which had escaped from France when the Germans occupied that country. These Polish army units were organized in France when the Nazis marched into Poland. Among these soldiers were a considerable number of Jews, who often suffered from the malice of the Polish sergeants who were poisoned with anti-Semitic venom. Were it not for Mr. Lados's protection, some of these Jews might not have survived. In addition, Mr. Lados tried to stem the vicious hatred against the Jews and to develop a measure of respect toward them. Before each Jewish holiday, Mr. Lados would send special greetings to the Jewish soldiers. Also, in his messages to the general army groups Dr. Lados would mention the suffering of the Jews at the hand of the common enemy so as to create a better attitude toward them. In order to elevate the image of the Jews in the minds of the Polish soldiers, Lados chose Dr. Kuhl, a Jew, to represent him with the army officers.

The help afforded by Alexander Lados went far beyond standard diplomacy for he backed the illegal immigration efforts of Recha Sternbuch and Dr. Kuhl, a position which frequently brought him into sharp conflict with the Swiss authorities, especially the anti-Semitic Alien Police. In the first chapter of this book we recounted the incident of the three young men for whom

Dr. Kuhl intervened with the Swiss police on behalf of the Polish consulate, and who were subsequently set free. When Heinrich Rothmund, the head of the Alien Police, discovered what had happened, he angrily demanded of Ambassador Lados: "Who rules here in Switzerland — the Swiss laws or your consul Dr. Kuhl?" This was hardly a minor incident, given Rothmund's virulence and the tensions of the time. However, Ambassador Lados, who was much respected in the higher Swiss echelons, somehow managed to contain the widening scandal. The aftermath, though, was that the Alien Police were convinced that a conspiracy existed between the Sternbuchs and the Polish

The wedding of Dr. and Mrs. Julius Kuhl, November 3, 1943, brought together a diverse group of guests: Jewish leaders of different persuasions, Orthodox Jews who were engaged in rescue projects, and gentile diplomats. The wedding took place at a time when Dr. Kuhl's mother was still in Siberia and Jews under Nazi rule were being exterminated every minute of the day. Therefore [perhaps to the disappointment of the gentile guests] there was no music, dancing, or speeches — only the chupa followed by a meal.

Among the guests in attendance (numbers correspond to those on photograph): 1. Mr. and Mrs. Sternbuch; 2. Mr. Ch. Y. Eiss, head of Agudath Israel in Switzerland; 3. Dr. A. Silberschein, member of the Polish Parliament; 4. Mr. Saly Mayer, head of 'Joint' and President of all Jewish communities in Switzerland; 5. Dr. George Brunschvig, President of the Jewish community of Bern, and his wife, Odette; 6. Ambassador Alexander Lados, representative of the Polish government in Bern; 7. Mr. S. Ryniewitz, First secretary of the Bern Embassy, and his wife; 8. Mr. S. Nachlik, custodian of the secret code of the Bern Embassy in Switzerland, and his wife; 9. Rabbi Dr. and Mrs. Eugene Messinger.

consulate. Although he did not want to wage a pitched battle with the Polish government-in-exile, Rothmund did attempt to have Dr. Kuhl restrained or removed. Ambassador Lados, however, did not budge. Indeed, he continued to encourage Dr. Kuhl's work with Recha Sternbuch.

Furthermore, Mr. Lados permitted his name to be used to encourage others to become involved in helping Jews in desperate straits. Strange as it may seem, Jews involved in rescue work often asked Mr. Lados to intervene with Swiss Jews on behalf of fellow Jews in trouble. This is clearly shown in an interesting document found in the papers of Dr. Kuhl. It is a letter from four rescue workers, headed by the well-known Hatzalah activist and Agudath Israel leader Mr. Chaim Yisroel Eiss, in which they ask Dr. Kuhl to intervene with the president of the Swiss-Israelite *Gemeindebund*, Saly Mayer, to increase his own activity for Jews in Poland. The letter was written to Dr. Kuhl, with the intent that it be used to persuade Mr. Lados to approach Saly Mayer. The letter writers were apparently convinced that the intervention of a Polish minister would inspire Mayer to do more than in the past, and events proved them right. Lados's personal visit to Saly Mayer had a great impact on him, as is seen from Mayer's subsequent letter to Kuhl, in which he writes glowingly of the Polish Minister's visit.

PERHAPS THE MOST IMPORTANT contribution of Mr. Lados was to place the communications system of the Polish embassy at the

Vital Communication Link

disposal of the Sternbuchs. Correspondence with the U.S. was very difficult once it had entered the war, and confidentiality was almost impossible. Furthermore, transferring funds from the U.S. to Shanghai, then under Japanese occupation, was illegal. Thus, the use of the communications system and its secret codes was of immense value. The Polish director of communications, Stanislaw Nachlik, was a vital collaborator in the work of the Sternbuchs. It was through this channel that telegrams were exchanged between the Sternbuchs and the organizations in the U.S. The Sternbuch cable on the Final Solution in the summer of 1942 as well as the alarming messages of Rabbi Michael Ber Weissmandel regarding the Germans' preparations to destroy Hungarian Jewry came through this channel. Funds necessary for the survival of the Shanghai refugees were transferred from the Vaad Hatzalah in New York to the Far East port of refuge via the Polish Embassy in Switzerland.

Dr. Kuhl's role as assistant to Ambassador Lados enabled him to disseminate atrocity news to the Sternbuchs and to the other important Jewish figures in Switzerland: Dr. George Brunschvig, a prominent lawyer and president of the Jewish community of Bern;

```
                POSELSTWO
       RZECZYPOSPOLITEJ POLSKIEJ
                 W BERNIE


       245/tj/43                              - 3 SEPT 1943
       SN                         Bern, den 31 August 1943.



           Sehr geehrter Herr Doktor,

              Meine längere Abwesenheit von Bern hat es mir leider un-
           möglich gemacht, den Empfang Ihres Schreibens vom 11 August
           1.J. schon früher zu bestätigen.

              Es freut mich, Ihnen mitteilen zu können, dass die beiden
           Telegramme bereits am 19 u.20 August aufgegeben worden sind.

              Ferner erkläre ich mich gerne mit Ihrem Vorschlag ein-
           verstanden, Herrn Dr.Julius Kühl, der mein volles Vertrauen
           geniesst, in allen Fragen, die das polnische Judentum be-
           treffen, zu meinem Vertreter gegenüber Ihrer Kommission im
           Sinne Ihrer Anregung zu ernennen.

                                   Mit vorzüglicher Hochachtung
                                       DER POLNISCHE GESANDTE


       Schweizerischer Israelitischer Gemeindebund
       Kommission für Nachkriegsprobleme
       z.H. Herrn Dr.Georg Brunschvig
       Marktgasse 51
           Bern.

                   Kopię otrzymuje do wiadomości Dr.J.Kühl
                                    w miejscu .
```

A letter from Ambassador Lados to Dr. George Brunschvig, informing him of the appointment of Dr. Julius Kuhl as his representative for Jewish organizations and of a number of clandestine messages that he had arranged to be sent to the United States via the code of the Polish Legation. Dr. Brunschvig was the chairman of the Jewish community in Bern and later chairman of all Jewish communities in Switzerland. He was one of the very few non-Orthodox Jewish leaders in Switzerland who warmly cooperated with the Sternbuch rescue efforts.

Saly Mayer of the Joint; and Dr. Abraham Silberschein of the World Jewish Congress. All of Dr. Kuhl's reports also found their way to the Jewish Agency in Jerusalem through its representative in Switzerland, Richard Lichtheim. Thus the Polish Embassy became a vital link in the struggle to rescue Jews.

When Mr. Lados went into retirement in Poland after the war, the Sternbuchs did not forget his unusual benevolence. Because of their profound gratitude, they maintained an intimate correspondence with him for many years, much as they would with a close relative. They continued to encourage him with warm friendship and help when he had become a forgotten relic in the reconstructed society of the People's Democratic Polish Republic. When he died, the Sternbuchs genuinely mourned him.

Similar feelings were expressed by Dr. Julius Kuhl, who still cherishes the memory of his former superior officer. "Mr. Lados," he says, "was a great humanitarian, one of the greatest I've ever met."

IN A LETTER to Mr. Jacob Rosenheim in which the Sternbuchs laud the help of the Polish Ambassador, Alexander Lados, they also

Philippe Bernardini

pay tribute to the warmhearted help of Monsignor Philippe Bernardini. They write:

> Our work has the support of the Papal Nuncio, Monsignor Bernardini. We visit him two or three times a week ... at any time we choose. Before he took the matter [i.e., the problem of Jews with the foreign passports] in hand, no consul wanted to lift a finger [on their behalf]. But he impressed upon the American Consulate and the Red Cross in Geneva [the importance of] initiating some steps. He sent a courier to Madrid and from there to Berlin. He influenced the Vatican to intervene with the South American governments to recognize the passports. He also interceded in Berlin to hold back the decree ...

In their correspondence, the Sternbuchs stress Bernardini's repeated intervention on behalf of the Jews with foreign passports who were interned by the Germans. However, his help extended to other areas.

Monsignor Bernardini enjoyed considerable influence in Switzerland. As the Papal Nuncio, he was automatically accorded the honor of being the dean of diplomatic corps in Switzerland.

Dr. George Brunschvig   Monsignor Philippe Bernardini

This gave him great prestige with the Swiss government as well as with many embassies and consulates, those of Catholic countries in particular. Therefore, winning his cooperation for the rescue efforts of the Jews in Europe was extremely beneficial to the Sternbuchs.

As with Ambassador Lados, the Sternbuchs' acquaintance with Bernardini was made possible by Dr. Kuhl. Bernardini was a close friend of Ambassador Lados, through whom he met Dr. Kuhl. Eventually, Bernardini and Kuhl became close friends — they even played ping-pong together every Sunday. Dr. Kuhl, in turn, introduced Recha Sternbuch to Bernardini. He also established a contact with Bernardini for other Jewish leaders of the Swiss Jewish community, such as Saly Mayer and Dr. George Brunschvig.

According to Dr. Kuhl, it was not only his personal friendship with Bernardini that influenced him to help Recha Sternbuch in her rescue activities. This only opened the door for the Sternbuchs. Other factors included Bernardini's generosity, goodness of spirit, and deep love for humanity, on the one hand; and, on the other, the overpowering personality of Recha Sternbuch.

MRS. STERNBUCH'S FIRST MEETING with Bernardini is a typical example of her influence. The Nuncio first invited her to sit down,

The First Encounter: "You Don't Even Know Me!"

and then asked her what she wanted. She requested a letter of recommendation. The Monsignor's response was: "Please tell me what to say, since I don't know the precise wording you need." He then wrote out the letter, in which he, the dean of ambassadors in Switzerland, vouched for everything that Mrs. Sternbuch said. Amazed at the affirmative response, quite beyond her expectations, Recha Sternbuch remarked, "But you don't even know me."

The veteran diplomat responded:

> You have to rely on my diplomatic skills and my acumen in knowing people. I immediately recognized you by the way you came in and the way you sat down. Your demeanor gave you away.

Bernardini, from the very first moment, felt a deep sympathy for the bitter fate that befell the Jews in Europe. He instantly displayed a readiness to help the victims of Nazi persecution. Moreover, he was impressed and overwhelmed by Recha Sternbuch's selflessness and self-sacrifice. As a deeply religious man, he respected her knowledge of the Bible and her piety. So great was Bernardini's admiration for Mrs. Sternbuch that in time he informed her that his door was always open for her; she could call him at any time, any hour, day or night.

Modest Beginnings

BERNARDINI'S AID WAS MODEST at first, as were the activities of the Sternbuchs. He frequently intervened on behalf of the Jews who arrived in Switzerland illegally. Quite often, he was able to gain reprieves for individuals or even entire groups who were threatened with expulsion and return to the Nazis. Recha Sternbuch convinced him that escaping illegally to Switzerland from the Nazis should not be considered a crime. The Nuncio accepted this and presented this defense to the Swiss government officials.

One incident in particular vividly illustrates Bernardini's great help in this respect. For a time Swiss authorities permitted entire families with small children of refugees to enter Switzerland, but turned away single people. While organizing this immigration of refugees Mrs. Sternbuch created "families" so that they could gain entry. Later, when the Swiss inspectors of the refugee camps noticed that such families did not live together, they felt betrayed. In their anger the Swiss authorities planned to send all these refugees back across the border to France, into German hands.

Desperate, Mrs. Sternbuch went to the Nuncio Bernardini who took immediate action. Not only did he officially intercede with the authorities but in a radio speech he openly defended the "treacherous hoax" ... Inasmuch as their lives were in danger — he declared — the "hoax" that they had perpetrated was perfectly moral and justified. In no way should they be punished. The defense of the refugees by a respected church dignitary made a tremendous impression on Swiss public opinion. The Swiss authorities abandoned any thought of deporting these refugees.

IN TIME, BERNARDINI went much further. At the request of the Sternbuchs he initiated the release of a number of Jews who were interned by the Swiss in specially designated detention camps for illegal aliens. (Among those whom he freed was the future secretary of HIJEFS, Mr. Herman Landau.) Bernardini's help in these affairs was not only important for the suffering individuals, but also created (in some circles) a friendlier climate for Jewish refugees in general. Through Bernardini, Recha Sternbuch became a *persona grata* with a number of government officials who previously had considered her a criminal for the many times she was caught in the act of smuggling in Jewish escapees.

From Criminal to Persona Grata

Bernardini's warm compassion for the victims of Nazi persecution had a number of other beneficial results. Through Bernardini, Recha Sternbuch befriended an influential Catholic woman, Mrs. Bolomey, the wife of a prominent colonel in the Swiss army. In the course of time, Mrs. Bolomey became part of Mrs. Sternbuch's team and one of the most important volunteers in her rescue endeavors. It was Mrs. Bolomey who acquainted her with the former president of the Swiss Bundesrat, Jean-Marie Musy. It was she who influenced him to undertake his mission to Himmler (see chapter on Musy Mission), through which a large number of Jews were saved from certain death in the last months of the war.

Bernardini rendered a most important service by placing the couriers of his diplomatic service at the disposal of the Sternbuchs.

This enabled them to maintain valuable contact with those countries with which the Polish government-in-exile and the Polish embassy in Bern ceased to have diplomatic relations — such as Czechoslovakia, Hungary, and Roumania. This was also important for some connections with Poland proper. Through Bernardini's diplomatic couriers, the Sternbuchs were able to communicate with the Jewish activists in those countries throughout the war years, receiving information regarding the Jewish situation there and transmitting various messages to them. With these diplomatic couriers, who were mostly priests, Dr. Kuhl was able to send a Polish passport for the Belzer Rebbe, Rabbi Aaron Rokeach, as described earlier. These same men brought to Switzerland many reports of the massacres in Poland, and even drawings of the German extermination camps near Lublin. In time, other Jewish rescue activists like Nathan Schwalbe of the *Hechalutz* group also made use of Bernardini's diplomatic couriers.

Rebuke in Rome

IN 1942, BERNARDINI personally intervened in order to ameliorate the situation of the Jews in Slovakia. According to a report sent from Bernardini's office to Dr. Kuhl, the Secretary of State of the Vatican, at the initiative of Bernardini, met with the Slovak representative in Rome and rebuked him for the persecutions the Jews of Slovakia were suffering. How strong that Vatican intervention was is hard to judge, for according to our knowledge, the Tiso government did not alter its anti-Semitic course. It is possible, however, that this intervention did have some effect, because in the summer of 1942, when Rabbi Michael Ber Weissmandel succeeded in bribing the Bratislava Gestapo Chief for Jewish Affairs, Dieter Wisliceny, to temporarily halt the deportations, the Slovak government also halted its demands that the Germans deport the Slovak Jews. This halt helped Wisliceny keep his promise to Rabbi Weissmandel. From the documents in our possession we can see that Monsignor Bernardini, at the request of the Sternbuchs, also intervened with the Vatican on behalf of Slovak Jews a number of times in 1944.

Other documents reveal that Bernardini's couriers were utilized many times during the war years by the Sternbuchs to help acquire visas for Jewish refugees to Brazil, Argentina, and other Latin American countries. A number of Jewish refugees stranded in Switzerland, Spain and Portugal, received such visas and were thus saved.

Bernardini played a major role in the Sternbuchs' rescue plan to save Jews by acquiring fictitious South American passports for them. (See chapter on South American passports.) Later, when the Germans began to question the validity of these passports, Bernardini worked with great devotion and intensity through the Vatican and the International Red Cross to obtain recognition of the documents by the South American governments. He succeeded to the point that the representatives of the respective countries intervened directly in Berlin for the bearers of such passports. Thanks to Bernardini's efforts with the Vatican, even the Spanish government, which was allied with the Germans, agreed to intervene with the German Foreign Ministry. Unfortunately, the recognition of the passports and the intervention came too late for the majority of the holders of these passports. The Gestapo refused to wait for a ruling of the Foreign Ministry, and most Jews with foreign passports in the special camp in Vittel were deported to the infamous Drancy concentration camp and from there on to Auschwitz, where they perished together with other Jews. Nevertheless, the belated recognition of the South American passports saved a number of Jews in other places.

Postwar Assistance

BERNARDINI'S HELP to the Sternbuchs continued even after the war, in an area where warm cooperation from a Church official could hardly be anticipated. Indeed, Bernardini may have even come into conflict with other Church representatives. It is no secret that many Church leaders were hesitant to release Jewish orphans who were saved from death during the war years by being placed in monasteries and other church institutions. They wanted to continue raising them in the Christian faith. However, when Mrs. Sternbuch undertook her journey to France in July 1945 to remove the Jewish children from such homes, Bernardini gave her a warm letter of recommendation to present to the French church leaders, which proved helpful. Through this recommendation, Recha Sternbuch befriended the Catholic priest Pierre Chaillet. Chaillet was helpful in the release of many children from Christian institutions. He even aided in bringing them to Paris, arranging their stay in Hotel Luteria, and later renting and purchasing villas in which to lodge these children.

Bernardini's recommendation also helped the Sternbuchs establish contact with the French government. With his letter of recommendation, Recha Sternbuch reached the office of the Foreign Minister George Bidault. There she made the acquaintance of the future Madame Bidault, who was his secretary at the time.

DECLARATION

Monsieur Josef Rottenberg, de nationalité polonaise, de Montreux et Anvers, a l'intention de se rendre dans différents pays pour des missions charitables comme représentant de diverses organisations humanitaires. Il se charge de négociations et d'organisations destinées à sauver et à aider surtout la population juive frappée par la guerre.

Le soussigné, Monseigneur Philippe Bernardini, Nonce Apostolique en Suisse, prie les autorités et représentants des pays étrangers de L'assister et de Lui faciliter, si possible, l'accomplissement de sa mission humanitaire.

Berne, le 10 octobre 1945

Letter of recommendation from Monsignor Bernardini for Mr. Josef Rottenberg (brother of Recha Sternbuch) in which he requests support for Mr. Rottenberg's mission, which was to take Jewish children out of non-Jewish homes

Dr. Reuben Hecht, who escorted Mrs. Sternbuch to France on this mission, related that Mme. Bidault even furnished them with diplomatic visas with which they were able to travel in the French-occupied zone in Germany to help the Jews who had been liberated from Hitler's concentration camps.

AT THE REQUEST of Mrs. Sternbuch, Bernardini gave similar letters of warm recommendation to other HIJEFS representatives who traveled on Recha Sternbuch's behalf all over Europe to reclaim such children wherever they were to be found. Righteous, broadminded and full of generosity, Bernardini did not share the attitude of other church leaders who wanted to keep the children in their grip. He fully recognized the claim of the Jewish people to its offspring, especially after the tragic decimation of its numbers.

Free the Children for Judaism

Bernardini's staunch support must be appreciated not only for what it contributed to each particular rescue project, but as a source of general encouragement for the Sternbuchs over those difficult years. As Dr. Kuhl put it: "At a time when we all felt abandoned and forlorn, facing a world which was at best indifferent to the fate of our suffering, dying brothers and sisters, Bernardini's compassion and constant help showed us that humane instincts had not yet come to an end. It gave strength to the Sternbuchs and all others to carry on their efforts to save as many Jews as possible."

The Sternbuchs, like many other Jewish leaders in Switzerland, naturally did not forget Bernardini's kindness and help in those difficult war years. In 1944, with approval of rabbinic authorities, the Sternbuchs presented him with the most beautiful Jewish gift in recognition of his good deeds, a Torah scroll.

On October 9, 1944 Mr. Yitzchok Sternbuch and Dr. Kuhl sent the following message to Bernardini:

> Since we had the honor of making your acquaintance, we were able to appreciate the spirit of humanity, justice and sacrifice with which you defended the cause of people in distress, particularly our unfortunate brothers.
>
> We wish to express to you our profound gratitude, and we beg you to please accept that which is dearest to us, the very reason of our existence throughout the centuries, a roll of parchment on which is inscribed our Torah.

Once again we express our heartfelt gratitude for your efforts on our behalf. May G-d be with you.

Dr. Kuhl recalls other Swiss gentiles who extended themselves to help save Jewish lives and to alleviate the plight of Jews who had found refuge in Switzerland. R. Crivelli, administrator of the University of Bern, Bundesrat Feldman of Bern, Colonel E. Ceresole, who was attached to the Polish Embassy as Switzerland's liaison to Polish prisoners of war interned in Switzerland; and Mrs. G. Kurz, both of Bern.

His experiences during the war in storming barricades of apathy and in treasuring the help of the few exemplars of the human spirit — such as Lados, Bernardini and the others — convinced Dr. Kuhl that people everywhere desperately need the living examples of such people. He feels passionately that every nation, especially those affected by Nazi brutality, should document the deeds of these heroes, Jew and gentile alike, who endangered themselves to save their fellow men from torture and death. Through everlasting memorials to these men and women of valor, Dr. Kuhl feels that future generations may be inspired to self-sacrifice in the service of morality.

CHAPTER SEVEN
Shanghai
— A Torah Outpost Saved With the Help of the Sternbuchs

SHANGHAI WAS A TEEMING METROPOLIS, a thriving industrial and commercial capital of China. Despite its population of four million people, until World War II it was scarcely worthy of mention in Jewish history books. However, during the war Shanghai assumed unusual significance as a haven for some 20,000 refugees from Hitler.

For religious Jewry, the importance of Shanghai looms even larger. Strange as it may seem, while the voice of Torah and the pursuit of Torah scholarship was almost stilled all over the world, the city of Shanghai became the world's primary center of Torah study. In fact, the rescue from Hitler's gas chambers of close to five hundred scholars to Shanghai turned out to be a major historical event which contributed to the revival of traditional Judaism after the Holocaust. Thanks to their rescue, many great new beachheads for Torah were established after the war. The Shanghai survivors became the leading spirit of almost every great Torah center in Israel, Europe, and the United States.

In this historical undertaking, too, the Sternbuchs played an important role.

When the Borders Closed

TO BETTER UNDERSTAND the Shanghai chapter in the Sternbuch saga, let us briefly describe how this distant, exotic port was transformed into a major Jewish refugee center.

In August 1938, at the time when the Swiss closed their borders to Jewish refugees, a Viennese Jew named Sebastian Steiner, along with his wife and children, booked passage on the *Conte Biancamano*, and set off for Shanghai. When they arrived, they were met by another displaced European, Mr. S. Gruenberg, who arranged the necessary customs clearance and escorted the Steiners to an apartment in the French section of the International Settlement. They were welcomed there by Rabbi Meir Ashkenazi, spiritual head of Shanghai's small Jewish community, which was comprised mainly of Russian Jews who had fled the Bolshevik Revolution. There was great relief and joy in the room, and the satisfied feeling of a job well done. No one present could have predicted that the arrival of the small Steiner family was in reality not the close of a minor episode, but actually the beginning of a Jewish refugee community that would soon swell to nearly 18,000.

Kristallnacht was the turning point. After the horrible events of the night of November 9-10 in 1938, many more thousands of German and Austrian Jews thought seriously of fleeing the Nazis — to any haven that would take them. As the Steiners had discovered earlier, Shanghai was in fact the only place in the world available to the refugees. This was an open city of four million Chinese, 100,000 foreigners, and *no* passports or visas were required for entry. That was the situation until August 1939, when the Japanese authorities who controlled the harbor of Shanghai started restricting free immigration. Although most European Jews had previously been reluctant to emigrate to an oriental capital — especially to one generally viewed as a symbol of vice and immorality — thousands of Jews from Germany and Austria who had nowhere else to go now came readily.

Perhaps the most unique group in this flight were the contingent of 2,000 Polish Jews who had escaped the German invasion of Poland by crossing the border into Lithuania and settling in Vilna. Among them were more than a thousand yeshivah students and their rabbis. Since Vilna was about to be taken over by the Soviets, this yeshivah population had the good fortune to obtain fictitious Curacaoan visas, which they were able to use to secure Japanese transit visas. These turned out to be a gift from heaven, for these papers enabled the refugees to book $200 Intourist train tickets for the overland trip through Siberia to Vladivostok, and then passage by ship to Kobe, Japan. There, about half of the 2,000 were able to obtain legitimate end-visas for the United States, Canada, and other western countries. (This group included the great Torah leader, Rabbi Aaron Kotler.) The Japanese were secretly preparing for war and sent the remaining 1,000 refugees to the open city of Shanghai just a few months before Pearl Harbor. The 1,000 included the remnants of a number of yeshivos — including roughly 80 rabbis, plus nearly 500 Torah scholars from Lublin, Lubavitch, Kletzk, and others. The Mirrer Yeshivah, consisting of over 250 students, represented the sole Eastern European yeshivah body that survived World War II virtually intact.

ALTHOUGH STRANGERS in an alien land, the Tamudic scholars immediately settled down to continue their studies as soon as they arrived in Shanghai in September 1941. With the warm assistance of Rabbi Meir Ashkenazi, almost every yeshivah succeeded in establishing its home. Maintenance, food, and shelter, although meagre, did not present too much of a problem. There was some help from the American Joint Distribution Committee, in addition to individual sources of help that the yeshivos had in the United States. The Vaad Hatzalah, which was founded at the beginning of the war in the U.S., also contributed to the yeshivos' needs. And so the yeshivos continued to function and the students studied Torah with the same fervor as they had before the war.

Scholars in an Alien Land

All this changed when the Japanese-American war broke out. Without warning, the Jewish refugees in Shanghai, and especially the yeshivah students, were cut off from all their sources of sustenance. The Joint, which until that time had been extremely generous in its support of the Shanghai refugee community, now followed its standard policy of not violating the American "Trading With the Enemy" laws — which forbade dispatching any communications, or the transfer of funds to enemy-occupied territory. The Joint simply refused to send further monies to Japanese-occupied China. In fact, just prior to Pearl Harbor, the Joint had encouraged Shanghai Jews to borrow money for six months, using the Joint as a guarantor, a fairly standard practice. Yet when the six months were almost over, the Joint representative

Rabbi Aaron Kotler

Rabbi Chaim Shmulevitz

in Shanghai, Laura Margolies, repeatedly cabled the United States further permission to borrow, with no response. Finally, on May 21, 1942, a cable from the Joint, routed through Paraguay, reached the Shanghai Jewish community: "All further communications will be discontinued." Margolies had borrowed money anyway on her personal "moral guarantee" that the Joint would repay the loan after the war (which, in fact, the Joint did). However, she was forced to curtail her aid to a bare minimum, and the yeshivos were the first to feel the pinch. Thus, a few weeks after the war started, the yeshivah students faced the threat of starvation.

IN THE PREVIOUS CHAPTER we mentioned briefly how Recha Sternbuch responded quickly to the call from these scholars in

Activating HIJEFS For Shanghai

Shanghai, and how she founded HIJEFS, initially only for the purpose of helping the yeshivos in Shanghai. For a while, this help was literally a lifesaver for the hundreds of Torah scholars. Switzerland was a neutral country and had no problem with sending money to Japan. As the Mirrer Rosh Yeshivah wrote to the Sternbuchs after the war:

> 8 Shvat, 5706
> With the help of the Almighty, your self-sacrificing work enabled us to overcome the worst of all times and to continue our holy task.
> (Rabbi) Chaim Shmulevitz

Rabbi Eliezer Silver   *Rabbi Chaim Ozer Grodzensky*

It is doubtful whether the Sternbuchs would have been able to sustain the yeshivos and their scholars by themselves, with funds from Switzerland alone. It certainly would have made it impossible for them to work on all other fronts of *hatzalah*. Fortunately, help came from the Orthodox Jewish community in the United States, whose leaders decided to overlook all legal restrictions, and rushed in with their help. At the helm was the Vaad Hatzalah.

THE VAAD HATZALAH in the United States was founded at the behest of the renowned Torah leader of world Jewry, Rabbi Chaim Ozer Grodzensky of Vilna. His call for the establishment of this organization was directed to Rabbi Eliezer Silver (president of the Union of Orthodox Rabbis of the U.S. and Canada, and of Agudath Israel of America) as soon as the scholars from the Polish-Lithuanian yeshivos arrived as refugees in Vilna. The response was immediate, with the founding of the Vaad Hatzalah in October 1939. To a great extent, the money sent by the Vaad Hatzalah to Rabbi Grodzensky for the yeshivos in Vilna played a vital role in enabling many scholars to reach Shanghai, via Japan. The Vaad Hatzalah also helped the yeshivos once they had arrived in Shanghai.

Vaad Hatzalah: on Order from Vilna

But the crucial role of Vaad Hatzalah started after Pearl Harbor. The leadership of the Vaad Hatzalah was joined by such

Rabbi Abraham Kalmanowitz

Mr. Irving Bunim

towering Torah personalities as Rabbi Abraham Kalmanowitz and Rabbi Aaron Kotler, and lay leaders like Irving Bunim, who were determined to use any possible avenue to save the yeshivos and their scholars in Shanghai.

Rabbi Kalmanowitz and the other leaders of Vaad Hatzalah in the U.S. (like the Sternbuchs in Switzerland) had no compunctions regarding use of illicit means in their rescue and relief work, since its goal was *pikuach nefesh* — saving lives. It was this common philosophy and partnership between the Vaad Hatzalah and the Sternbuchs that really saved the yeshivos and their scholars in Shanghai.

IN THE BEGINNING, because it was illegal to send money from the United States directly to Japan, the Vaad Hatzalah dispatched **Coded Messages through the Poles to Shanghai** coded messages to the Sternbuchs asking them to borrow money in Switzerland and transfer it to Shanghai. These messages were sent from the Polish consulate in New York (through contacts established by Dr. Isaac Lewin) to the Polish embassy in Bern (the contacts here were established by Dr. Kuhl with the help of Ambassador Lados).

In reality, though, this too was illegal. We know of two grants of $20,000 which were dispatched by this relatively simple method. The Joint turned down the invitation of the Polish embassy to use this method, and refused to transfer funds without prior State Department official approval. In its own words, the Joint stated: "We, as an American organization, cannot be involved in anything that has the remotest taint of trading with the enemy."

Eventually, the Vaad Hatzalah succeeded in legalizing its money transfers to Shanghai. The State Department finally agreed to issue a license for sending money to the Polish government-in-exile, for the benefit of Jewish refugees overseas who were Polish citizens. This money, given to the Polish consulate in New York, was legally transferred to the Polish legation in Bern, Switzerland. Then, through the good offices of Ambassador Lados and Dr. Kuhl, the money was handed over to the Sternbuchs who sent it, via the International Red Cross, the Swiss consul in Shanghai, or other means, to Rabbi Chaim Shmulevitz, Rabbi Meir Ashkenazi, or other Orthodox leaders in Shanghai. In cooperation with the Vaad Hatzalah, this channel was later also used by the Zeirei Agudath Israel of America and its indefatigable leader, Mr. Elimelech Tress, and others to send aid money to Shanghai, as well as for other *hatzalah* projects.

Transferring the money from America to Shanghai was not an easy task. Along with the money came daily coded messages from the Vaad Hatzalah in New York detailing how the money should be distributed. These messages had to be decoded and then relayed to Shanghai. The Sternbuchs had to maintain contact with not one, but a number of groups and institutions, each vying for its share of the funds, and each with its particular needs and emergencies, which in turn had to be relayed back to the Vaad Hatzalah. The

The Mirrer Yeshiva in Shanghai

Right: Rabbi Shimon Kalish, the Grand Rabbi of Amshinov, who was one of the major spiritual and intellectual leaders of the Shanghai refugee community. He came to the United States after the war where he helped infuse the embryonic Torah community with his warmth and wisdom.

Left: Rabbi Meir Ashkenazi, the rabbi of Shanghai, whose help and intervention was vital to the settlement and survival of the refugees. One of them, Rabbi Hirsh Milner, became the rabbi's son-in-law and is now a respected Torah scholar and businessman in Forest Hills, New York.

messages to the yeshivah leaders in Shanghai had to be sent in code as well, for although it was legal for them to receive money from a neutral country, the yeshivah leaders did not want the Japanese to find out that in reality the money came from an enemy land, i.e., the United States.

THE PREOCCUPATION with the community of scholars in Shanghai was by no means limited to the transfer of money. It also entailed protecting the general well-being of the refugees. The Germans were prodding the Japanese to take brutal action against the Jews under their jurisdiction; only the vigilance of the Sternbuchs, acting through the International Red Cross, restrained the Japanese from inflicting any harm on them. The care for the Jews in Shanghai was a yeoman's task. It required constant effort, and had to be handled with great care. One must also bear in mind

More than Money Dealings

that the Sternbuchs were engaged in many other projects as well. Undoubtedly, the mere fact that they helped sustain the world's only existing haven of intensive Torah study, in a remote corner of the globe, and the realization that they had saved the lives of so many Torah scholars, filled their hearts with satisfaction, and inspired them to work with greater patience and love.

Throughout the war, the study of Torah in Shanghai did not cease for a moment. Not only did the scholars continue to study, they even published books and Torah journals. They founded a Talmud Torah and a Beth Jacob school for the hundreds of refugee children. In the words of Rabbi Chuna Hertzman, a refugee scholar who had spent the war years in Shanghai with the Mirrer Yeshivah:

> The bulk of our time ... was devoted to Torah study, and we listened eagerly to *shiurim* by Rabbi Chaim Shmulevitz ... We *davened* slowly — carefully — one word at a time. If at times a plaintive note could be heard, it was the anguish we felt for our dead mothers and fathers ... The *mussar shmuessen* were given by Rabbi Yechezkel Levenstein (later *Menahel Ruchani*, spiritual guide, in the world-famous Ponevez Yeshivah in Bnei Brak, Israel). His words lifted us out of our daily preoccupation with sustaining our bodies and healing our ailments. The warmth of his thoughts and their profound simplicity, carried us above our troubles and helped us to overcome the anguish of knowing that we had become orphans in a hostile world ...

The spirit of Mir in Europe ... lived on, none the worse for its transplantation on Museum Road in Shanghai, China.

ALL IN ALL, through the partnership of the Vaad Hatzalah and the Sternbuchs, close to a million dollars reached the yeshivos and

Dividends of the Partnership

their scholars, as well as the other institutions of the Orthodox Jewish community, during the four years of the war. This aid saved almost one thousand refugees from starvation and also contributed to a wholesome spiritual life. This was true even after February 1943, when the Japanese established a ghetto for those who had entered Shanghai after 1937. After the war, this outpost of Torah spawned scores of institutions throughout the world, and provided the means of imparting Torah to tens of thousands of disciples.

CHAPTER EIGHT
Two Cables from Europe — Two Cries for Help and Their Difference

BY THE BEGINNING OF 1942, the well-oiled wheels of mass destruction of Europe's six million Jews started to turn — this was shortly after the Wansee Conference, near Berlin, where the plans for the Final Solution were adopted. Yet, it was not until December 17, 1942 — after more than a million Jews had perished — that the Allied governments who were at war with Nazi Germany openly condemned the Nazi massacre of the Jews and warned of retribution for the mass killings.

Most historians attribute this turnabout in attitude, which also marked the beginning of the United States' interest in the fate of Jews in Europe, to the telegram that Dr. Stephen S. Wise, American Jewry's most prominent spokesman, received on August 28, 1942 from Dr. Gerhardt M. Riegner, the Geneva representative of the World Jewish Congress. Dr. Riegner had wired Wise that a plan was under consideration at Hitler headquarters to exterminate all of European Jewry with poison gas.

However, the truth is that it was a different cable — one sent by Recha and Yitzchok Sternbuch — that helped arouse Jewish and American public opinion to the horrible events, and eventually led to some action on behalf of European Jewry.

LET US EXAMINE both cables and the subsequent events, and then permit them to speak for themselves.

Riegner and the Wise Response

The cable from Dr. Riegner, which Stephen Wise received on August 28, 1942, read:

RECEIVED ALARMING REPORT THAT IN FUHRER'S HEADQUARTERS PLAN DISCUSSED AND UNDER CONSIDERATION ACCORDING TO WHICH ALL JEWS IN COUNTRIES OCCUPIED OR CONTROLLED GERMANY NUMBERING 3½ FOUR MILLION [excluding Jews in the Soviet Union] SHOULD AFTER DEPORTATION AND CONCENTRATION IN EAST BE EXTERMINATED AT ONE BLOW TO RESOLVE ONCE FOR ALL THE JEWISH QUESTION IN EUROPE STOP ACTION REPORTED PLANNED FOR AUTUMN METHODS UNDER DISCUSSION INCLUDING PRUSSIC ACID STOP WE TRANSMIT INFORMATION WITH ALL NECESSARY RESERVATION AS EXACTITUDE CANNOT BE CONFIRMED STOP INFORMANT STATED TO HAVE CLOSE CONNECTIONS WITH HIGHEST GERMAN AUTHORITIES AND HIS REPORTS GENERALLY SPEAKING RELIABLE
                                                                       RIEGNER

What did Wise do after receiving the Riegner cable? Almost nothing. He did not contact President Roosevelt; he did not call a press conference to alert the public; and he did not mobilize anyone for action. He referred its contents to the State Department for confirmation, and nothing more.

The Sternbuchs sent their cable just six days later, on September 3, addressed to Mr. Jacob Rosenheim, president of the Agudath Israel World Organization. It arrived via the Polish Consulate in New York to Dr. Isaac Lewin who delivered it to Rosenheim on the day of its arrival. The cable read:

ACCORDING TO RECENTLY RECEIVED *AUTHENTIC INFORMATION*, THE GERMAN AUTHORITIES HAVE EVACUATED THE LAST GHETTO IN WARSAW, BESTIALLY MURDERING ABOUT ONE HUNDRED THOUSAND JEWS. MASS MURDERS CONTINUE. FROM THE CORPSES OF THE MURDERED, SOAP AND ARTIFICIAL FERTILIZERS ARE PRODUCED. THE DEPORTEES FROM OTHER OCCUPIED COUNTRIES WILL MEET THE SAME FATE. IT MUST BE SUPPOSED THAT ONLY ENERGETIC REPRISALS ON THE PART OF AMERICA COULD HALT THESE PERSECUTIONS.

After recounting the fate of the 100,000 Jews deported from Warsaw, Sternbuch further advised Mr. Rosenheim:

> DO WHATEVER YOU CAN TO CAUSE AN AMERICAN REACTION TO HALT THESE PERSECUTIONS. *DO WHATEVER YOU CAN TO PRODUCE SUCH A REACTION, STIRRING UP STATESMEN, THE PRESS, AND THE COMMUNITY. INFORM [STEPHEN S.] WISE, [ABBA HILLEL] SILVER, LUBAVITCHER [REBBE], [ALBERT] EINSTEIN, [JACOB] KLATZKIN, [NAHUM] GOLDMANN, THOMAS MANN, AND OTHERS.*
> [Emphasis added]

Not a Moment's Hesitation

IN CONTRAST TO STEPHEN WISE, Rosenheim did not hesitate for a moment. Immediately upon receipt of the tragic news, Rosenheim notified all the Jewish and non-Jewish notables listed in the cable, including Wise and Thomas Mann, the great liberal German novelist, who was a non-Jew. (Mann publicized this news that same month in a BBC broadcast.) By 9:00 P.M. that evening, Rosenheim had also sent the details of the Sternbuch cable to President Roosevelt, adding to it his personal plea:

> I dare, in the name of Orthodox Jews all over the world, to propose for consideration the arrangement by American initiative of a joint intervention of all the neutral states in Europe and America expressing their moral indignation.

Mr. Jacob Rosenheim further requested that the President act to halt the massacres, and that the Allies take collective action against Germany.

The President did not even acknowledge the cable; after three weeks, he sent it on to the State Department. Rosenheim, unaware of the President's failure to react, was not content with his message to him. The next day, September 4, 1942, Rosenheim requested a separate meeting with FDR on behalf of the World Agudath Israel movement. The meeting never took place, but Rosenheim's demand testifies to the urgency and seriousness with which the Sternbuch cable was received and acted upon.

A CLOSE EXAMINATION of the text reveals also a marked difference between the cables of Riegner and Sternbuch. Riegner

*Letter from the Polish Consulate in New York to Dr. Isaac Lewin
informing him about the coded Sternbuch cable
for Mr. Jacob Rosenheim, president of the World Agudath Israel,
with the tragic news of the mass deportations and annihilations in Poland.*

Moreinu Yaakov Rosenheim

Reading the Differences speaks of a "plan" to exterminate the Jews, of which he was not sure; the Sternbuch cable contains clear information about the mass murders that were going on for weeks and the deportation of a hundred thousand Jews from Warsaw.

There is little wonder that the Sternbuchs were the first to learn of the terrible fate of the Jews under the Nazis. In contrast to the other Jewish leaders in Switzerland, including Riegner, they were not sitting at their desks waiting for news to arrive. As mentioned previously, they were in close contact (as much as humanly possible under the war conditions) with Jews in all occupied countries. They were in daily touch with the Polish Legation in Bern where news arrived from the Polish underground. When the various communiqués confirmed that mass killings were indeed taking place, they felt it their obligation to inform and alert anybody that could be of some help.

ONE OF THE STERNBUCHS' informants was Mr. J. Domb, a Jew living in Warsaw. According to the Sternbuch family and a **The Domb Source** number of Warsaw Ghetto survivors, Mr. Domb was in possession of a Swiss document through which the German authorities recognized him as a Swiss citizen. As such, he could move in and out of the Warsaw

Ghetto at will, and he was able to make use of the postal services between occupied Poland and Switzerland. Indeed, many Warsaw Jews sent messages to the free world through him, via the Warsaw main post office. Through this mail, Domb sent a stream of messages written in an original Hebrew code, to the Sternbuchs — whom he knew from the years that he had lived in Switzerland before the war — informing them of all that was happening in Warsaw.

As Mr. Eli Sternbuch recalls, Mr. Domb first contacted the Sternbuchs when he heard that they were sending Latin American passports to individuals in Warsaw. Mr. Domb was not restricted to the ghetto, and had the freedom to live anywhere in Warsaw. Nonetheless, he was probably afraid that the Germans might start questioning his Swiss papers and discover his true Jewish identity. Soon he began pleading in his letters for a Latin American passport not only for his friends in the ghetto, but also for himself. Then, beginning in July 1942, when the Germans initiated their mass deportations from the Warsaw ghetto, Mr. Domb's letters became a source of information for the Sternbuchs regarding the true nature of these deportations.

NOT ALL OF MR. DOMB'S letters can be found, but two letters in our possession, which were sent to Mr. Eli Sternbuch in St. Gallen, **"Uncle Gerush" at Work in Warsaw** clearly indicate that the Jews of Warsaw were being deported and then murdered. In the letter of September 4, 1942, Mr. Domb first pleaded for a Paraguayan passport, and then writes:

> I spoke to Mr. *Jager*. He told me that he will invite all relatives of the family *Achenu* (with the exception of Miss Eisensweig) from Warsaw to his countryside dwelling *Kever*. I am done here. I feel lonely. As to the citrus-fruit, I hope I will receive them in time, but I do not know whether I will then find any of my acquaintances. Uncle *Gerush* also works in Warsaw. His friend *Miso* works together with him and is a very diligent worker ... Please pray for me.

This letter makes it quite clear what was going on. Mr. *Jager* — lit., Mr. Hunter — refers to the Germans. *Achenu* means "our brother" Jews, whom the Germans will "invite" to the "grave" (*Kever*). The citrus fruit refers to the *esrog* for Succos that the

Sternbuchs had promised to send him. Mr. Domb indicates that he is not sure if by then he will be able to find anybody to use it, since Uncle *Gerush*, meaning deportation, and *Miso*, death, are working very effectively in Warsaw.

In a subsequent letter, dated September 12, Mr. Domb very clearly indicates that *Achenu* died and he will not have anybody to whom to give the citrus fruit. (In fact, we know now that during the week beginning September 4, vast numbers of Jews were deported, and by September 12, the majority of the Jews of Warsaw had already met their death in Treblinka.)

THESE LETTERS together with additional information from the Sternbuchs' usual sources, stirred them into action, and gave them

No Rest for the Concerned

no rest. Only a day after they had sent their cable via the Polish Legation in Bern to Rosenheim, Mr. Sternbuch succeeded in getting a telephone call through to Rabbi Abraham Kalmanowitz in Brooklyn, to whom he related the latest information from Warsaw. According to Rabbi Alex Weisfogel, his secretary, Rabbi Kalmanowitz fainted after just a few words from Mr. Sternbuch, and Rabbi Weisfogel retrieved the phone to hear the remainder of the message.

But the Sternbuchs did not stop there. As one can see in Arthur D. Morse's work, *While Six Million Died*, the Sternbuchs circulated the letters to all prominent Jewish leaders and to representatives of the major Jewish world organizations, so they should be informed and disseminate the news. One of them was Dr. Riegner, who later, on September 28 (according to Mr. Morse), presented these letters to the American Consul, Paul Chapin Squire, to forward to the American authorities in Washington. (Riegner never told Morse that these letters originated from the Sternbuchs. Like most secular Jewish leaders and representatives of large Jewish organizations, Dr. Riegner was probably jealous of this Orthodox Jewish couple who were more active and accomplished much more for Jewish rescue than all of the others.)

On their own, the Sternbuchs also gave these letters to Mr. Sam Woods, the American commercial attaché in Zurich, who often sent reports directly to Secretary of State Cordell Hull. But their main efforts were concentrated on directing the news from Poland to Orthodox Jewish leaders in the United States and Great

Britain, through the code department of the Polish Legation in Bern. As Dr. Kuhl recalls:

> In the summer and autumn of 1942, when the tragic news came from Poland, the Sternbuchs — mainly Recha — kept us busy day and night, especially our code expert, Professor Stanislaw Nachlik, who sometimes personally tapped the telegraph keys late into the night, sending the Sternbuch messages to the United States.

Although the Polish Legation, through the good offices of Dr. Kuhl, made the cable accessible to all Jewish representatives, only Recha Sternbuch took advantage of it because use of another country's code was illegal under American law. No one else would violate this simple diplomatic regulation, except the woman who sacrificed all else to the Torah dictate of *pikuach nefesh* — saving lives, which overrules all other considerations. (Even after the creation of the War Refugee Board in January, 1944, which then offered telegraphic communication for HIJEFS and others, the Sternbuchs continued to use the Polish cable for secret messages — especially when the messages were related to rescue tactics that American representative Roswell McClelland would not have condoned.)

The U.S. Reaction

NOT ONLY WERE THERE stark differences between the tone and substance of the Riegner and Sternbuch cables, there was a dramatic difference in the reactions of the two corresponding communities in the United States upon receipt of their messages.

By September 4, Mr. Rosenheim and Rabbi Kalmanowitz took the lead, and arranged a preliminary meeting in the office of the Union of Orthodox Rabbis. They invited several prominent Jewish leaders, including Dr. Wise, and Dr. Arye Tartakower and Dr. Arye (Leon) Kubowitzki of the World Jewish Congress. Mr. Rosenheim and Rabbi Kalmanowitz read the Sternbuch message to them and urged them to take immediate steps, without any delay whatsoever, to mobilize the entire Jewish community for action. After some arguing, Rabbi Kalmanowitz and Mr. Rosenheim prevailed. Their pleading also moved Wise, who previously had not reacted to Riegner's telegram. On September 5, Wise telegrammed the leaders of the thirty-four major Jewish organizations, inviting them to an emergency meeting the

following day. The wire read:
    (sample)
    Sept. 5 PM 2:30
    Rabbi A. Kalmanowitz
    HORRIFYING NEWS OF MASS MASSACRES OF JEWS HAS JUST RECEIVED US [SIC]. INFORMATION SO APPALLING AND IMPLICATIONS FOR FUTURE SO GRAVE THAT WE ARE CALLING SPECIAL MEETING OF LEADING JEWISH BODIES TO CONSIDER TOGETHER ACTION WHICH CAN AND SHOULD BE TAKEN. MEETING WILL BE HELD TOMORROW SEPTEMBER 6 AT 1:00 PM, ROOM 809, 330 WEST 42 STREET. INVITE YOU TO BE REPRESENTED IN BEHALF AGUDAH HARABONON [SIC]

                        Stephen S. Wise,
                                President
                    American Jewish Congress

Mr. Jacob Rosenheim, Dr. Isaac Lewin, and Mr. Meir Shenkolewski represented Agudath Israel, while Rabbis Kalmanowitz and Shabse Frankel attended on behalf of Vaad Hatzalah. But the meeting resulted in failure. At the meeting Wise accused the Orthodox of spreading *gruelmarchen*, or atrocity myths. Against the rabbis' vehement protests, he convinced a majority of the Jewish leaders to agree to avoid public disclosure of the Nazi massacres, unaware that the Sternbuch cable had already been sent to the President.

Isolating the "Hysterical" Orthodox

THE FEW POWERLESS Orthodox rabbis and leaders of Vaad Hatzalah and Agudath Israel — most of them recent refugees to American shores, unversed in English — were deliberately ignored by the Jewish establishment as an anachronistic element soon to be extinct. Yet their sense of mission and burning brotherly concern gave them no rest. As cable after cable arrived, further verifying the heart-rending facts of the initial Sternbuch cable (they had not been informed of the Riegner cable), they could not contain their impatience. On the other hand, they refrained from alarming the world because, at both meetings with them, the leaders of the secular Jewish establishment threatened "excommunication" upon whomever would reveal the tragedy to the press. All were sworn to silence. The establishment's cooperation was needed and the rabbis of Vaad Hatzalah and

Agudath Israel remained too weak to challenge Stephen S. Wise, the most powerful American Jewish leader of his time; who even had the ear of the President.

During those weeks of silence, cables continued to arrive, verifying and reinforcing the accuracy of the original cable with phrases such as "deportations, mass slaughter, emptied ghetto" or "unknown destination for those shipped away."

After several weeks of such confirmations, a small committee convened once more, for a third time. Again, Wise enjoined them to silence while they awaited the imminent arrival of an important European figure bearing accurate reports — Myron Taylor, FDR's envoy to the Vatican.

THE ORTHODOX LEADERS, however, were not silent. Dr. Isaac Lewin published a number of articles in the Yiddish press in which he urged:

"What Will You Answer?"

Let [the tragic news] be revealed [at least] in the Jewish circles of America! Let the conscience of the world be shaken, first of all that of the Jewish world!

And he concluded his cry with a warning to the Jewish leaders:

> We ask the leaders of the American Jewish organizations: What will you answer on the "day of retribution"? What will you answer should someone someday request an accounting of what you did at a time when the blood of your brothers flowed in rivers!?

While waiting for a response from the State Department, a series of confirmative cables and letters arrived at the offices of Wise and his fellow Zionist leaders. Most of them came directly from the Swiss representatives of the Jewish Agency and the World Jewish Congress. Richard Lichtheim, who worked closely with Riegner, sent numerous reports that were especially pessimistic and accurate. On September 26, for example, he cabled Arthur Lourie of the American Zionist Emergency Committee in New York that, "the total destruction of the Jewish communities in Belgium and Holland is nearly complete."

Still, six weeks later, on October 9, Goldmann, Wise, and Perlzweig cabled their English colleagues,

PROBLEM RECEIVING CONSIDERATION HIGHEST AUTHORITIES WHOSE GUIDANCE IMPERATIVE. STOP.

[STATE] DEPARTMENT DEEPLY SYMPATHETIC AND COOPERATIVE. STOP.

But, as the historian Walter Laqueur pointed out in his book, *The Terrible Secret:*

> This information about the 'highest authorities' was quite simply false — neither the President nor the Secretary of State was giving consideration to the problem.

STEPHEN WISE CONTINUED to keep his silence, until November 24. It was then that the State Department informed Wise that it had "confirmed his worst fears," and that he had their approval to make the information public. And it was then that he held a news conference to announce that the Nazis had murdered half of the four million Jews in German-occupied Europe. (The *New York Times* saw fit to print this terrifying news in a small article on page ten, since its publisher, Arthur H. Sulzburger, feared bringing up the "Jewish problem." Previously, he had refused to publish earlier atrocity reports, sent by the Jewish underground via the Polish government-in-exile, including the Bund Report of June 1942, which reported the mass murder of 700,000 Jews!)

November 24: The Twelve Week Silence is Broken

It was only after the State Department confirmed the Riegner cable, and even more, the Sternbuch cable, that the ad hoc subcommittee of the Special Conference on European Jewish Affairs, which was formed as a result of the September 6 meeting, could finally seek a public response from the President. The committee members asked chairman Stephen S. Wise to arrange such a meeting, and on December 2, Wise urged the President to meet with Jewish leaders concerning the great tragedy suffered by the Jews.

In his response, the President agreed to Wise's request, designating December 8 as the date for meeting with the Jewish delegation. Members of this delegation, Dr. Stephen S. Wise of the American Jewish Congress, Henry Monsky of B'nai B'rith, Rabbi Israel Rosenberg of the Union of Orthodox Rabbis, and a representative of the American Jewish Committee, prepared two memoranda for this meeting: a brief one to be read to the President, and a longer one that detailed and substantiated the terrible facts about the mass murder.

AT THE MEETING with the President, however, instead of reading the prepared memorandum telling of all the atrocities, Wise simply said:

The Meeting vs. the Press Release

Mr. President, we also beg to submit details and proofs of the horrible facts. We appeal to you, as head of our government, to do all in your power to bring this to the attention of the world and to do all in your power to make an effort to stop it.

In turn, the President monopolized the conversation at this, his only meeting with Jewish leaders, by addressing the delegation for twenty-three out of twenty-nine minutes. There are interesting differences between Wise's press release on this meeting and the minutes of this meeting taken by the chairman of the Jewish Labor Committee.

In his press release, Wise noted:

> In responding to the statement of the delegates, the President said he was *profoundly shocked to learn* that two million Jews had, in one way or another, perished ... [emphasis added]

Wise wanted the American public to believe that the President was appalled at hearing these horrible facts even though, among other sources of information, Roosevelt had already received a copy of the Sternbuch cable from Rosenheim and readily admitted knowledge of the systematic murder of Jews. As the minutes of the meeting indicate:

> The President replied: 'The government of the United States is very well acquainted with most of the facts you are now bringing to our attention. Unfortunately, we have received confirmation from many sources. Representatives of the United States government in Switzerland and other neutral countries have given us proof that confirm the horrors discussed by you.'

Undoubtedly, Wise altered his version of the event to again protect the President. By intentionally making him appear unaware of the tragedy that was befalling the Jewish people, Wise preserved an image of FDR that would suffer if the public knew the stark truth — that Roosevelt had full knowledge of the atrocities in Europe and did nothing about it.

BUT THE MEETING, nevertheless, did bear some results. For the first time, in response to mounting public pressure, a declaration by the Allied Powers issued on December 17, 1942, included a condemnation of the murder of the Jews. This marked the first public statement that the Jews were specifically targeted by Hitler and were not merely victims among the casualties of all the other nationalities.

The Public Condemnation

Beyond its symbolic value, this declaration had important consequences of both immediate and long-range significance. First, hitherto inactive Jewish organizations were moved to undertake some relief and rescue efforts, resulting in the evolution of the ad hoc Conference into the "Joint Committee for European Jewish Affairs." This more permanent rescue body included, among others, delegates of the Zionist American Jewish Congress, the socialist Jewish Labor Committee, the American Jewish Committee, the Orthodox Agudath Israel, and the Union of Orthodox Rabbis' Vaad Hatzalah.

ALTHOUGH IT CANNOT be said that the Joint Committee accomplished much, or that the major secular Jewish organizations were mobilized for great accomplishments, the public awareness of the plight of European Jewry indirectly helped the rescue work of the Orthodox Jewish leaders in the United States. It lent more prominence to the Vaad Hatzalah, which was at least able to mobilize the Orthodox Jewish community to some major efforts for rescue activities. It also gave more public credence to the Peter Bergson group, led by Peter Bergson (alias Hillel Kook), Samuel Merlin, Yitshak Ben-Ami, and Ben Hecht, which diligently worked to focus public attention on the plight of European Jewry. All of this eventually culminated in the establishment by the U.S. Government of the War Refugee Board, which did accomplish some significant rescue work in later years, some of it in conjunction with the Sternbuchs in Switzerland.

A New Public Awareness and its Consequences

A longer-lasting consequence of the Declaration, as pointed out by British historian John P. Fox, was that

in the postwar Nuremberg trials of Nazi war criminals, crimes against Jews became a specific part of the Allied indictment — Section B of Count 4 (Crimes Against Humanity) specifically referring to the persecution and extermination of European Jewry by Nazi Germany.

Thus, the atrocity reports of 1942 and the consequent Allied Declaration of December 17, 1942, decisively influenced a change in the international law to include crimes committed "against any civilian population," i.e., even Jews who were not nationals of the country in which the crimes were committed. In addition, the Sternbuch cable, especially its follow-up by Agudath Israel and Vaad Hatzalah in America, and the additional reports sent to America in the fall of 1942, helped to create an atmosphere for rescue during the war and to establish Nazi guilt in the Nuremberg trials after the War.

CHAPTER NINE
Latin American Passports — Another Avenue of Escape

The Steel Trap

FOR MORE THAN THREE YEARS, from 1938 to 1941, Recha and Yitzchok Sternbuch worked feverishly to take Jews out of Germany and Austria. Later their efforts were also directed towards saving Jews from France, Belgium and Holland, when the Germans occupied these countries. As more and more Jews became endangered, and as their suffering increased, the Sternbuchs' efforts to save as many Jews as possible from the bloody hands of the Germans became more intensive.

Understandably, as the urgency of rescuing Jews from German-occupied territories grew, so did the means for saving them become more difficult and more complicated. Earlier we related how Recha Sternbuch had smuggled thousands of Jews into Switzerland. But Switzerland toughened its restrictions and reinforced its border patrols, and it became even harder to smuggle in Jews, except for a few individuals.

In 1941 another far more serious problem arose. In earlier years, Germany had willingly permitted Jews to leave since her policy was simply to rid Germany of the Jews as quickly as possible. After the invasion of Russia in mid-1941, they formulated a strict policy of not permitting Jews to leave Germany or their occupied territories, but instead to deport them to the

Eastern annihilation camps. And, so, almost all rescue efforts came to a halt. Even if there was a place to settle the Jews, it was now impossible to get them out of Germany.

Yet Recha and Yitzchok Sternbuch would not yield, and continued their search for new ways to break out of this steel trap. Following the adage of the sages that "no obstacle stands against one's will," they hit upon an original idea, in 1941: to supply Jews within the German territories with Latin American passports.

The Paraguayan Ploy

THE STERNBUCHS DISCOVERED that in 1939, when the Russians occupied part of Poland and it became difficult to leave the Soviet-occupied zone, a number of Jews in free countries had supplied relatives trapped in Poland with passports from South American countries. Later, when the Germans invaded Eastern Poland and Russia, the German authorities, oddly enough, recognized the passports and considered the possessors of such passports as foreign citizens with all their rights and privileges, as dictated by international law. In all likelihood the Germans did so because of their interest in protecting the many thousands of German agents and spies living in Latin America. The Sternbuchs recognized the implications of this fact and saw it as offering a fresh approach to saving a number of Jews with such foreign passports.

Through the good offices of Dr. Kuhl in the Polish consulate in Bern, they found a friendly consul from Paraguay, a Mr. Hügly, who agreed, on his own responsibility — and for a price — to issue a number of such passports, which the Sternbuchs then sent on to individuals in Poland and France. Before long, the Sternbuchs found that the Germans did indeed recognize these passports. Its owners were able to move around somewhat more freely and avoid deportation. The Sternbuchs immediately immersed themselves into the new venture of obtaining foreign passports.

In a short time they succeeded in obtaining a few hundred Paraguayan passports from the consul in Bern; they also tried to obtain such passports from other South American consulates. Other rescue activists such as Chaim Yisroel Eiss, Mathew Muller of Agudath Israel, and Dr. Alfred Silberschein of RELICO (another Jewish rescue organization in Switzerland) followed suit and succeeded in obtaining similar documents from Peru, Costa Rica,

Honduras and especially El Salvador, whose Jewish Secretary General, George Mantello, freely dispensed many such papers. Also, some private Jews in Switzerland were able to obtain such passports for their relatives in various countries under German occupation.

FOR A PERIOD OF TIME, the Germans continued to recognize the Latin American passports. Their possessors were not deported, but, instead, were later interned by Germans in special camps for citizens of foreign countries. Such camps for foreign citizens were maintained in Vittel and Gurs (France), and in Timaning and Bergen-Belsen (Germany). Red Cross representatives had access to these camps and the internees could correspond with relatives in neutral countries.

Dead End at Drancy

The author and historian Dr. Hillel Seidman who was saved from the Warsaw Ghetto when he received a South American passport from the Sternbuchs told us about his subsequent internment in Vittel:

> The abrupt transfer from the depth of despair of the Warsaw ghetto to the German internment camp in Vittel, one of the most luxurious resorts in France, stunned us into stupor. The one obvious conclusion we were able to grasp was this: Here we are, a people with the most tremendous spiritual achievements and gifts of the world, but without a state. Therefore, we are condemned to total and cruel disgraceful death. As soon as Paraguay, one of the banana republics that contributed little to the world, recognizes us as its citizens we are again treated deferentially as human beings whatever the reasons. This lesson, which I shared with the other Jews from Warsaw, was never erased from my mind.

By the end of 1943, the Sternbuchs had supplied hundreds of Jews in Poland, Belgium, and France with such documents. They compiled lists of many more Jews to whom they were about to send such foreign passports.

The Sternbuchs were very hopeful about the prospect of this new rescue project. But by April 1944, the Germans who were supervising the Vittel camp began questioning the legitimacy of these passports. According to some opinions, this was the result of an informer among the internees. But according to Dr. Hillel Seidman, the Germans were well aware from the outset that these

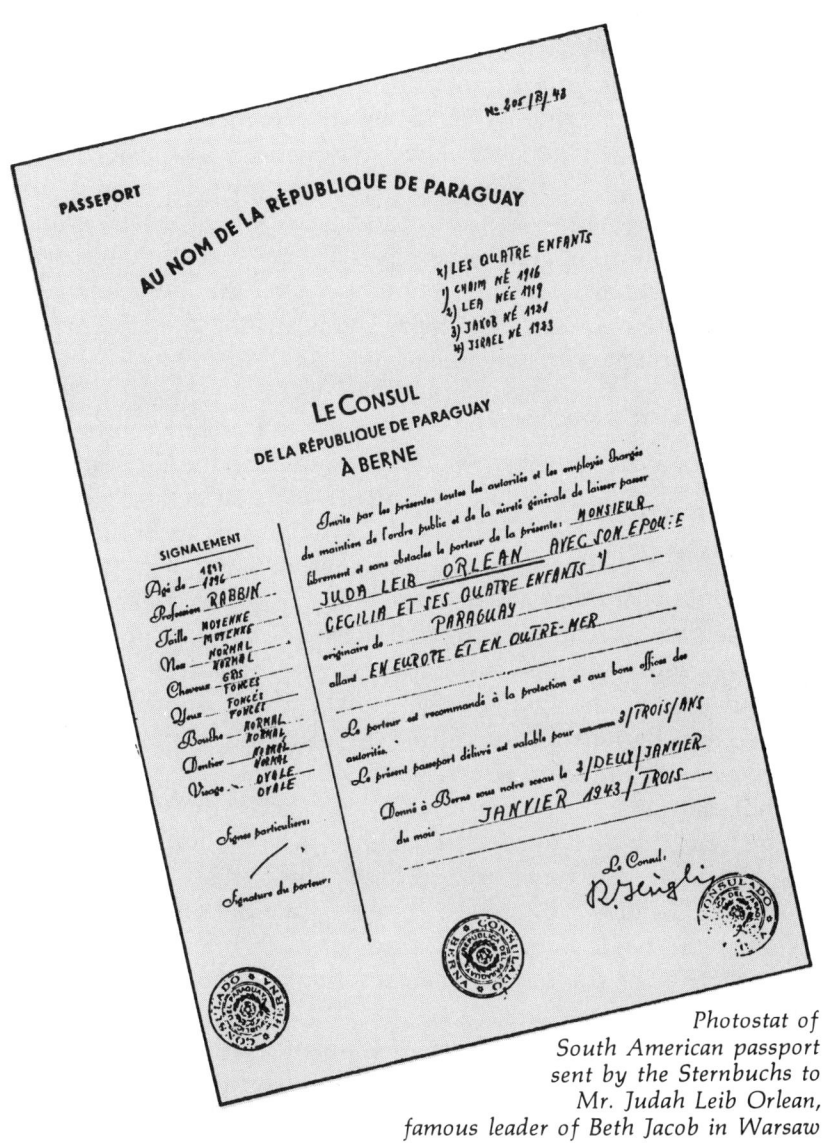

Photostat of
South American passport
sent by the Sternbuchs to
Mr. Judah Leib Orlean,
famous leader of Beth Jacob in Warsaw

passports were fictitious. They had recognized them only because they had hoped that they would be able to exchange the holders of these passports for their own citizens. When this hope failed, they decided to treat the holders like all other Jews, and annihilate them. Sure enough, on the day after Pesach 1944, they rounded up almost all Jewish holders of the Latin American passports except those who were in the Vittel hospital, and a few who had hidden in this large camp — and deported them to the infamous concentration camp in Drancy, near Paris.

One can imagine what a severe blow this was for the Sternbuchs and their efforts. The Sternbuchs had known that they were on weak ground, since these passports were issued at their initiative by the Latin-American consulates in Switzerland without the authorization of their governments. However, they refused to resign themselves to the situation. On the contrary, they intensified their activity, leaving no stone unturned, in their efforts to save the owners of the passports.

FIRST THEY ATTEMPTED to influence the governments of the South American countries to officially declare these passports as valid. This was not a simple task, especially since the Spanish and Swiss consuls in Berlin, which represented these governments, also questioned their validity, and refused to intervene. To attain recognition for the passports, the Sternbuchs mobilized the support of the Polish ambassador, Mr. Lados, and Papal Nuncio Bernardini. Mr. Lados in turn sought the help of the Polish government-in-exile and Monsignor Bernardini succeeded in convincing the Vatican to intercede with the Latin American governments — mainly strongly Catholic countries. The Sternbuchs also alerted the Vaad Hatzalah in the United States to seek the help of the War Refugee Board in Washington. Actively involved in this effort were Rabbis Abraham Kalmanowitz, Shabse Frankel, and Baruch Korf. Finally, by June 16, 1944, the American government intervened with the governments of the Latin American countries to recognize these passports.

Knock on Every Door

When one reads the many documents from those days, one can see that these efforts truly constituted a mammoth undertaking. Many hundreds of letters and telegrams were sent by the Sternbuchs to everyone who could possibly be of any assistance. In their race against time, they knocked on the doors of all embassies whose governments exerted some influence. Eventually, they were able to persuade the Latin American governments to officially recognize their passports. But that was not enough.

Even with this official recognition, the Sternbuchs had yet to influence the Spanish and Swiss representatives in Germany to intervene with the German Foreign Ministry in Berlin. That too was not enough. It was also necessary to gain assurances from the American government that it would inform the Germans that the possessors of the documents were candidates for an eventual exchange for Germans in the Allied countries. Only then were the Spanish and Swiss governments ready to intervene with the German government.

UNFORTUNATELY ALL THIS came too late for the majority of the internees of Vittel, who in the meantime were deported from Drancy to Auschwitz. After the Latin American countries had recognized their passports, the German Foreign Ministry claimed that their holders were now in the hands of the Gestapo in whose activities the Foreign Ministry could not interfere, and that they therefore did not know of their whereabouts. The truth is that in the meantime these unfortunate Jews had met their death in the gas chambers of Auschwitz.

Too Late for Too Many

For a long time Recha Sternbuch grieved for the victims of Vittel, especially since much of her family, headed by her father, the famous rabbi of Antwerp, Rabbi Mordechai Rottenberg, was among those deported from Vittel to Auschwitz. Nonetheless, the project of saving Jews with these passports can still be considered a great accomplishment. Many Jews with foreign passports who were not yet deported from Bergen-Belsen, and a number from smaller internment camps, were saved. Moreover, as a result of the recognition achieved by the efforts to save the internees of Vittel, thousands of Jews were saved in various countries, especially Hungary, because they held Latin American papers. Thus, though their frantic efforts failed to save most of Vittel's detainees, the Sternbuchs had the consolation of knowing that thousands of others survived because of the precedents they helped establish.

CHAPTER TEN

Extraordinary Schemes — A Plea to Bomb Auschwitz and a Ransomed Train

DURING THE LAST YEAR of the Holocaust several attempts were made to save the surviving Jews under Nazi occupation, particularly the last sizable group — Hungarian Jewry. These efforts included the work of Rabbi Michael Ber Weissmandel and his plea to bomb Auschwitz; the Joel Brand mission; the so-called Kastner train; and the Musy negotiations, (which will be the subject of a later chapter). The Sternbuchs played a significant role in all of these efforts.

BY THE MIDDLE OF 1944, Auschwitz was a name familiar to all who were concerned over the plight of the Jews in occupied Europe. During 1941 and 1942, the Sternbuchs had already come in contact with Auschwitz. As mentioned previously, they had a list of Jews imprisoned in Auschwitz to whom they sent food packages, for which they initially even received confirmations. During those years, Polish inmates were on occasion freed from Auschwitz and so the knowledge of the situation in the camp was sometimes available. When Auschwitz became an extermination camp in 1943, all communication with Auschwitz stopped. No one was ever set free, and no stranger — except for the German guards

The Auschwitz Protocols

or trusted Nazi personnel — ever entered its compound. The Nazis sealed the camp so tightly that no information whatsoever leaked out.

A breakthrough occurred in April 1944, when two daring young men from Slovakia, Alfred Wetzler and Rudolph Vrba, succeeded in escaping from Auschwitz. After a few days, they reached Rabbi Michael Ber Weissmandel, head of the Jewish rescue committee in Bratislava. Wetzler and Vrba, one of whom had known Rabbi Weissmandel since childhood, gave him and his associates, known as the Working Group, a full report of the horrors in Auschwitz — its gas chambers, crematoria and torture blocks where thousands upon thousands were dying daily.

Since 1942, Rabbi Weissmandel had been sending alarms to the Jewish leadership in the free world to save European Jewry. He was familiar with Auschwitz, but did not know that it had become the main death camp in all of Europe. Now he learned from Wetzler and Vrba that it had the capacity to exterminate well over 10,000 Jews a day! After the Working Group interrogated the two escapees, Rabbi Weissmandel managed to draw a map of Auschwitz and its facilities and environment.

Based on the report of these two escapees, he drew up a Hebrew version of what was known as the "Auschwitz Protocols" which he immediately sent off to Switzerland and Istanbul, in his own code, with the urgent request that it be transmitted to American Jewry, to the Jews in Palestine, to the international Jewish leadership, and to the world at large.

Change for the Worse in Hungary

RELEASE OF THIS detailed knowledge about Auschwitz coincided with another event that made the "Auschwitz Protocols" even more urgent. Just a few weeks earlier, on March 19, 1944, the Germans invaded Hungary and replaced the collaborationist Kallay regime with a new puppet government that enabled the Germans to rule Hungary by themselves. As could be expected, the annihilation of Hungarian Jewry was of the highest priority on their agenda. Within a few days the Nazis ordered most of the Jews all over Hungary into cramped ghettos, and by late April, they started transporting the Jews to Auschwitz. By the middle of May, transports of some 12,000 Jews were going to Auschwitz daily.

Rabbi Weissmandel, from his outpost in Bratislava, started alarming the Jewish world even more vigorously than before, urging them to take swift, decisive action. Although he believed in attempting to negotiate and bribe the Germans (he was quite successful in halting the deportation of Jews from Slovakia for more than two years), he knew that time was of the essence. He therefore devised a plan to appeal to the Allied powers to bomb the railway lines leading from Hungary to Auschwitz. In his coded messages he even pinpointed the exact location of the targets where the railroad could be successfully interrupted for a longer period of time ... Every day of delay would mean slowing down the machinery of death, saving 12,000 souls per day.

Bringing the Message to the Allied Powers

AS WOULD BE EXPECTED, the Sternbuchs tried, with the greatest sense of desperation, to bring the message to the Allied authorities. Although the records of the War Refugee Board in Washington identify the first cable to plead for the bombing as arriving on June 2, 1944, it was by far not the earliest. The first dated document, with Rabbi Weissmandel's plea, is dated May 16, 1944. One of the pleas was addressed to Nathan Schwalbe of the Swiss *Hechalutz* organization. We simply do not know what Schwalbe's response was to this momentous plea because his papers are still not open to historians. Most likely it was sent, along with ten other copies of the "Auschwitz Protocols" and the plea to bomb Auschwitz received by the Jewish Agency from different sources, to the *Moatza* (Committee) of the Vaad Hahatzalah — Rescue Committee of the Jewish Agency in Istanbul. We do know that Dr. Jacob Griffel had received the first communication from Rabbi Weissmandel with his plea (in code) in the regular mail from a post office in Bratislava, signed "Dr. Michelbeer." It was he who then promptly delivered the plea to the *Moatza* in Istanbul. But what the *Moatza* did is not known.

The Sternbuchs, however, did not work so slowly. On the very day that they received the plea — some time in May — they began working on it. Mr. Landau recalled that it was on a Friday. Since it was written in a strange code for which they had no key, they spent six hours deciphering Rabbi Weissmandel's message. He had noted particularly that if the two key bridges along the

Kosice-Presov rail lines were bombed, it would halt the deportations for at least six months, saving over 300,000 lives from certain death.

AS SOON AS THE MESSAGE was clear — it was already Sabbath — Mr. Sternbuch and Mr. Landau traveled to Bern and there together with Dr. Kuhl tried to alert the military attachés of the U.S., Great Britain and Russia to this plan to save lives. It was after office hours, but this did not stop them. For the opportunity to save lives, they had the audacity to visit these diplomats at their private residences. One of these diplomats, Sternbuch later told Landau, greeted these two anxious Jewish visitors in his shorts! Dr. Kuhl's diplomatic credentials no doubt eased the way for such "highly undiplomatic" meetings. Moreover, their unquestionable sincerity helped bring home the urgency of their important humanitarian plea. All three attachés promised to convey the contents of the Weissmandel cable to their respective governments.

Undiplomatic Desperation

The Sternbuchs were not content with their own interventions. While trying to personally influence the Allied representatives in Switzerland, they simultaneously sent urgent coded messages to the Union of Orthodox Rabbis in the U.S. and the president of the Agudath Israel World Organization, Jacob Rosenheim.

As we now know from many documents of the War Refugee Board and other U.S. government agencies, Mr. Rosenheim was the first to approach the U.S. government with this plan and he indefatigably badgered the authorities for months on end. By the end of June 1944, Chaim Weizmann, president of the World Zionist Organization, sent a similar request to the British Foreign Office. But the Allied response was one of delay, leading to ultimate disappointment.

A FEW WEEKS went by. The Sternbuchs continued to cable Washington, but all they heard from Washington was that Mr. Rosenheim and others were trying to move the U.S. government. After many weeks, the Americans responded verbally that the two bridges lay beyond their spheres of aerial activities. Now, however, we know that the Buna Rubber Works, five miles from Auschwitz and

Two Bridges from Life

Chapter 10: EXTRAORDINARY SCHEMES / 109

staffed by inmates from that camp, was bombed many times by the Allies, and the bridges could have been bombed with no appreciable change in flight patterns. The English responded with: "We conduct the war according to strategic, rather than humanitarian, considerations." (Quote by Landau)

But this Allied response was not the only disappointment the Sternbuchs suffered during these years. Many more were in store for them. Nonetheless they did not tire, and ultimately also achieved many successes. A case in point was their next effort to save the Hungarian Jews — the so-called Kastner train — which resulted in the rescue of close to 1700 Hungarian Jews.

The Kastner Train

SHORTLY AFTER the Nazis marched into Hungary on March 19, 1944, S.S. Major Dieter Wisliceny, Adolf Eichmann's assistant in carrying out the Final Solution, contacted two Jewish groups with letters of "recommendation" from the rescue activists group of Rabbi Weissmandel and Gisi Fleischmann. (Rabbi Weissmandel had halted the deportation of Slovakian Jews in the summer of 1942 by bribing Wisliceny. After this, Rabbi Weissmandel negotiated with him a plan to halt all deportations of Jews in Europe, a plan which the World Jewish leadership was reluctant to accept.) One group Wisliceny approached was the Zionist relief and rescue committee, called the *Vaadat Ha'ezrah Vehahatzalah*, or *Vaadah* for short, headed by Otto Komoly, chairman of the Zionist Organization of Hungary. The other was the Jewish Council of Budapest, whose leaders were Samuel Stern, head of the *Neolog*, or Reform community, and Philip Freudiger, the head of the Orthodox community.

The letter presented by Wisliceny to Freudiger was written in Hebrew by Rabbi Weissmandel. In it, he indicated that now it was the turn of Hungarian Jewry for the Final Solution, and he suggested that his earlier scheme, the "Europe Plan" — to rescue the remaining Jews under the Nazis for two million dollars — be proposed to Wisliceny. Freudiger along with others, such as Gyula Link, an Orthodox merchant, tried to negotiate this ransom of all Hungarian Jewry, and for a while, it seemed to offer some hope, but then it all came to nought, when the Nazis confiscated all Jewish bank accounts, turning most Hungarian Jews into paupers.

Rabbi Michael Ber Weissmandel

At the same time, negotiations with the Zionist group, conducted by Komoly's deputy, Dr. Rudolph Kastner, a bright journalist from Cluj, the representative of the Jewish Agency, and Joel Brand, his associate, seemed to carry greater weight with Eichmann. So the Freudiger group was eased out of the broader picture, although it continued to maintain steady contacts with Rabbi Weissmandel on one hand and the Sternbuchs on the other, to explore other possible rescue plans.

Wisliceny, who was Freudiger's contact, was sent to the provinces to implement the ghettoization programs as a first step to deport Hungarian Jews to Auschwitz. At this stage Kastner and Brand took over as the sole negotiators for the fate of Hungarian Jewry, but they never took the trouble to confer with any non-Zionist leaders or even to keep them informed. The first stage of their negotiations yielded a concrete proposal; the S.S. would allow the *aliyah* (immigration) of 650 holders of Palestine Certificates for a large sum of money. The quota was then increased to 750.

THESE NEGOTIATIONS, however, soon assumed a broader scope, and developed into what became known as the Brand Mission. On

Blood for Money, Money for Blood

April 25, Eichmann called in Brand to send him on a mission to the Jewish leaders in Jerusalem to negotiate for the lives of one million Jews in exchange for ten thousand trucks and some vitally needed goods. (The meeting and the conditions were described by Brand in his memoirs, entitled *Desperate Mission*.) After Brand was led to the Eichmann headquarters at the Majestic Hotel he was told the following:

> I expect you know who I am. I was in charge of the actions' [i.e. deportations] in Germany, Poland and Czechoslovakia. Now it is Hungary's turn. I have got you here so that we could talk business. I have already investigated you and your people of the Joint and the *Sochnut* [Jewish Agency] and I have verified your ability to make a deal. Now then, I am prepared to sell you one million Jews ... Blood for money; money for blood. You can take them from any country you like, wherever you can find them ... I can let a million Jews go. We want goods, however, not money ... I'm going to Berlin day after tomorrow, and I'll discuss the matter again with our leaders [i.e., Himmler].

After a second meeting on May 8, following Eichmann's return from Berlin, Brand got very specific guarantees from Eichmann:

> If you return from Constantinople and tell me that the offer has been accepted, I will close Oswiecim and bring ten percent of the promised million to the frontier. You can take one hundred thousand Jews away, and afterward bring me one thousand trucks ... A thousand trucks for one hundred thousand Jews. You can't ask for anything more reasonable than that ...

Brand went to Istanbul (Constantinople) with letters of recommendation from the Jewish Council of Budapest, the Zionist *Vaadah*, the Zionist youth movement *Hechalutz*, and from Rabbi Weissmandel. But he failed. The reason why Joel Brand failed to return to Budapest is debated by many historians. Some say that it was the British who refused any deal. Others contend that it was the negligence of the Zionist leadership and even worse, their active sabotage, that thwarted his mission. All we know for sure is that Brand was arrested by the British and detained for over four months in Cairo before being permitted to go to Jerusalem in

The Satmar Rebbe

Rabbi Yonasan Steif

October, when he could do no more.

WHILE NO NEWS seemed to be forthcoming from Istanbul, Kastner in the interim kept up the original negotiations with Gestapo agent Krumey, whereby the 750 Zionists would be permitted to leave via train for a neutral country such as Spain or Allied territory, as long as it was not Palestine. (It seems that Hitler had promised the Grand Mufti, Amin el Husseini, his Arab collaborator from Jerusalem, not to send any Jews to Palestine, and the Gestapo agents in Budapest were reluctant to violate this promise.)

Train of Uncertain Destination

In addition to the Zionists who were selected according to lists of the different Zionist parties, such as Poalei Zion, *Hechalutz*, Mizrachi, Revisionists, and so on, there were special groups that could be added, including several hundred of Kastner's friends and relatives, and prominent Jews from his hometown of Cluj. In addition there were seats sold to wealthy Jews and converts who had managed to hide their jewels and valuables and now brought them forth. Freudiger, with the help of Link, also bribed Wisliceny to allow eighty prominent Jews to join this transport. This last group was mostly Orthodox, and included the rabbis of Satmar and Debrecin, and Rabbi Yonasan Steif. Very soon the train of 750 became 1200, and with several authorized and unauthorized additions, including 450 Jews from a nearby labor camp who climbed aboard, the human cargo added up to a total of 1,684 Jewish lives. Incidentally, at the same time, for the sum of over a million U.S. dollars in Hungarian pengos, Eichmann approved the transfer of 30,000 Jews to Austria (of which only 18,000-20,000 were sent) to be "kept on ice" as possible tradeoffs at a later date.

THE ONLY CATCH to the departure of this train from Budapest was the Nazis' unwillingness to continue the negotiations until they received some positive response to their more ambitious deal. Kurt Becher, the Gestapo agent in charge of "legally" confiscating the wealth of Hungarian Jewry, demanded more than the $2 million paid for by Budapest Jews. Again, it was the Orthodox Weissmandel-Freudiger-Sternbuch connection that enabled this train to leave safely. Rabbi Weissmandel, who had desperately sought any way to keep the negotiations going, utilized his pseudonym "Ferdinand Roth" as a ploy to fool the Nazis. With a cable on stationery sent from Switzerland signed by that name, he notified Wisliceny, Eichmann's assistant, through Freudiger, that 250 trucks were available for him in Switzerland. Freudiger passed on this plan to Sternbuch requesting 750,000 Swiss francs to pay for at least 40 trucks (or tractors) immediately so that the train could continue from Budapest to Spain. Sternbuch cabled back that he only had 150,000 Swiss francs at hand and he asked Saly Mayer to provide the balance from Joint funds. Mayer, true to his convictions of not dealing in ransom, refused. He informed the War Refugee Board representative Mr. McClelland about this, and quickly put a stop to the deal. Further, since Mayer was under the mistaken notion that the transport consisted of all rabbis, he noted that "rabbis are like captains; they have no right to save themselves." This made Eichmann send the train to a special section of Bergen-Belsen where they were "put on ice" for further negotiations.

Jew on Ice

It is hard to know what would have happened to these people if the Sternbuchs had not stepped in to save them. In desperation, Yitzchok Sternbuch used whatever money he had, and placed a deposit for a letter of credit for 10 tractors. While it came too late to divert the whole train, at least it enabled 318 of the 1,684 to be taken out of Bergen-Belsen to Switzerland in August, about six weeks later. At the same time, Rabbi Weissmandel's offer of trucks through the Sternbuchs was the key to continuation of negotiations which later enabled the rest of the 1,684 to leave Bergen-Belsen for Switzerland. In fact, this scheme eventually saved about 18,000 Jews whom Eichmann "stored" in Austria. As U.S. Ambassador Harrison wrote to the State Department on August 21, 1944:

> ... the affair of the 40 tractors which Sternbuch brought to our attention ... was part of the deal which [Gyula] Link with Freudiger of the Orthodox group at Budapest negotiated and relayed to Sternbuch ...

This, in turn, bore other favorable results, as the Ambassador continued:

> On the basis of these offers, the Gestapo in Budapest refrained from sending to Auschwitz ... the following groups totalling 17,290 souls.

These included:

> 1,690 [actually 1,684] ... sent later to the camp of Bergen-Belsen, ... approximately 15,000 [actually 18,000] ... sent to an unknown destination in Austria to be kept "on ice," ... and 600 persons [that] are still confined in Budapest.

CHAPTER ELEVEN
The Kuhl-Sternbuch Mission — to France and Belgium

Saving the Survivors

IN THE AUTUMN OF 1944, while the war was still raging, and Recha and Yitzchok Sternbuch were deeply involved in all sorts of rescue plans, they simultaneously took a deep interest in the rehabilitation and well-being of those Jews who had the good fortune to survive the Holocaust.

The successful Allied invasion of the European mainland, which was launched on June 6, 1944, brought about the swift liberation of large parts of France and Belgium and the Sternbuchs immediately turned their attention to the needs and problems of the liberated Jews in these two countries. Their correspondence bears vivid testimony to this activity.

Among the various coded messages that the Sternbuchs sent to the leaders of the American Vaad Hatzalah through the Polish Embassy in Bern, we find the following communication, dated October 14, 1944, only two months after Belgium and most of France were liberated from the Germans.

> We are making an effort to send Dr. Julius Kuhl, the head of the refugee division of the Polish Embassy in Switzerland, to France and Belgium for a short time, to become better acquainted with the situation; Dr. Kuhl's task will also be to find out how many Jews were deported and to where they were

sent. We have the support for such a visit from the Polish Ambassador, Mr. Lados. Dr. Kuhl is especially suited for this task since he possesses a diplomat-service passport and it would be easier for him to obtain the necessary visas. The Polish Ambassador trusts him and he has accomplished much for our work. He will be accompanied by Mr. Eli Sternbuch and their mission is of special value since we were just informed that some of the internees of Vittel were transferred to Lewen (Belgium) by the Germans. The possibilities of contacts with Belgium are limited. Hence, Dr. Kuhl's trip can be of great significance.

DR. KUHL'S TRIP to France and Belgium, which he undertook only a few days later, was fraught with overwhelming difficulties.

Dangers and Disappointments Although the parts of France and Belgium that he was to visit were already liberated from the German Army, the roads still posed a host of dangers. There were rumors that scattered in the forests, small armed bands of the decimated German Army were still operating. The train connections between Switzerland and France were not functioning yet. Also, there were almost no hotels available in France and Belgium. Food was in short supply, and there was almost no kosher food to be found. Because the war was still in full operation, most French cities were partly under a martial curfew and the war-time blackout was still in force. The German Air Force was not yet completely eliminated, and the roads in France and Belgium, crowded with transports of the invading Allied armies, were in constant danger of being bombarded by the Luftwaffe. Yet, all of these difficulties and dangers did not deter Dr. Kuhl or Mr. Eli Sternbuch (brother of Yitzchok Sternbuch who worked with the Sternbuchs on all aspects of rescue and relief projects) from undertaking this mission. Eli Sternbuch did not possess a passport from an Allied government, only the one from Switzerland, a neutral country, and could therefore be suspected of being a spy at many Allied checkpoints. Under the circumstances, Eli Sternbuch's joining Dr. Kuhl was certainly a most daring and courageous act.

Dr. Kuhl's and Eli Sternbuch's trip did not meet all of the expectations of the Sternbuchs. In some respects, the trip was a disappointment. They had hoped that Dr. Kuhl would find alive the Jews with foreign passports, whom the Germans had previously kept in a special detention camp at Vittel. On his very first stop in Aix-Les-Bains, Dr. Kuhl was informed that most of the Jews previously detained in Vittel as foreign citizens had been deported to Auschwitz. Despite all the diplomatic efforts by the Sternbuchs (described in Chapter 9), the S.S. refused to recognize most of these passports.

The mission was laced with personal disappointments for Dr. Kuhl as well. Among others, Dr. Kuhl was searching for the mother of the world-renowned Polish Jewish artist, Bronislaw Huberman. Just a few months before the liberation of France, Huberman — who lived in Switzerland — heard that his mother was alive in a concentration camp at Gurs, and he begged Dr. Kuhl to visit her. On his arrival in Gurs, Kuhl found out that the Germans deported the inmates to Auschwitz prior to their retreat. From the litter on the floor of the camp, Dr. Kuhl picked up a list of those Jews who were sent from Gurs to the Auschwitz extermination camp before the arrival of the Allied liberation troops. The list included the name of his friend's mother.

YET OTHER ASPECTS of the trip can surely be considered as successful and significant for the liberated Jews. This was the first mission of a Jewish aid organization in the liberated countries for the purpose of becoming acquainted at first hand with the situation of the survivors, their needs and problems.

The Positive Aspects: "They Know We're Here!"

After his return to the Polish Embassy, Dr. Kuhl submitted a report of nearly thirty pages to HIJEFS and to Saly Mayer, the leader of the Joint in Europe which recorded his visits to Aix-Les-Bains, Grenoble, Nice, Marseilles, Montpelierre, Ferfigan, Toulouse, Limoges, Aredat, Paris, Brussels and Antwerp. Dr. Kuhl and Eli Sternbuch also visited the sites of a number of former German concentration camps. The Germans had planned to take the inmates of the camps along with them, and only the rapid march of the Allied invasion army saved these Jews from certain death.

All of the cities and camps that Dr. Kuhl and Eli Sternbuch visited were populated with many survivors from all parts of Europe. Almost all of them were in dire need of help, although

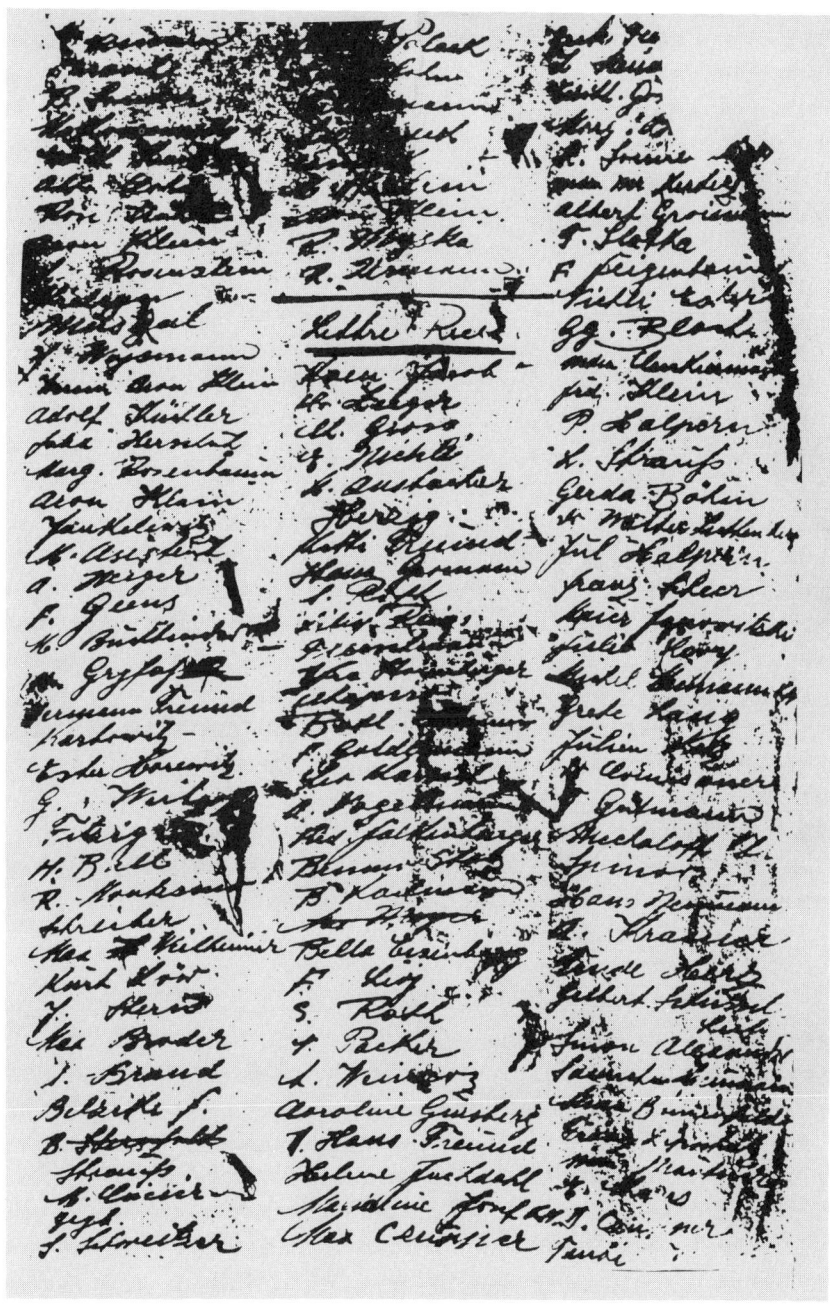

A list of camp inmates who were deported by the Germans to Auschwitz. Dr. Julius Kuhl found this list on the site of a German internment camp for foreign citizens in Gurs, France, after the Germans retreated from France

Chapter 11: THE KUHL-STERNBUCH MISSION

some of the communities had already managed to some degree to organize for self-help.

The mere appearance of Dr. Kuhl and Eli Sternbuch on the scene greatly encouraged the local Jewish leaders. Until then, these leaders, overwhelmed with so many problems, were not successful in establishing contact with overseas Jewish aid organizations. Simply the fact that a delegation of Jews from free countries came to them with the intent of gaining first-hand knowledge of their situation, boosted their morale and was a source of courage to continue their own work of organizing their Jewish communal life anew. Their long isolation was finally coming to an end; there were actually people "out there" who recognized their agony in living in the Valley of Death, people who would make it their business to help relieve their anguish and suffering.

The Kuhl-Sternbuch visits especially encouraged the few surviving rabbis and religious leaders who were struggling to renew the religious life of the survivors. These leaders had many difficulties to contend with, including opposition from other Jews, especially those who had fallen under the Communist influence during the war years. The leftist Jews, having gained prominence by participating in the revered resistance movements, attempted to dominate newly-established Jewish communal life after the liberation. They had no interest, however, in the resurgence of a national-religious Jewish life within the Jewish community. In fact, they did their best to obstruct any efforts for the revival of religious Judaism. Dr. Kuhl and Mr. Sternbuch strengthened the hand of the battlers for religion.

IN ADDITION TO BOOSTING the morale of the Jewish leaders and creating contacts between the survivors and HIJEFS and other aid organizations of the free world, the Kuhl-Sternbuch mission can also be credited with many practical achievements on the spot for both community leaders and individual survivors.

Establishing Equality

In the first place, Dr. Kuhl's mission succeeded in alleviating the poverty and deprivation that marked the daily lives of the survivors in France and Belgium. Anti-Semitism is a highly contagious disease, and as a result some of the new authorities and civil servants, even if not personally anti-Semitic, had become accustomed during the Nazi occupation to treating Jews as second class citizens at the very best. It was therefore extremely important to impress upon them that, following the Nazi defeat, they not only had the obligation to restore their Jewish neighbors to full citizenship, but they also had a moral duty to give more consideration, as compensation, to the Jews who had suffered so much durng the war.

Dr. Kuhl and Mr. Sternbuch conveyed this message in their many visits with the mayors, police chiefs and leading civil servants in a number of cities in France and Belgium. The intervention of Dr. Kuhl, who possessed a diplomatic service passport, carried significant weight with those in authority.

Dr. Kuhl's visas to visit different parts of France and Belgium

Mr. Eli Sternbuch with Rabbi Shmuel Yaakov Rubinstein in Paris

Finding the Children

FURTHERMORE, DR. KUHL and Eli Sternbuch assembled invaluable information regarding the whereabouts of many Jewish children who were saved from the Germans by being hidden in gentile homes, monasteries and other church institutions. As will be shown later, the spiritual rescue and the transfer of these children to their parents or to Jewish homes became one of the most important activities of the Sternbuchs for several years.

Of no less importance, was their personally visiting these children's institutions. They met with their leaders, among them church dignitaries, expressing the deep interest of the Jews around the world in the welfare of the orphaned survivors. Dr. Kuhl was armed with a warm letter of recommendation from Nuncio Bernardini. His arguments backed with his credentials had great influence on some of the Christian leaders. The more decent members of the clergy were made aware by these visits that the Jewish war orphans or children in Christian homes were not abandoned by world Jewry and that the churches should not consider them as their own charges. These children still belonged to the Jewish people.

Polish Homecoming

IN HIS VISITS WITH THE THOUSANDS of Polish Jewish survivors in France and Belgium, Dr. Kuhl accomplished a great deal towards fulfilling some of their immediate as well as long-term needs. At every stop, Dr. Kuhl met with the local representatives of the Polish government-in-exile and persuaded them to give more consideration to the needs of the Polish Jews in France and Belgium. His standing as a staff member of the Polish Embassy in Bern carried great weight with these functionaries.

During his trip, Dr. Kuhl took great interest in opening up opportunities for many Polish Jews in Switzerland who had fled from Belgium and France to be able to return to their previous homes. Most of these refugees had no permanent residence or legal employment privileges in Switzerland and lived off charity. Some of them were still in refugee camps. For all of them, returning home was a primary goal.

Dr. Kuhl and Eli Sternbuch returned to Switzerland with lists of Jews who had survived, Jews who had been deported, and Jews who had perished. These lists aided the relief organizations as well as many thousands of individuals in the free world, who for years had been eager to learn of the fate of their closest relatives under the brutal Nazi regime. They also gathered important documents on the Nazi atrocities in France and Belgium, which they delivered to the Jewish organizations and to the legations of Allied countries in Switzerland.

Of vital importance, Dr. Kuhl's visit paved the way for the later activities of the Sternbuchs in France which evolved into a great relief center for survivors of many countries. On their visit to Aix-Les-Bains they found a small institution of Jewish children headed by Rabbi Moshe Lebel. Later, as we will see, the Sternbuchs converted this institution into the first yeshiva in postwar Europe and into a rescue center for surviving Jewish children. Thus, many of the most notable achievements of the Kuhl-Sternbuch mission paved the way for further accomplishments of the highest significance.

CHAPTER TWELVE
Triumph and Disappointment in Rescue
— The Musy Mission

THE MOST IMPORTANT of the Sternbuchs' rescue efforts in the last year of the war has come to be known as the Musy Mission, as it involved the former president of Switzerland, Dr. Jean-Marie Musy, in negotiations with S.S. Chief Heinrich Himmler. The goal was no less than the release of all of the remaining 300,000-800,000 Jews under Nazi control. The mission stretched over 8 months and can be considered both the Sternbuchs' greatest triumph as well as their greatest disappointment.

IT ALL BEGAN IN THE FALL of 1944 when the War was winding down. Although many Jews had been saved through the timely **Eight Months** help of the Sternbuchs and others, the **of Frustration** annihilation continued. Recha Sternbuch was keenly aware that hundreds of thousands of Jews were still under Hitler's thumb and were facing death by gas or starvation. She could not rest. Moreover, the successful conclusion of the Kastner train deal proved to her that there were definitely similar ways to save the remaining Jews. The Musy Mission was one such ray of renewed hope.

The mission, which lasted for roughly the last eight months of the War, began in September 1944. It started when Recha Sternbuch was desperately searching for the Jews deported from Vittel. She discovered through a Catholic friend (whom she met through Monsignor Bernardini) that for 10,000 francs and through connections with high-echelon Nazis, Dr. Musy had been able to free a Jewish couple from a concentration camp. It was well-known that Dr. Musy, the arch-conservative publisher of the pro-Nazi newspaper *La Jeune*, had a long-standing personal friendship with Himmler. In their typically unpredictable fashion, the Sternbuchs took note of this information to consider Musy a prime candidate to help them. The Sternbuchs, who followed the traditional Torah attitude towards the rescue of Jewish lives, were always willing, and indeed they felt obligated, to deal with anyone in order to save lives. Therefore, Musy's pro-Nazi sympathies were quite irrelevant. For secular Jews, such considerations made a crucial and tragic difference.

THROUGH HER FRIEND Mrs. Bolomey, Recha Sternbuch set up a meeting with Dr. Musy. Initially she only hoped that he would travel to Berlin to locate and then secure the release of the Vittel inmates — who included much of her family. After several meetings with Dr. Musy at Friburg, however, the Sternbuchs began to consider what was previously unthinkable — that they might be able, through Musy, to effect the release of *all* the Jews still in Nazi hands. Dr. Musy sent a letter to Himmler, and an affirmative response came through the German Legation, inviting him to Berlin.

Considering the Unthinkable

It must have been a remarkable sight in October 1944, with the Allies regularly bombing German cities, and the War closing in on both fronts to see the 75-year-old dean of Swiss politics, a fascist and Nazi-sympathizer, being driven to Berlin, with his son Benoit, a Swiss Air Force officer, at the wheel of the new Mercedes bought for them by the Sternbuchs. A large red cross was painted on the rooftop of the car, in the hope of preventing Allied Air Force strafing. With the promise of 60,000 francs — to be followed by more — for expenses and bribes, Dr. Musy was set for the first leg of what would become a journey of 30,000 kilometers. His mission was certainly ambitious: the release of more than three-hundred thousand Jews from Nazi concentration camps.

Chapter 12: TRIUMPH AND DISAPPOINTMENT / 125

Himmler: Eager to Negotiate

IT BEGAN WELL. Right after his first meeting with Himmler, and with General Walter Schellenberg, head of the united S.S. and military intelligence, Himmler's closest associate, Musy was able to reduce the original ransom demands from 20 million Swiss francs ($5 million) in various goods (notably trucks) to a more manageable 5 million francs ($1 million). The main incentives for the German negotiators were not money and goods, however, but the so-called "good will" and "political" benefits for Germany. Although Musy had to indicate to Himmler that he and he alone had access to and control of the $1 million — this accomplished through a statement from a bank where he was a trustee — all the parties seemed to realize that good will was Himmler's main objective. Himmler's desire for "good will" posed no problem for the Sternbuchs. The Germans were obviously losing the war, and no amount of good will would help them reverse the military tide. For the cause of saving several hundred thousand Jews, the Sternbuchs were quite willing to let Himmler and Schellenberg play the role of humanitarians who saved Jews.

Saly Mayer, however, was of a totally different mind. After ousting the Weissmandel-Freundiger-Sternbuch group from the negotiations, Saly Mayer, together with Rudolph Kastner, continued to deal with two of Himmler's other associates, Colonel Kurt Becher and General Ernst Kaltenbrunner.

While responsible for bringing the second part of the Bergen-Belsen train to Switzerland, the further Mayer-Kastner negotiations with the Germans were doomed to failure because of their shortsighted approach. Mayer had no intentions of giving the Nazis anything — money, goods, or "good will." He had hoped only to stall for time with vague promises, convinced that the war would come to an early end. In addition, he was still committed to keep from bringing more Jews to Switzerland out of fear of anti-Semitism. As a result, Mayer never requested the release of the Jews, but preferred to keep them in German concentration camps under the supervision of the International Red Cross.

When Musy returned from Berlin with the good news that Himmler was interested, indeed eager, to negotiate — Yitzchok Sternbuch used the Polish diplomatic cable service to send a message to the Vaad Hatzalah in New York, stating in part that Himmler would release 300,000 Jews at the rate of 15,000 persons a

In 1944 the arch-butcher Heinrich Himmler was ready for a deal to free the Jews. Recha Sternbuch tried it and partially succeeded.

month for appropriate amounts of cash to be deposited in Swiss bank accounts. "In principle," Yitzchok Sternbuch wrote, "we have accepted this proposition."

YET, AFTER ALL THIS TIME, the Sternbuchs knew very well the feelings of other Jewish leaders toward ransom, and so Yitzchok Sternbuch added a plea to his report: "We beg you," he implored, "not to demand of us any collaboration with the Joint ... the antireligious attitude and seeming patriotism of [Saly Mayer] the Swiss representative of the Joint is a hindrance for any collaboration with him. The Swiss and American authorities favor him because he rarely troubles these officials." As a reminder,

Who Will Put Up the Ransom

Sternbuch also cited the previous "collaboration with the Joint" in the "tractor deal" — "the result of which," he added, "was catastrophic."

All Yitzchok Sternbuch's fervent pleas notwithstanding, the Vaad Hatzalah did not comply with this request because they couldn't. Simply, the Vaad Hatzalah was financially powerless, and couldn't raise $1 million on the spur of the moment to meet Himmler's demands. Yet they were not going to let such an opportunity pass, so they applied pressure on both ends: on the Joint to lend them the money, and on the Sternbuchs to share their plans with Saly Mayer. The results in Switzerland were sadly predictable: Mayer refused to coordinate rescue efforts with the Sternbuchs, refused to grant the Nazis "good will," refused in fact to consider the ransom plan at all. Undaunted, Yitzchok Sternbuch went over Mayer's head — to the otherwise sympathetic Dr. Joseph Schwartz, European head of the Joint — hoping that he would supercede Mayer to cooperate. Schwartz also declined the offer.

Nevertheless, the Sternbuchs still tried to coordinate efforts. They met in late December with Mayer ally and Jewish Agency representative Rudolph Kastner and presented their plan but Kastner refused. They offered him the use of the Polish diplomatic code so that he could bypass Mayer and the War Refugee Board; he still refused. Literally in tears, they pleaded with him for hours to drop Mayer. Again Kastner refused. As a last bargaining chip, a Sternbuch representative said that the entire Musy mass-rescue operation could continue under the aegis of the Joint — as long as it went ahead. This, too, failed to move Kastner. But the real tragedy was two-fold; Mayer and Kastner not only did not want to cooperate in rescue efforts, they went to all lengths to undermine the efforts of the Sternbuchs, as will be shown.

ALTHOUGH THE STERNBUCHS seemed hamstrung by the refusal of the Joint and others, the Musy negotiations went ahead — and achieved some results. In his conversations, Himmler, among others, promised to stop further mass killings of Jews in the concentration camps, and in early January, 1945, after Musy's second trip to see Himmler, Himmler played his first card. Realizing that he could gain nothing from the futile talks with Mayer, Himmler decided to deal seriously with Musy. As a sign of good faith, Himmler would

Himmler's First Move

send a trainload of roughly 1,200 Jews from the Theresienstadt concentration camp to freedom in Switzerland. Indeed, on February 7, 1945, he did so.

There was a price, of course — one involving Himmler's clearly-conceived public relations campaign for a better postwar image of Germany. To begin with, the Swiss had to agree to accept the 1,200 refugees, and the United States had to support and eventually relocate them, and the $1 million had to be established as a guarantee for Reichsfuhrer Himmler that Musy — and the "rabbi Jews," as he called the Sternbuchs — were indeed serious. Most important, though, was that Germany's image in the press — seriously affected by the earlier published "Auschwitz Protocol" be mitigated. To this end, for example, Recha and Yitzchok Sternbuch told the Vaad Hatzalah in early February, 1945 (again via the secret Polish cable,) that "it is imperative ... following the release of the first train, that five or six major American newspapers declare that in this respect Germany was very favorably inclined." The Sternbuchs included specific directions — copies of the newspapers by courier, names and summaries by cable for Musy's presentation to Himmler. "Should you fail," Sternbuch added ominously, "then don't expect another train." Through a great deal of effort by the Vaad and Agudath Israel, and the cooperation of Yiddish journalists and the sympathy of some major American newspapers such as the New York City *Times*, *Sun*, and *Herald Tribune*, this too was successful.

Good Press for the Nazis

WHEN THE WORD CAME from Dr. Musy that the train would soon arrive from Theresienstadt, Sternbuch-aide Dr. Reuven Hecht conferred with Swiss President von Steiger to formulate an official Swiss communiqué in reference to the arriving refugees. This was a relatively easy task given the War Refugee Board's prior agreement to support the newly-released Jews, yet a highly important one considering Himmler's great concern for Swiss acceptance and American attitudes. Then, as soon as the train arrived, Dr. Hecht personally embarked upon a ten day tour of all major Swiss newspapers, and the foreign press, to convince the world that "all is well." The ultimate irony was that the very people who had worked so strenuously to paint an accurate picture of the Nazis and their atrocities now sought to convince scores of reporters and editors that the Germans were performing a worthwhile action to abate — at least in part — the ongoing annihilation of Europe's Jews. The press, in fact, was prepared for Hecht's visit, due to the Sternbuchs' timely mailing of information sheets on the Musy mission and the Theresienstadt train. Indeed, the vast majority of the editors and reporters contacted by Hecht were favorably impressed, with both the efficiency of the operation as well as with the condition of the prisoners. It also did not hurt matters any that the ransom terms, an anathema to most, were not touched upon. As a last bit of optimism, the Sternbuch information packet claimed that future releases of Jews were expected. The strategy worked — and worked so well, in fact, that Hecht had to hire a clipping service to keep track of the volume of favorable notices.

BUT ALL WAS NOT WELL. Although President von Steiger warmly welcomed the trainload of Jews to Switzerland, the prospect now existed that the Nazis might free 800,000 Jews, and he voiced the long-standing Swiss fear that the country would be flooded with refugees. Von Steiger's concern prompted the Sternbuchs to send a cable to New York on February 16, 1945, asking Vaad Hatzalah to use its influence in securing American approval to periodically move Jewish refugees in Switzerland to countries such as Portugal or Spain — a move that would enhance Swiss willingness to permit the expected future (and larger) transports. In all, the Sternbuchs were optimistic about the proposed weekly transports of Jews. Indeed, arrangements had already been made for a HIJEFS representative (in all likelihood Recha Sternbuch herself) to meet with French officials concerning transit through France. "It appears," Yitzchok Sternbuch cabled New York on February 18, "that a change in Germany's treatment of the Jews is in the makings after all." The Swiss, too, had everything to gain from cooperating; one substantial dividend would certainly be the softening of their somewhat harsh image, engendered by the previous *refoulement* policy, which eventually resulted in an official investigation of its wartime policy.

THE STERNBUCHS' OPTIMISM, however, was short-lived. The

Swiss Fears: Flooded with Jews?

Short-lived Optimism

separate Kastner-Mayer negotiations caused problems for the continuing Musy negotiations — in part, because confidants like Colonel Kurt Becher tried to convince Himmler that the Joint was far more powerful than the Union of Orthodox Rabbis, the supporters of the Vaad Hatzalah and the Sternbuchs. Some well-coordinated and vicious attacks on Himmler in the Swiss socialist press hindered matters further. Worse, the general Swiss Jewish community was often intractable. For example, when Yitzchok Sternbuch pleaded with the editor of the *Israelitisches Wochenblatt*, a leading Jewish newspaper, to tone down his heavy criticism of Germany, the entreaties were ignored. One excuse given to Sternbuch was that the articles were already set in type and that it would involve great expense to change them. When the Sternbuchs offered to cover any extra expense the newspaper might suffer, they were flatly turned down. Only after the first trainload of Jews actually arrived in Switzerland did the paper change its stance.

Similarly, Roswell McClelland of the War Refugee Board, who would not consider ransom at all, was dubious both of Musy and the negotiations. You will remember that McClelland was staunchly against any form of ransom. The Sternbuchs had informed him that Musy would need a considerable sum of money to cover various expenses. Sternbuch did not want anyone to know that the money would really be used for necessary bribes. Yitzchok Sternbuch also pointed out to the Vaad Hatzalah, that McClelland simply did not like the Sternbuchs or their tactics. It hardly came as a surprise, then, that at a key juncture, McClelland recommended that the War Refugee Board *not* participate in a joint $1 million bank account with Musy — even though Musy had just engineered the release of the 1,200 Theresienstadt Jews, and that future releases seemed at hand. Besides, McClelland, a Quaker relief worker tapped by Franklin Roosevelt to be the WRB representative in Switzerland, simply favored Mayer's plan to keep the Jews interned under International Red Cross supervision and therefore preferred to wait for the end of the War — then but a few months away. In all, that was a much easier tactic than bringing hundreds of thousands of refugees into crowded Switzerland.

TWO THINGS MADE MATTERS even worse. First was the absolute necessity that the Sternbuchs work through McClelland —

The Insurmountable Obstacles

because American guarantees were an essential part of the plan, both for the Swiss as well as for Himmler. Second was the inability of Vaad Hatzalah in New York to raise the $1 million on its own to transfer it secretly via Swiss depositers. If the $1 million — Himmler's requisite "hand money" — were to be raised at all, it would have to come from the Joint with the permission of the American government, which was inalterably opposed to ransom efforts of any kind. So while the early stages of the Musy mission were handled independently by Musy and the Sternbuchs, this independence ceased after the arrival of the February transport from Theresienstadt. From that time on, virtually all phases of the mission had to pass through Roswell McClelland.

By the time Musy made a third trip to Germany on February 19 to negotiate further transports, events in Switzerland seemed almost out of control. Wild rumors circulated everywhere — rumors which (given Nazi nervousness) threatened further success. Some said that the Sternbuchs paid 1,000 francs per refugee; others said that Switzerland obligated itself to accept Nazis for postwar asylum — one for every Jew released. Ransom talk was all the rage in Swiss cafés, and the Socialist press particularly proved as difficult as ever. Overall, the favorable effect of the press notices which the Musy mission had created just weeks before was now disappearing — and with it was disappearing the Nazi belief in the Sternbuchs' ability to create the favorable image which they desperately sought.

On the other side of the Atlantic, things were also faring none too well. Vaad Hatzalah representatives Rabbi Aaron Kotler and Irving Bunim came before the Joint to ask for the necessary one million-dollar loan to free the remaining Jews in the camps, and came away empty-handed until they put pressure on the Joint with the help of a few big Orthodox donors. Then, of course, the money had to be declared and channelled via the restrictions of the WRB and McClelland. Events continued to work against the Sternbuchs' efforts. When, for example, the Vaad Hatzalah called upon the Sternbuchs to send a representative to plead their case before the Joint, they agreed on Reuven Hecht, and later both Hecht and Recha Sternbuch. Hecht, however, was unable to obtain the necessary visas, and the trip was cancelled. The press did not help matters either. The Socialist-Zionist PALCOR News Agency in Switzerland, under the influence of Mayer's friend Nathan Schwalbe, brought up the ransom issue, and also indicted the Sternbuchs for using Musy, a known fascist, as their negotiator. Yitzchok Sternbuch's response was the transmission of urgent cables to Jewish allies in New York, London, and Istanbul, asking for assistance in curbing the harmful PALCOR reports. Sternbuch eventually got the help he requested, but by then it was too late.

IN MANY WAYS, then, Dr. Musy's third trip to Berlin was doomed from the outset — and perhaps Recha Sternbuch knew it, for she

The Third Trip: Doomed from the Outset
volunteered to accompany him, despite the fact that she was Jewish, despite the repeated Allied bombings, which at one point had overturned Musy's car. Her husband forbade the trip, citing her safety, and for once Recha

Translation of the above hand-written note of former Swiss Federal Councilor Jean-Marie Musy, sent from Kreuzlingen, March 6, 1945: "To the European Executive Council of the Union of Orthodox Rabbis of the U.S.A. and Canada, Montreux ... Last week I was told in Berlin: 'You may thank Mr. Saly Mayer, that no convoy of Jews of German camps reached Switzerland.' Kreuzlingen, March 6.
J.M. MUSY.

Chapter 12: TRIUMPH AND DISAPPOINTMENT / *133*

Sternbuch agreed that a mission was indeed too dangerous. Although the Germans had already prepared a second transport of roughly 2,000 Jews — another 1,200 from Theresienstadt plus 800 more from Bergen-Belsen — a long-standing yet unforeseen obstacle had sprung up to prevent its success: Saly Mayer. On March 3, 1945, Yitzchok Sternbuch, again via the Polish diplomatic cable, flatly told the Vaad Hatzalah in New York that "S. Mayer through his agents in Berlin undertook steps to make impossible bringing over of refugees." Instead, Sternbuch wrote, "he strives to keep the Jews alive, but he doesn't care to take them out of Germany." Other factors, in Germany, also worked against Musy's success.

According to a testimony by General Schellenberg, Himmler's adjudant who was with him at the Musy negotiations, General Kaltenbrunner was jealous of Musy's success and wanted to sabotage the talks. Kaltenbrunner presented Hitler with a collection of "critical" articles from the Swiss socialist press about the Himmler-Musy negotiations and especially the nasty rumors that the deal involved Swiss asylum for 250 Nazis. The enraged Hitler then ordered that "not a single Jew should be allowed to leave Germany."

Last Attempts at Saving Survivors

DESPITE THE TRAGIC OUTCOME of the Musy negotiations for releasing all the incarcerated Jews from the camps — due to the obstructions of Mayer, Kastner, Becher, and Kaltenbrunner — the Sternbuchs together with Musy and his son Benoit kept up their unceasing efforts to retrieve as many lives as possible in those last hellish weeks of the Holocaust.

Of major concern was the need to assure the safe transfer of the concentration camps to the Allies. In the next chapter we describe how in October 1944, the Vaad Hatzalah learned of the Nazi plans to exterminate every last Jew, and how General Eisenhower's warning that followed had some effect on many Nazi officers. Some elements among the Gestapo, however, especially General Ernst Kaltenbrunner (chief of the Reich Security Main Office), who followed Hitler's diabolic line of exterminating the Jews as priority number one, as well as some vicious camp commandants, were eager to ignore Himmler's orders on behalf of the Jews. The prisoners themselves recall rumors of the camps being surrounded by flame-throwers, ready to destroy every last vestige of life and evidence of Nazi brutality.

Benoit Musy made several more trips into Berlin — almost

Musy train arrival in Montreux, Switzerland in February 1945. Herman Landau (top right) greets concentration camp inmates released from Theresienstadt

until the last days of the bitter fighting when the Russians were at the outskirts of Berlin — to negotiate the last concessions from Himmler via General Schellenberg. He also traveled to several of the camps, including Theresienstadt, Ravensbrück, Matthausen and Buchenwald, to assure last-minute cooperation. On a trip to Berlin on April 8, 1945, both the elder and younger Musy negotiated the key demand for the peaceful transfer of the camps to the Allies. Himmler had demanded assurance that the guards would not be shot on the spot. Instead, they would merely be tried as regular members of the Wehrmacht for specific crimes as long as they wore the uniforms of the Wehrmacht.

McCLELLAND, WHO WAS ASKED by Sternbuch and Musy to convey this message to the American government, did so immediately and was cabled a swift, affirmative reply. Musy said he had seen a report with an order to deport all internees. In fact, some of the internees were taken out on a forced march, the kind that had taken a heavy toll. When the Sternbuchs found out about this breach of agreement, Musy and Recha Sternbuch went to Bergen, across the Austrian border, to deal with an important Gestapo agent, while Benoit Musy returned to Berlin. Communications were already cut off from Berlin. Benoit Musy's car was hit, exploding the gas tank, and the tires were slashed. Fortunately, Benoit found a mechanic who fixed the car. He made it to the capital amidst vast destruction and met again with Schellenberg. Schellenberg immediately got in touch with the commanders of Buchenwald and Bergen-Belsen and warned them not to disobey Himmler's orders. Actually it had been Kaltenbrunner's nefarious role that was responsible for such disobedience. At any rate, Buchenwald and Bergen-Belsen were handed over to the Americans.

Negotiation under Fire

The younger Musy also participated in the negotiations for 15,000 women in the Ravensbrück camp, of whom about 2,000 were Jewish. Most of the latter were evacuated to Sweden with the help of the International Red Cross because Schellenberg had also been working with Count Bernadotte, head of the Swedish Red Cross, since the release of the Theresienstadt train in February, 1945, to help in further releases.

Benoit Musy then went on to Stockholm, Sweden, where he assisted with the arrangements for the Ravensbrück inmates, which were made possible through negotiations with the help of Hitler's physical therapist Felix Kersten and the representatives of the World Jewish Congress, Hillel Storch and Norbert Masur.

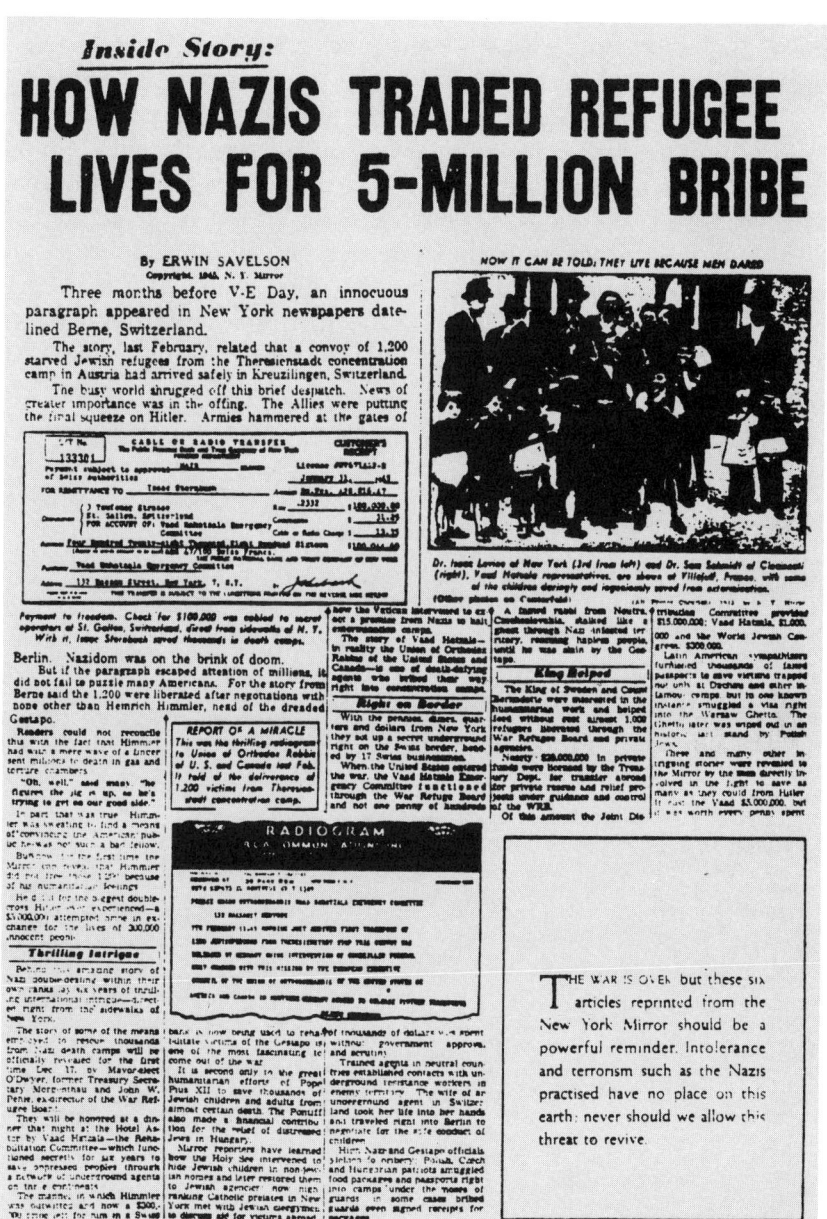

The Musy mission was widely reported in the American press after the war

Thus, while the major goal of the release of all the camp inmates was obstructed, at least three camps were handed over to the Allies intact and about one hundred thousand additional inmates were saved. For Recha Sternbuch this achievement did not mean that she could rest on her laurels. She had far too many urgent tasks ahead — mainly to assure proper care for the survivors at this critical hour — a challenge that she met head-on, as usual.

When the war was over, the Musy affair was concluded for all concerned except for one more sad, telling incident. A full year after the end of the war, the Swiss government charged the Sternbuchs with the unauthorized use of roughly 200 liters of rationed gasoline donated by a kind distributor, and used by Musy on his trips to Germany. There is no evidence of how the case was resolved, but given Musy's multiple missions, and the lives he helped save in the most trying and difficult circumstances, the charge speaks for itself.

CHAPTER THIRTEEN
Last Minute Rescue Efforts — Eisenhower's Warning and Red Cross Shipments

THE MUSY ACTION was by no means the only initiative of the Sternbuchs to save the remaining Jews in the final months of the war. Numerous other desperate steps were taken in order to discourage the Germans from murdering the last of the Jewish inmates in the face of the advancing Allied armies.

ON OCTOBER 5, 1944, the Sternbuchs cabled the following message to the Orthodox leadership in the U.S.:

Desperate Cable to New York   A number of reports indicate German intentions of murdering all remaining Jews and thus liquidating all the concentration camps at the last minute. Such plans are presently being finalized by Himmler personally, together with Hess, the commandant of Auschwitz. It is vital that a strong warning be issued by the U.S. to Germany that they refrain from such a violent act.

The source of this information concerning the intentions of the Germans was the Polish Embassy in Bern. The following is an excerpt from a confidential letter dated October 1, 1944, from Dr. Julius Kuhl at the Polish Consulate in Bern to Saly Mayer, representative of the Joint Distribution Committee in Switzerland:

c/o
Polnisches Konsulat

Bern, den 1. Oktober 1944.
Thunstrasse 21

Herrn Saly Mayer,
Postfach 262,
St. Gallen.

V e r t r a u l i c h !

Sehr geehrter Herr Mayer,

Ich komme zurück auf Ihr Schreiben vom 6. l. Mts. und teile Ihnen mit, dass Schritte via unsere Gesandtschaft unternommen wurden in Zusammenhang mit der bestehenden Gefahr, dass die Insassen der verschiedenen Lager, im letzten Augenblick umgebracht und die Lager liquidiert werden.

Folgendes Telegramm wurde mir via unsere Presseabteilung unserer Gesandtschaft, aus London überreicht:

"On mande de Pologne que les Allemands ont l'intention de liquider
"des les camps de concentration en massacrant tous les detenus et
"rasant les bâtiments, afin de faire disparaître les traces de leurs
"crimes. En premier lieu doivent ainsi être liquides les camps d'Os-
"wiecim, Brzezinka (Birkenau) et Buchenwald. Le chef du camp d'Os-
"wiecim, Hoss, ami de Himmler, a a prouvé le plan de destruction du
"camp de Brzezinka, elabore par le chef de celui-ci- Mille. Ce plan
"prevoit une action combinee d'une division motorisee S.S. avec artil-
"lerie et une escadre de bombardiers pour detruire rapidement tout le
"camp et faire disparaître les traces même de celui-ci, dès que l'ordre
"en sera donne par Berlin. Les malheureux detenus en appellent à la
"conscience du monde pour empêcher ce crise. Il se trouve actuellement
"16.727 hommes et 39.125 femmes au camp de Brzezinka. Dans celui de
"Plaszow près de Cracovie, des executions en masse de Polonais ont
"lieu actuellement.

Es ist nicht ausgeschlossen, dass ich auf Grund meines Dienstpasses, nächstens für kurze Zeit nach Frankreich und Belgien reise. Diese Mitteilung bitte ich Sie aber vorderhand streng vertraulich zur Kenntnis zu nehmen.

In der Beilage erhalten Sie die Wiedergabe einer Anzahl Besprechungen, die ich mit verschiedenen Gesandtschaften in den letzten Tagen hatte, betr. Rückwanderung unserer Flüchtlinge.

Letter from Dr. Kuhl to Saly Mayer informing him about the threat of annihilation facing the Jewish inmates in German concentration camps while the Germans were retreating from the onslaught of the Allied armies

> From London our Embassy just received the following message:
>
> We were informed from Poland that the Germans intend to liquidate the concentration camps, murdering all the prisoners and destroying all the facilities so as to erase all traces of their crimes. First [on the list are] the Camp of Oswiencim-Brzezinka [Auschwitz-Birkenau] and Buchenwald. The chief of the Oswiencim Camp, Hess, friend of Himmler, has approved the plan of the destruction of Camp Brzezinka [Birkenau]. The plan foresees a combined action by one motorized S.S. artillery division and a squadron of bombers to destroy the camp and to make all traces disappear, the minute the order is given in Berlin. It is important to appeal in behalf of the unfortunate prisoners to the conscience of the world, to impress upon the Germans to refrain from this crime. There are 16,727 men and 39,125 women in the Camp of Brzenzinka. At the camp of Plaszow near Cracow, a mass execution of Poles [meaning here Polish Jews] is now taking place.

We are not aware of the reactions of other American Jewish leaders to this shocking communication; however, based on available documentation, we do know that the leaders of the Vaad Hatzalah in New York, who received this urgent message from the Sternbuchs, took immediate action.

The day the message was received in New York, Rabbi Abraham Kalmanowitz rushed to the U.S. War Department, and again, several days later, he met with John J. McCloy. On October 13, the following response was issued by the War Department to Rabbi Kalmanowitz:

> As I stated at our meeting, the problem which you have brought to my attention is under serious consideration. I am assuming that you are bringing the other aspects of this problem to the attention of proper government departments, whose sphere of interest would be more involved than that of the War Department.

Indeed, the Vaad Hatzalah as well as the leadership of the Union of Orthodox Rabbis intervened with the State Department and other government agencies. Nevertheless, pressure was still brought to bear upon the War Department for some drastic action, and with *some* success, as documents indicate.

LESS THAN ONE MONTH LATER, General Eisenhower issued the following strong message "to German people":

The Eisenhower Warning

Germans! You have in your midst a great many men in concentration camps and forced labor battalions.

Germans! Do not obey any orders, regardless of their source, urging you to molest, harm or persecute them, no matter what their religion or nationality may be.

The Allies, whose armies have already established a firm foothold in Germany, expect, on their advance, to find these people alive and unharmed. Heavy punishment awaits those who, directly or indirectly, and to whatever extent, bear any responsibility for the mistreatment of these people.

May this serve as a warning to whoever at present has the power to issue orders.

This statement by the Supreme Commander of the American forces was printed onto leaflets and dropped all over Germany by American planes, in advance of the U.S. Army's relentless march into that country. The impact of these leaflets is, of course, difficult to assess. It does appear likely, however, that numerous atrocities were averted as a result of this warning. Many camp survivors recall a degree of mellowing on the part of some S.S. officers in the final months prior to the liberation. We may assume that many officers of the S.S., previously known for their indiscriminate brutality to Jews, were suddenly frightened by the stern message of the commander of the advancing American Army.

ANOTHER SERIOUS PROBLEM that troubled the Sternbuchs in the closing months of the war was the threat of virtual starvation of

Saving the Starving Inmates

Jewish inmates in the various German concentration camps.

Although hunger and malnutrition were not new to them (hundreds died daily as a result of hunger and related diseases, for they usually received less than one thousand calories of nutrition a day) the situation worsened toward the end of the war. As German cities and roads came under increasingly heavy Allied bombardment, severe food shortages came to be felt even by the civilian German population. Faced with this dire situation, the S.S. command decided to allocate even less food to the camps. To be sure, the death toll in the concentration camps grew each day.

Complicating matters even more was the fact that the Jewish inmate population of many camps began to grow toward the end of the war. As the Germans retreated before the Allied armies, they evacuated all of the small concentration camps in the path of their retreat and deposited the human cargo in the larger camps. For example, from November to December 1944, Theresienstadt's inmate population more than tripled, as did those of Bergen-Belsen and Buchenwald. Even if their captors had been more humane, it would have been difficult to feed the prisoners properly. Of course, the Germans' complete lack of compassion made the plight of the Jewish inmates disastrous. Many thousands perished daily from hunger, as we know from the heaps of corpses that "welcomed" the liberating Allied forces some time later.

Moving the Red Cross

THE STERNBUCHS REALIZED that time was running short and turned to the International Red Cross for help. Throughout the war the Sternbuchs had struggled many times with the International Red Cross, pleading with them to bring relief to the Jews inside the concentration camps. The Red Cross, however, had always been extremely reluctant to involve itself with Jews in the camps. Its leadership in Geneva, led by Professor Carl J. Burckhard, often explained to Jewish delegations that due to the intense German enmity towards Jews, any Red Cross intervention on behalf of the Jews would only jeopardize the lives of thousands of Allied prisoners of war, who were protected by international law.

Needless to say, the Sternbuchs never accepted this explanation and continued pressing the International Red Cross to find ways to include Jews on their relief programs. Although they failed to effect an official IRC policy change, they did succeed frequently with individual Red Cross officials in bringing about direct or indirect help for some Jews in some parts of Nazi-occupied territories.

Taking their cue from the Sternbuchs not to give up, some other Jewish groups joined in pressuring the IRC; the long-awaited policy change of the IRC finally came in 1944, when a special (though small) Jewish Division was established, headed by a sympathetic official, Mr. Marcel Leclerc. Through this department, the Sternbuchs now succeeded in sending substantial food shipments to various concentration camps, including

From the voluminous correspondence between the Sternbuchs and the headquarters of the International Red Cross in Geneva concerning help for Jews in Europe

Theresienstadt. In November, 1944, a transport with ten thousand kilos of sugar and spaghetti arrived, via the Red Cross, in Theresienstadt. The delivery was officially acknowledged by Drs. Benjamin Israel Mermelstein and Raphael Levi of the *Altestenrat* at the camp.

IN DECEMBER 1944, the food situation was deteriorating rapidly in the camps, while the Allied forces were penetrating the frontiers

Trucks of the Lifeline of the Third Reich. Due to this predicament, Dr. Reuben Hecht, the Sternbuchs' liaison with the Red Cross, increased his pressure on the IRC to transport more food for the Jews into the concentration camps. Dr. Hecht spent many days in Geneva conferring with the leadership of the International Red Cross. Some time later, HIJEFS even put a number of "camions" (special transport trucks) at the disposal of the IRC, to bring food to the camps. Although the Red Cross leadership continued to feel obliged to give preference to the Allied prisoners of war, Hecht persistently pressed them to include food shipments for Jews in their transports to Germany, and they went along with this.

Of course, in some concentration camps this was to no avail. Brutal S.S. commandants of certain camps did not allow the shipments to reach the Jewish inmates. In other camps, however, the relief shipments were delivered. Moreover, starting from January 1945, in some camps — such as Buchenwald — Jewish inmates who had previously been excluded from receiving any food packages from the Red Cross were no longer restricted from receiving such gifts. We could not establish the reason for this policy change, but we can assume that this had something to do with the change of policy on the part of the Red Cross, whose representative grew bolder and asked the Germans not to exclude the Jewish prisoners for whom these gifts were destined.

The close ties between Dr. Hecht of HIJEFS and the officials of the International Red Cross at the end of the war had other beneficial effects as well. Through Red Cross officials stationed or traveling in Germany, the Sternbuchs and other Jewish leaders in Switzerland came to learn vital information of the goings-on within various camps. In addition, the IRC was involved in last-minute rescue efforts on behalf of Slovakian and Hungarian Jews. Finally, Hecht's contacts with the IRC proved exceedingly significant after the war, when the Red Cross actually volunteered to bring first aid to the liberated Jews in Germany and Austria.

CHAPTER FOURTEEN
After the Liberation — Reviving the Survivors

IN APRIL AND MAY OF 1945, the historical turning point that the entire world was awaiting, finally took place: Hitler's Empire was crushed and defeated. In its wake came the liberation of about half a million Jews in what had been Nazi-occupied Europe.

This joyous event, however, was intermingled with immeasurable pain and tragedy. The liberated Jews were relieved of only one threat: death — either in the gas chambers or from starvation and hard labor. At the same time, however, as a result of the Holocaust in all its facets, almost all of them were despondent and, tragically, burdened with countless problems.

AMONG THE PROBLEMS faced by those whom modern Jewish history designates as *She'eris Hapleitah* — the generation of survivors — were:

A Galaxy of Problems

- Most liberated inmates (who became known as D.P.'s for "displaced persons") were weak and undernourished; some were little more than living skeletons. All needed food and clothing, and many were in desperate need of medical attention after years of deprivation and disease.

Liberated Jews in Buchenwald

- Almost all of them were emotionally shattered by their experiences and by the loss of family and relatives. The survivors were husbands without wives, wives without husbands, children without parents, and parents without children. Some relatives were thought to be lost, yet were alive, and help was needed to reunite families.
- Almost all survivors were homeless and they were painfully aware of it. Those who were liberated in Germany, Austria, and Italy knew that they could not return to their homes; those liberated in Poland, Czechoslovakia, Hungary and Roumania soon realized that — even if they could regain their homes — they could not remain in those countries. On the other hand, all the

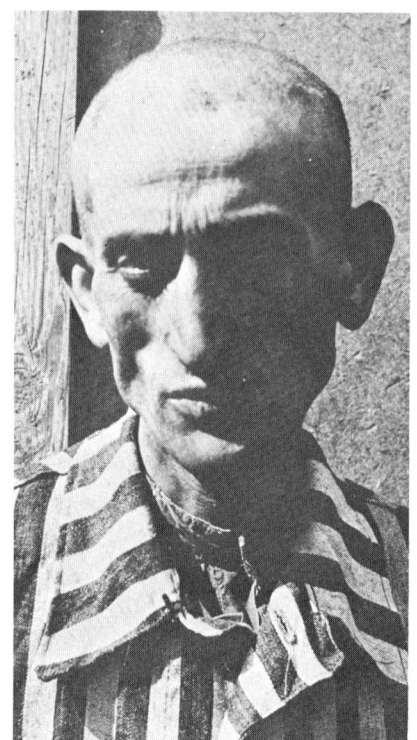 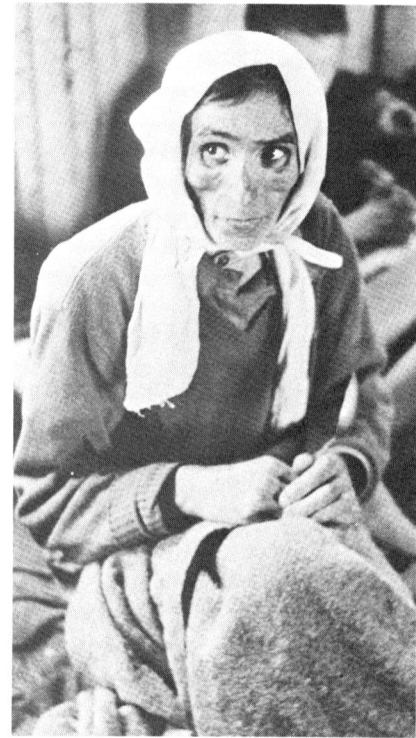

Liberated Jews in Dachau

gates to the free world, including *Eretz Yisrael*, were sealed. Very few could hope for a British certificate to Palestine or an immigration visa to other free countries. Jews who had fled to Russia during the war and now returned to Poland were faced with the same problems.

- Those who were eager to renew their religious way of life had special needs. First they required kosher food, which UNRRA, the agency that took care of the immediate needs of these liberated inmates, did not initially bother to provide. Also needed were religious articles, such as *tefillin, taleisim,* religious books and so on — all essential for the resumption of a full Jewish life.
- Many of the survivors were youths who had been torn away from their parents' home and from religious surroundings. They faced the danger of being severed from their Torah upbringing. It was imperative that proper homes, with a Jewish religious atmosphere, be created for them. Moreover, they needed capable educators and counselors. These needs also had to be met in

neutral Sweden, where temporary homes had been found for a large number of Jewish girls who had been saved during the last months of the war or who had been liberated in the camps.
- The young survivors also included some children who could not have received any substantial education before the war. They needed schools, yeshivos and religious girls schools, as well as teachers. This problem was especially severe for religious survivors, since the various survivors' centers and D.P. camps supplied only a general secular education with no provisions for a traditional Jewish one. That problem became even more acute in 1946 when many Jewish children returned to Poland, Germany, and Austria from Russia, where they had fled with their parents at the beginning of the war.

A separate problem marked by tragedy was the fate of thousands of Jewish children who were saved from death when they were placed in non-Jewish homes, Christian institutions, and even convents and monasteries. Some church leaders and other non-Jews, assuming that the parents of the children in their hands had perished, decided to adopt the children and bring them up as Christians. This was especially the case in regard to Jewish war orphans in Christian institutions, particularly in Poland and in France. Obviously, swift action had to be taken to get them out so that they would not be lost to Judaism.

In addition to all these problems, there were the many hundreds of yeshiva students and their rabbis in faraway Shanghai, whose needs the Sternbuchs had dealt with for the entire duration of the war. When the war ended in Europe, the war in the Pacific was still on and the Sternbuchs still had to care for them. Following the capitulation of Japan, it was essential to take these refugees out of Shanghai.

All of the above problems — and many other related ones — suddenly became the problems of the Sternbuchs and their HIJEFS organization in Switzerland, which in the meantime had become the representative of the Vaad Hatzalah of America. In their rescue efforts, the Sternbuchs also partially represented the Agudath Israel organizations in America and England, as well as all other Orthodox groups in the free world that wanted to help the survivors.

WITHIN A FEW DAYS after the liberation of each country in

Myriad Tasks, Few Shoulders

Europe, the HIJEFS office of the Sternbuchs was already in contact with the survivors to inquire about their needs and to look for ways and means of helping them. When one examines the many thousands of telegrams, letters and other documents of that period, which are in the archives of Dr. Julius Kuhl, Herman Landau, the Sternbuch family, and Agudath Israel, as well as *The History of Vaad Hatzalah* by the renowned historian, Moshe Prager, one is overwhelmed by the myriad of tasks undertaken by the Sternbuchs after the liberation. The relief work of HIJEFS after the war encompassed twelve countries: Germany, Austria, Italy, Poland, Czechoslovakia, Roumania, Hungary, France, Belgium, Switzerland, Holland and Sweden; each country with its vast problems and specific needs. In the first year after the war, and in some cases even for four or five years thereafter, the rabbis and Orthodox leaders in these countries had only one address, HIJEFS in Montreux, which in reality meant Recha and Yitzchok Sternbuch. The staff of HIJEFS in Montreux, under the able and

A rescue conference of Orthodox Jewish leaders took place at the home of the Sternbuchs in Montreux in the winter of 1946. In the picture are Chief Rabbi Isaac Herzog, Yitzchok Sternbuch, Benjamin Mintz, Rabbi Chizkeyahu Mishkowsky, Rabbi S.P. Wohlgelernter, Rabbi Zev Gold, Moshe Shapiro, Herman Landau, Dr. Shaul Weingort, Hugo Donnenbaum, Moshe Botchko, Rabbi Mendel Stern, Chaskel Rand, Ruthie Mandel Rottenberg, Chiel Brand

devoted leadership of Mr. Herman Landau, was very small; and it is almost impossible to comprehend — looking back today — how the Sternbuchs managed to handle all of these problems and to accomplish so much.

OF COURSE, IN THEIR WORK the Sternbuchs were assisted by many outstanding Orthodox personalities the world over. Rabbi Eliezer Silver and Rabbi Abraham Kalmanowitz, Dr. Samuel Schmidt, Dr. Isaac Lewin, Rabbi S.P. Wohlgelernter, Rabbi Simcha Wasserman, Mr. Elimelech Tress, and Stephen Klein were among many other distinguished emissaries who came from the United States to help in their valiant efforts. Chief Rabbi Isaac Herzog, Rabbi Chizkeyahu Mishkowsky, and Mr. Binyomin Mintz came from *Eretz Yisrael*. Dr. Jacob Griffel, who did outstanding rescue work during the war in Istanbul, Turkey, now came to Central Europe. Mr. Heinrich Landau was another important figure who joined the Sternbuch team. In some of the above-mentioned tasks, the Sternbuchs found exceptional help on the part of the Chief Rabbis Council of Great Britain, created by Rabbi Solomon Schonfeld. From within the ranks of the survivors, too, a distinguished group of great relief activists arose to help their fellow Jews.However, examining the documents of that postwar

International Task Force

Vaad Hatzalah conference in Montreux 1946. From left to right: Rabbi S.P. Wohlgelernter, Rabbi Eliyahu Botchko, Rabbi Chizkeyahu Mishkowsky, Chief Rabbi Herzog, Moshe Shapiro, Jacob Herzog, Mr. Elinson

Dr. Samuel M. Schmidt

period, one can easily see how in the center of almost all activities and achievements, it was Recha Sternbuch who directed the work, as will be demonstrated in the chapters that follow.

Dr. Jacob Griffel

Mr. Elimelech (Michael) Tress

CHAPTER FIFTEEN
Recha Sternbuch in D.P. Camps in Germany

AS AN INDICATION of how keenly sensitive the Sternbuchs were to the needs of the survivors, one need only look at a telegram which Recha Sternbuch sent to America concerning the Jews who had been liberated from Buchenwald and Bergen-Belsen in April 1945.

Only two days after the first news reached her about the liberation of these infamous camps, Recha Sternbuch appealed to the American and British Occupation Authorities for permission to visit Buchenwald and Bergen-Belsen. When she was refused on the grounds that the war was still raging and all the roads were shut to civilian traffic, Recha Sternbuch refused to accept this. She immediately sent an alarming telegram to America, in which she wrote:

> CANNOT ASSURE HELP FOR SURVIVORS UNLESS WE GET PERMISSION TO VISIT BERGEN-BELSEN AND BUCHENWALD IMMEDIATELY. PLEASE TRY YOUR UTMOST TO PROVIDE US WITH SUCH A PERMIT FROM THE ALLIED HIGH COMMAND.

IT SEEMS THAT EVEN the intervention from America did not help. The Allied Occupation Authorities assured her that for the time being they themselves would be taking care of the immediate needs of the survivors, and any additional aid would have to wait until the war operations were over.

Unsatisfying Assurances

But these assurances did not satisfy Recha Sternbuch, who fom far away felt the agony of the weakened, half-starved survivors. She understood that they were in need of much more than a portion of bread. For many survivors more immediate help was essential just to keep them alive, and the army was not capable of effectively handling their problems.

Recha Sternbuch was even more alarmed when her fears were confirmed by a number of letters she received from the liberated concentration camps — mainly Matthausen. She was informed that in some places the Allied Army provided only little food and that, because of this as well as inadequate medical care, which was almost non-existent in the camps, many survivors were dying daily.

In a letter of May 25, 1945, to Mr. Katsky of the American Legation in Geneva, she bitterly complained:

> It is just incomprehensible that although there is enough food here available to be sent to the camps, there are no means available to ship it. Is it right that the few survivors should still suffer, or even die, from want of food? We repeatedly tried to send food to the camps, but we were told by the International Red Cross that they still cannot get the permission from the Military government for such transports. Please, you must do everything to avoid catastrophe!

The Sternbuchs, however, did not wait for permission or official help. During April and May they succeeded in finding a number of avenues for bringing some help to the liberated Jews. By July 1945, Recha Sternbuch finally succeeded in getting a permit for a longer visit to the D.P. camps in Germany in order to orient herself to the situation and to map out a program of help for the needy survivors. She came to Germany in the company of another great rescue leader, Dr. Jacob Griffel, who then specialized in dealing with war-orphaned Jewish children in non-Jewish nomes. Accompanying them was Rabbi Moshe Lebel, the head of the children's home in Aix-Les-Bains in France.

On-Site Visits — A Hazardous Task

UNDERTAKING SUCH VISITS in those trying days was no simple task. Germany was in ruins and there was only sporadic train transportation. Many tried to dissuade her from the difficult trip, suggesting that a representative go in her stead. Recha Sternbuch refused such advice.

During her four-week trip, Recha Sternbuch visited Munich and neighboring D.P. camps: Feldafing, Landsberg, Fernwald, St. Otillien and Gauting, as well as some smaller centers for the liberated Jews. From Munich she traveled to Frankfurt, where she visited the large D.P. camp in Zeilsheim. She traveled from one location to another, and also visited smaller centers of survivors in the American and British-occupied zone.

Carrying an official UNRRA document, she periodically received special automobile transportation facilities from the offices of that relief organization. If this was not immediately available, however, she did not wait, but traveled with whatever mass transportation was available, in vehicles which were invariably primitive and overcrowded. Traveling in those days in packed buses and trains sometimes involved risks to one's life, but Recha Sternbuch was racing against time in her drive to do something for the survivors.

Moreover, she passed up the relatively decent living quarters in the hotels that the American and British military governments had put at the disposal of the UNRRA personnel (which was a status her document entitled her to). Recha Sternbuch insisted on joining the female Jewish survivors, sleeping in a bunkbed in their barracks. Mrs. Sternbuch's actions were recorded in the memoirs of Mrs. Rivka Pinkusewicz, a well-known Beth Jacob leader both before and after the war, who currently resides in Antwerp. Mrs. Pinkusewicz came from Cracow, where the Beth Jacob movement's headquarters in Poland were located. During the war she had been in Auschwitz and other camps, and after the liberation she met with Beth Jacob students and encouraged them to start life anew, in the spirit of Beth Jacob of the past. In an article published in *Hamodia* after Mrs. Sternbuch's passing Mrs. Pinkusewicz writes:

> Who doesn't remember Recha Sternbuch's visit to Camp Zeilsheim shortly after the war! ... She could have lived in full comfort in one of the American hotels, but she deliberately

chose to live with our girls in the D.P. camps on primitive hard camp beds. There she shared with the others whatever she had brought along. At the end of the visit, with motherly love, she left for the others all of her own personal belongings which she had brought along; she traveled back with empty suitcases. She asked everyone what they needed and then sent packages to their camps. She even supplied wigs for brides who requested them ...

Courage for the Despondent

POIGNANT MEMORIES OF HER VISITS to the camps in Germany are cherished to this very day by many survivors who came in contact with her in those days. Most survivors were despondent and apathetic. For them, her mere presence in the camps brought a ray of new hope.

Rabbi Abraham Ziemba was a young leader of the religious community in the Feldafing D.P. camp who helped establish several institutions to strengthen the religious spirit among the young survivors. He wrote:

> We had thought that the entire Jewish world, and surely Judaism itself, was gone. Indeed, many lost their faith in the future of religious Judaism. Her appearance in the camps, her deep interest in reviving Judaism among the survivors, kindled fires of faith ... Her interest in our situation — and in all our physical and spiritual needs — let us know that we were not alone, that world Jewry had not forgotten us, G-d forbid.

Similarly, Recha Sternbuch is remembered to this day by the former Rabbi of Munich (from 1945 till 1952), Rabbi Baruch Leizerowski, who is now the rabbi of Congregation Bnei Yaakov in Philadelphia. He told us:

> Not only for the masses of the D.P. camps but even for us, the few surviving rabbis, Mrs. Sternbuch's visits meant a new start in life. Meeting this *Eishes Chayil* was a sign to us that our efforts to renew religious life were not in vain.

Practical Accomplishments

THE RENEWED COURAGE which Recha Sternbuch instilled into broken Jewish hearts was essential. Also of great importance were her practical accomplishments in the camps, and the important results that later emerged from them. Among her many achievements in the D.P. camps in the summer of 1945 were:

- She contacted relatives in the free world for hundreds of survivors. At that time there was still no postal service between Germany and America, England, Palestine and other countries. She took out of Germany several suitcases full of letters from survivors to mail from Switzerland to destinations around the globe. (These suitcases, which she had brought into Germany full, became empty because she had given away all her personal belongings to the survivors in the camps, as mentioned above).
- In almost all the D.P. camps, she intervened successfully with the camp commanders of the military government, as well as with the UNRRA personnel, to deal with the religious needs of the survivors with more understanding — to help them erect synagogues, establish kosher kitchens, and so on.
- At each location she encouraged the establishment of religious committees to work with the camp directors, to strengthen and broaden the religious life in the D.P. camps.
- She participated in a series of conferences with a few surviving rabbis under the leadership of Rabbi Samuel Snieg of Kovno, held in a sanatorium in Ganting, near Munich. She encouraged them to found a Union of Orthodox Rabbis of the D.P. Camps, which later became the Union of Orthodox Rabbis of Germany, and played a vital role in the revived religious life among the Jewish D.P.'s in West Germany.
- Her visit also brought her to the Klausenberger-Sanzer Rav, Rabbi Yekusiel Yehudah Halberstam, perhaps the only great Chassidic leader among the survivors. This contact later helped the Klausenberger-Sanzer Rav when he established the first yeshiva in the D.P. camps in Fernwald.
- She encouraged the Orthodox lay leaders in the camps, especially the young activists, to establish homes for young religious survivors and also *hachsharot*, or *kibbutzim*, for those who wanted to emigrate to *Eretz Yisrael*. She was able to give financial aid to some of these projects.

This initiative later developed into many youth homes and *kibbutzim* in the camps known as *Chofetz Chaim* for men, and *Ohel Sarah* (after the founder of the Beth Jacob movement, Sarah Schenirer) for girls. Most of them were under the sponsorship of either Agudath Israel or the Mizrachi. One cannot overestimate the effect of these religious homes in renewing the religious spirit among the youthful survivors.

The Klausenberger-Sanzer Rebbe, Rabbi Yekusiel Yehudah Halberstam

- She also gave close attention to many individuals who needed special aid. Recha Sternbuch brought a number of extremely sick survivors who could not find proper medical care and rehabilitation in Germany, to reputable hospitals and sanatoriums in Switzerland.

Creating Channels for Help

NATURALLY, THIS WAS ONLY the beginning. From the time of her initial visit until Vaad Hatzalah established its own office in Munich under the devoted and capable leadership of Rabbi Naftali Baruch from New York, she kept in close contact with the D.P. camps in Germany, and she extended help through various channels.

To provide this help — mainly food, clothing and religious

articles — was no simple task. Transportation to Germany continued to be extremely difficult, and even available transportation was complicated by red tape on the part of the occupation army. These factors also hindered the American Jewish Joint Distribution and indeed, it took many months before it could start functioning in Germany to extend wider help to survivors in the D.P. camps.

But Recha Sternbuch's work during the war had accustomed her to devising all sorts of clandestine operations and she quickly found ways to deliver help to the D.P. camps. She succeeded in getting some transportation through the International Red Cross. In addition, she used the good offices of individual Allied Army officers who were traveling between Switzerland and Germany to deliver her help to various D.P. camps.

Of great importance, she mobilized a number of Jewish chaplains of the U.S. and French Armies, who could more readily come to Switzerland and travel freely around Germany. In the Sternbuch archives we find more than 150 communications from the period between July through December 1945, with just one chaplain, Captain Robert Monheit of the French army — all concerning help for the Jewish D.P.'s in Germany!

Mrs. Sternbuch's visits to Germany also paved the way for the visits of other religious personalities on behalf of Vaad Hatzalah and Agudath Israel. Her visits laid the foundations for the important aid and relief work that the Vaad Hatzalah provided in Germany for over five years, until 1951, when most D.P. camps were liquidated and the majority of the Holocaust survivors, spiritually rehabilitated, emigrated to Israel, the United States or other countries.

CHAPTER SIXTEEN
Recha Sternbuch and the Jewish Exodus from Poland

THE JEWS WHO SURVIVED the war in Poland or who returned there from concentration camps faced situations that were more complicated and difficult than those of their brethren in German D.P. camps. Western Germany was controlled by the U.S., England and France, whose governments felt some moral obligation to help the victims of Nazi persecution. However, neither Poland's government nor her people harbored any friendly sentiments towards Jews — not even to Holocaust survivors. On the contrary, they considered Jews who survived a burden.

Polish Hospitality: Hatred and Resentment

Moreover, survivors in Poland did not receive any help from UNRRA or similar aid agencies. Nor did the Polish government offer any special help to the Jews who returned to Poland from the camps. The American Jewish Joint Distribution Committee, which resumed operations immediately after the end of the war, did offer aid, but it was inadequate, leaving the survivors desperate for help.

Wherever Jews appeared, they were met with hatred and resentment. The homes that the Jews had left behind fell into the hands of Polish gentiles, who would not consider returning them to the Jews. In some smaller towns, Jews attempting to return to their previous dwellings were set upon by organized Polish bands, as a warning to other Jews not to try to claim their homes or belongings. As a result, most survivors concentrated in the big cities, where they were also unable to reestablish normal lives. By the middle of 1946, it became clear that Jews could not remain in Poland. On the fourth and fifth of July, 1946, scores of Jews were massacred in a bloody pogrom in the city of Kielce while the Polish security forces did nothing to stop the violence.

The Sternbuchs were keenly aware of the precarious situation of the Jews in Poland by early 1946, and they felt it imperative that the Jews leave Poland as quickly as possible.

TO AGGRAVATE THE SITUATION, the Polish government did not officially allow the Jews to leave. Most likely this was due to the Communist mentality of the new leaders in Poland, who, like their Soviet counterparts, considered any exodus an affront to their system. It may also be attributed to the influence of the Jewish Communists in Poland who still believed, naively, that Jews could expect a better life, and even enjoy full equality under the Communist regime. Whatever the reason, Poland did not officially permit any mass exodus of her Jewish citizens.

Exit Impossible

Again, Recha Sternbuch appeared as an angel of mercy. In fact, immediately following the liberation, the Sternbuchs, representing the Vaad Hatzalah, sent kosher food, clothing and other such assistance. From afar, Mrs. Sternbuch encouraged the establishment of youth homes, kosher kitchens and other aid centers in Poland. These relief projects helped revive religious life among the Jewish survivors, which had been interrupted during the war years.

Once it became clear, however, that such aid was not sufficient and that it was more important to get the Jews out of Poland, Recha Sternbuch decided to travel to Poland to help take out as many Jews as possible.

MRS. STERNBUCH AND VAAD HATZALAH were not the first organization to be active in this field. At the end of 1945, *Bricha* (Hebrew for "flight") was organized to bring East European Jews to Germany, Austria, and France as a step toward illegal immigration to Palestine (as Israel was then known). *Bricha*,

Avoiding the "Bricha" Route

however, was a Zionist project concerned mainly with young people and others interested in *aliya*. Initially, *Bricha* almost totally ignored the emigration needs of the elderly or those interested in emigration to America. The Sternbuchs and the Vaad Hatzalah felt that all Jews should be helped in leaving Poland regardless of their intended destination.

Mrs. Sternbuch decided to become actively involved in exodus activities rather than to leave them in the hands of *Bricha*. This was especially important in regard to the homeless youth, because of religious considerations. *Bricha* policy was to transfer all youth into the hands of the *Aliyat Hanoar* (Youth Aliya) of the Jewish Agency. *Aliyat Hanoar* arranged living quarters in Germany, Austria and Italy, where the youths were indoctrinated in Zionist ideology, to prepare them spiritually for settlement in Palestine.

The Sternbuchs knew from their experience during the war years that they dare not entrust the surviving youth to the *Aliyat Hanoar*, where the youngsters would certainly be subject to anti-religious propaganda. The Sternbuchs thus had a twofold thrust to their relief activities. They wanted to get these youths safely out of Poland and, most importantly, arrange for them to live in religious homes where they would be educated in a religious atmosphere.

OTHER PROBLEMS EXISTED in Poland. In the beginning of 1946, many Jews who had escaped to Russia at the outbreak of the war now returned to Poland. Among them were a number of rabbinic scholars and young men who had studied at various yeshivos in Poland and Lithuania. They expected to rebuild their old yeshivos or join others that had been re-established in America and *Eretz Yisrael*. The Sternbuchs recognized the importance of keeping the members of these groups together so they could emigrate as a unit and establish the yeshivos again.

"Returnees" to Poland from Russia

The Sternbuchs were faced with yet another problem. The "returnees" from Russia included a number of Orthodox Russian Jews who had left Russia under the guise of being Polish citizens. These Jews had hidden their identity illegally, and faced great mortal danger in Poland, for if discovered, they could have been sent back by the Communist Polish authorities to Soviet Russia, where they would face harsh punishment of many years in Siberia.

Those Jews had to be sent out of Poland without any delay.

In addition, there were many Jewish children who were in non-Jewish hands, in the homes of individual Poles or in Christian institutions. The Sternbuchs had involved themselves in the rescue of children in such situations following Dr. Kuhl's visit to France and Belgium in October-November 1944. (See chapter on Kuhl-Sternbuch mission.) Now that Mrs. Sternbuch learned of a similar situation in Poland, extraction of these children from non-Jewish hands also became a priority project. She realized that the local Jewish leaders were totally occupied in providing immediate aid to still the more insistent cries for help, and were not even aware that a problem existed with the children. For all the above reasons, Mrs. Sternbuch found it necessary to quietly travel to Poland in the beginning of 1946.

ONE OF THE TOP LEADERS involved in reorganizing religious life in Poland was the religious author, Mr. Yechiel Granatstein, who

Headquarters in Lodz survived the war by joining a partisan group in the woods of Lublin (he is currently residing in Jerusalem). Following the liberation of Poland in February and March 1945, Mr. Granatstein was among the first to organize Agudath Israel and Poalei Agudath Israel in Poland with headquarters in Zachodnia Street 66, in Lodz. The Sternbuchs were in contact with him from the first day the Agudah headquarters opened. Thanks to the aid and encouragement of the Sternbuchs in Switzerland, the Agudah headquarters did much to help the survivors renew their religious life. For many survivors, Zachodnia 66 became the first Jewish address they reported to when they returned to Poland. In Poland's larger cities, homes and *kibbutzim* were established, as were other important institutions that infused life into the survivors in Poland.

In the HIJEFS archives we find a number of communications from the Sternbuchs to Mr. Granatstein in Lodz; Dr. Kuhl's archives contain a copy of the telegram in which Recha Sternbuch informed Mr. Granatstein of her arrival in Poland. The telegram reported:

    TANTE RECHA ARRIVING TUESDAY
                UNCLE ISAAC

A group of children taken by Mrs. Sternbuch from Poland to Paris via Prague

On the other hand, Granatstein's writings indicate that Recha Sternbuch's arrival was a surprise:

> All of a sudden, on a winter evening in 1946, in our office on Zachodnia 66, the headquarters and head *kibbutz* for the girls, a woman appeared — a woman not from our pain-ridden world. Dressed in a fur coat and a fur hat, a pair of gloves on her hands — who saw something like that in those days? She asked for 'Herr Granatstein.' They pointed to me. Then she told me that she wanted to speak to me privately. She came into my office and related who she was and that she came to me from Vaad Hatzalah. What was her plan? 'Does not the Polish government want to get rid of the Jews in Poland?' If so, she was ready to finance the Emigration Passports.
>
> Negotiations were held with the government officials, but they dragged on and on. The Foreign Ministry and other officials changed their minds every day; they agreed and then revoked the agreement. Ultimately, not many passports were issued, so, lists were drawn up, first of old men with beards, and children who could not emigrate with *Bricha*, then younger people ... How many left Poland? Many hundreds, thousands, and perhaps more ... [with the help of Mrs. Sternbuch]
>
> This religiously observant, elegant European lady risked

her life and labored day and night. She traveled from place to place, from city to city, sleeping every night somewhere else, staying in cheap hotels so as not to draw attention. Warsaw, Lodz, Katowice, Bielsko were the places where emigration lists were drawn up. My wife, who was the head-counselor of all the girls' *kibbutzim* in Poland, worked diligently with her. They slept together in one bed in a hotel in Katowice. We were also together in Bielsko where we spent Shabbat in the house of Abale Rapaport (the son of a well-known Orthodox Jewish industrialist before the war), since children were transported from there. Moreover, she wanted to consult with us about various technical matters, away from the tumult and noise at the headquarters in Lodz.

Mrs. Sternbuch also concerned herself with our girls for whom she gave lectures on Judaism. She was filled with Jewish pathos and strong faith, and she was wise to see the reality. In short, she was part of our work and life as long as she was with us.

I am certain that under these conditions, facing numerous difficulties in every direction, no human being could have accomplished what she did. She was indeed a woman, a phenomenon, with a strong will and supernatural determination to help — and there were so many to help ...

Yet, her visits to Poland were never mentioned in the numerous news reports of the Vaad Hatzalah. In her humility, Mrs. Sternbuch never recorded her accomplishments and, certainly, did not relate how she succeeded. In her communications to the headquarters of Vaad Hatzalah in America, she transmitted only bare facts and results, e.g., "400 Jews taken to Czechoslovakia," "300 Jews taken to France," and no more,

What we know of her accomplishments in physically and spiritually aiding the Jewish survivors has been gleaned from documents that were written by others and from interviews we have conducted with those who were with her at that time.

The Orenstein Report

ONE OF THOSE IS Rabbi Samuel Orenstein, Rabbi of Congregation Ahavas Chesed in Manhattan. A former student of the Kamenitz Yeshiva, Rabbi Orenstein saved his life by spending the war years in Siberia, Russia. In 1946, he returned to Poland, residing in Katowice, in Polish Silesia. As a member of the committee

A children's home established by Poalei Agudath Israel in Poland with the help of Recha Sternbuch.

that represented Jewish scholars and yeshiva students for the Vaad Hatzalah, Rabbi Orenstein worked with Recha Sternbuch during her visit to Poland. He summarized his opinion of Mrs. Sternbuch in a short sentence: "She is certainly the greatest woman I have ever met."

Rabbi Orenstein has much to tell about Recha Sternbuch. First, about her help for the Jewish scholars in Poland: "Thanks to the funds which she brought to me, or sent through Rabbi Abraham Isaac Winkelstein (who later established the famous children's institution, *Achiezer*, in Haifa), I could distribute support to the Jewish scholars on a weekly basis." When some people warned her against the risks of bringing dollars into Poland, and suggested that she rather send it through others, she was insulted. If it is so dangerous to smuggle money into Poland for relief, why should others assume the risk and not she?

"I remember," tells Rabbi Orenstein, "that after the pogrom in Kielce, she insisted on visiting that city to determine how she could help the Jews there. We attempted to dissuade her, warning that it was too dangerous to visit that city. But she could not understand. 'If Jews are being killed there because they are Jews, one must risk one's life in order to help,' she retorted.

"Mrs. Sternbuch worked on two fronts," according to Rabbi

Orenstein. "On the one hand, she constantly traveled from Katowice to Warsaw to obtain passports and permits for Jews to leave. (In 1947, she established Katowice as her headquarters, because it was closer to the German and Czech borders and, hence, easier to transport Jews out of Poland.) On the other hand, she quietly supported every effort to smuggle Jews out of Poland. She occasionally succeeded in Warsaw, even though the official policy of the Polish government was not to permit Jews to leave the country. A number of government officials were deeply impressed with her dedication, and treated her with great respect. Presumably, they were unaware that Mrs. Sternbuch was also quietly and actively taking Jewish children out of gentile institutions and homes. She employed several people for this purpose. Most importantly, she was wonderfully in control of all of these activities, on all fronts."

To this very day, Rabbi Orenstein is in awe of her selflessness and humility, and how she never sought any recognition for her successful work. He relates a characteristic episode: "When Chief Rabbi Herzog visited Poland, he succeeded in taking out a large transport of Jewish children with him, with the permission of the government. Mrs. Sternbuch utilized the opportunity to send along with this same transport a substantial group of children from a children's home in Poland, which she had previously helped to establish. I suggested that she travel along with the transport. 'Otherwise, Rabbi Herzog will get all the credit, while nobody will even remember how much effort you exerted to save these children,' I told her. She would not — even for a moment — hear my arguments. 'I'm not at all interested in who will get credit for saving the children. I have to do my duty, and I still have to remain here. There are still so many Jews to be saved,' she insisted.

"Every time she came to Katowice, she was received with great enthusiasm by everyone. It is impossible to describe the benevolence and respect she accorded anybody who turned to her for help, especially Jewish scholars. Hundreds of people would come. She differed from most other relief emissaries; she handled the needy with heart and soul, and that was exactly what most people needed at that time. So many broken-hearted people felt encouraged after meeting with her. She would give aid in a noble fashion; nobody felt degraded ... and as religiously observant as she was, while handing out relief she would never make any

Children brought from Poland by the Vaad Hatzalah — HIJEFS arriving in Prague, 1946

distinctions between the observant and non-observant. The more I think of her significance for the Jews at that time, the more I am overwhelmed — even today — by this holy and noble woman," Rabbi Orenstein told us.

MR. BENJAMIN SCHACHNER of Brooklyn also tells of Mrs. Sternbuch's activities in Poland. Following the liberation, Mr. Schachner became one of the Orthodox leaders of the religious Jewish community in Reichenbach, which was originally East Germany and had become part of Poland in accordance with the Yalta Treaty.

Escape from Reichenbach

Many survivors settled in Reichenbach; a large number of them were repatriates returning to Poland from Russia. There Mr. Schachner founded a children's home, ran a *kibbutz* for youth, and helped found the local Orthodox community. One of his most important activities, however, was to smuggle out Jews. And this was financed by Recha Sternbuch.

Reichenbach was near the border city of Klacko, from where Jews were smuggled in to Czechoslovakia. "Recha Sternbuch gave us the money, and every morning, before sunrise, we would send twenty people over the Czech border. Recha Sternbuch gave us money to bribe the Polish border officer. She was always interested in how the work was moving ahead."

Schachner also told us how he and a group of his Orthodox friends had, with the encouragement of Recha Sternbuch, spirited a number of children from the Jewish Children's Home (*Dziecko-Sad* in Polish), which was run by Jewish Communists. "Initially the Jewish Communists would not hear of handing over the children to us. We pointed out to them that some of the children came from religious homes and were still observant. A little later they finally realized that Communist Poland holds no paradise for Jews. They began to be receptive to the idea of transferring a number of children to *Bricha* and *Aliyat Hanoar*. Naturally, we would not permit that. We wanted to get the children, raise them in our religious homes and transport them with the other children.

"What did we do? We planted our own teacher in the children's home. The teacher then took the children for a hike in the woods for a day. We did not need more. With the help of Mrs. Sternbuch, a bus was awaiting these children and we drove them to the border. A few days later the children were taken to the Orthodox Children's Home of Poalei Agudath Yisrael in Ulm, Germany."

The Zakopane Caper

A SIMILARLY DARING ACT of "stealing" Jewish children out of non-Jewish homes was undertaken by Recha Sternbuch at Zakopane, a Polish resort, with the help of a few Orthodox activists who headed the Poale Agudath Israel Organization in Lodz. The story was told to us by the late Mr. Simon Zucker, a well-known leader in postwar Poland and author of the book *The Unconquerable Spirit*. Mr. Zucker told us:

> When Mrs. Sternbuch came to Poland, interested in saving Jewish children, she learned of an orphanage in Zakopane, a well-known resort in the Polish Alps, with well over one hundred Jewish children. She insisted on taking them out but there was no way to do it. The orphanage was under the management of a few assimilated Communist Jews, whom we did not dare approach. But Mrs. Sternbuch did not give us any rest. She continued to insist that a way must be found to save them, and that with money this certainly could be done. Finally she won.

On the Polish-Czech border, Mrs. Sternbuch meets a group of activists who helped her in her mission of saving children from Poland.
Seated: Mrs. Recha Sternbuch, Mr. Simon Zucker, Mr. Benjamin Mintz, Mr. Yechiel Granatstein, Mr. Hershel Reisman.

Several of us came to Zakopane ostensibly for a vacation. We used to visit the orphanage almost daily and bring along candy for the children. This led to a friendship with one, then two of the head teachers. To avoid arousing suspicion, we moved very slowly. When we felt that we were ready we openly offered the teachers $10,000 — a large sum of money. After much hesitation the teachers agreed to cooperate. A plan was worked out whereby the teachers would approach the administration with a plan to arrange a vacation trip to the Czechoslovakian border. There, we thought, we would lure the children over the border, where Mrs. Sternbuch would prepare a transit home. This plan — actually Mrs. Sternbuch's idea — worked perfectly. On a sunny day, the children, accompanied by the "friendly" teachers, took a trip to Zablice. Mrs. Sternbuch had bribed the border guards there, and after four hours the children were already on the other side where they were taken over by Mrs. Sternbuch's agents.

That same evening, the children were on a train to Paris, and after 24 hours they were at one of the Jewish children's homes that Mrs. Sternbuch had founded and maintained in France.

This daring operation became widely known and had reverberations all over Poland. The government initiated a

Vaad Hatzalah Conference in Montreux 1946. From left to right: Yitzchok Sternbuch, Herman Landau, Recha Sternbuch, Rabbi S.P. Wohlgelernter, Rabbi Eliyahu Botchko

Mrs. Sternbuch with Chief Rabbi Herzog and Jewish children from Poland who were rescued with her help.

Chapter 16: RECHA STERNBUCH AND THE JEWISH EXODUS / *171*

thorough investigation. Fortunately, the authorities had no idea of Recha Sternbuch's involvement. Although she had been in Zakopane many times and even visited the orphanage, nobody knew her. During her brief visits, she never said a word since she did not know any Polish. But the other organizers of this operation were known and the police were searching for them. In fact, after this event Mr. Zucker never returned to Poland.

Typical of Recha Sternbuch, Mr. Zucker told us, was that she did not consider this operation a full success. While she succeeded in saving about one hundred children, she mourned the fact that six or seven children had been unable to join the trip because of temporary illness, and remained at the home in Zakopane. Mr. Zucker told us that even a year later she still talked about the remaining children and kept asking what could be done about locating them (they had since been transferred to another home) and taking them out of Poland.

How many times did Mrs. Sternbuch visit Poland? It is difficult to make an exact determination from our research of documents, but the available correspondence and various personal testimonies indicate that she was in Poland very frequently in January and February of 1946. She also visited in July of the same year (soon after the pogrom of Kielce) when she transported a large group of scholars from Poland to France, and helped them establish the Yeshiva of St. Germain near Paris. She returned to

Jewish orphans' home in Bits, Poland, founded by Mrs. Sternbuch

```
                Telegramm – Télégramme – Telegramma
                    32290 PARIS 23198 141 20/10 23.45
```

ELT = MR AND MRS STERENBUCH
CARE HIJEFS
GRANDRUE 84 MONTREUX

AS THE MOTHER OF THE ALL POLISH AND LITHUANIAN JESHIVOTH AS
THE ONLY ONE WHO SHOWED THE UTMOST EXERTIONS AND MOTHERLY
DEVOTION TO THE GRANUL OF TORAH WHICH REMAINED ALIVE AFTER THE
DISTRUCTION WHOM YOU HELPED TO SAVE FROM POLAND AND LITHUANIAN
WE HAVE THE PLEASURE IN THE NAME OF THE FIVE HUNDRED BNEJTORAH
TO INFORM YOU THAT WEDNESDAY EVENING WE HAPPILY REACHED PARIS
AND ARE WAITING FOR YOUR VISITING US TO ENJOY WITH US
TOGETHER YOUR FRUITFULL WORK STOP IN THE MERIT OF YOU
INEXHAUSTIBLE WORK LET HEAVEN ELEN (((160)))
YOU WITH LONG LIFE HEALTH AND HAPPINESS AND IN THE MERITS
OF YOUR GOOD DEEDS LET THE JEWISH NATION GET BUILT UP AS
BY ONE OF OUR GREAT MOTHERS SARAH RIVKA ROCHEL AND LEJA =
ROBBIS TROP LEWOWITZ MOWSZOWITZ WASERMAN LONDINSSKI NEWINANSKI

Telegram to the Sternbuchs from the heads of the Polish Lithuanian Yeshivos in Paris thanking them for Recha Sternbuch's help in taking out their young Torah scholars from Poland and bringing them to Paris.

Poland at least three more times, at the end of 1946, at the beginning of 1947 and in the autumn of that year. However, *Bricha* and her other aid projects for the Jews in Poland continued until much later. She maintained her contact with the religious leaders in Lodz, Warsaw, Katowice, and other cities until all the Jews who wished to leave Poland had succeeded in doing so.

CHAPTER SEVENTEEN
Help for the Transition Centers — Czechoslovakia, Austria and Italy

CZECHOSLOVAKIA WAS ANOTHER main center of Recha Sternbuch's rescue and relief work after the war. Jews who were saved or had returned to their homes from the concentration camps after the war had acute needs, especially in Slovakia, where liberated Orthodox Jews tried to reestablish their personal and communal life. Even before those Jews in Slovakia turned abroad for help, the Sternbuchs tried to establish contact with the Jews in Bratislava to determine their situation and identify the myriad problems facing them.

ON JUNE 6, 1945, less than a month after the liberation and only a few days after the Orthodox Jewish Council (the *Kehillah*) in Bratislava reestablished itself, Mrs. Sternbuch's HIJEFS office cabled Mr. Max Weiss, the president of the *Kehillah*, in reference to their needs. A lengthy letter was dispatched from Montreux on June 16 in which the Sternbuchs, offering help, asked for many details: the number of Jews who returned; the number of rabbis and children; their conditions and health; as well as all other possible needs and problems facing the Orthodox Jewish community there. In the letter they also asked for

"How Can We Help You?"

information about a number of individuals regarding whom they had received inquiries. They asked for a telegraphic response, since regular mail connections between Czechoslovakia and Switzerland were not yet restored. In the same letter, they also offered help to individuals interested in emigration.

From the extensive correspondence between the *Kehillah* in Bratislava and HIJEFS in the years 1945-47, it is clear that the HIJEFS office in Montreux provided the *Kehillah* and their institutions with substantial aid: food, clothing, medicines and also funds for various activities. For example, they provided Bratislava with 44,000 pounds of *matzah* for Passover 1946.

The Sternbuchs were also instrumental in interesting the Joint in the needs of the *Kehillah*, especially in providing help for the Jewish hospital in Bratislava.

Soon the aid from HIJEFS was broadened to include a number of other Jewish communities in Slovakia that attempted to restore their Jewish communal life. This is reflected in correspondence between the Sternbuchs and Rabbi Sholom Ungar of Nitra, Rabbi Raphael Blum in Kosice, and others.

Short-lived Rehabilitation

THE HIJEFS AID CONTRIBUTED substantially to the rebuilding of a fruitful Jewish life in Bratislava and elsewhere in Slovakia after the war. The Bratislava *shul* was renovated, the Jewish hospital reopened, and the Jewish cemetery repaired. The famous Pressburg Yeshivah renewed its learning and a number of impressive educational institutions were established in a few other Slovakian communities. Recha Sternbuch tried to help each of them with the Vaad Hatzalah funds at her disposal.

All this came to an end when Czechoslovakia was completely overtaken by a Communist regime in 1948, and the Slovakian Jews realized that they would have to seek other havens. However, it does not minimize the importance of Recha Sternbuch's help to the Orthodox Jewish community in Slovakia. Thanks to this help, many Jews, especially young Jewish boys and girls, who later left Czechoslovakia and emigrated to *Eretz Yisrael* or the West, found their way back to a fuller Jewish life.

The main thrust of Recha Sternbuch's personal work in Czechoslovakia was the assistance she extended to the Jews (mainly Jewish children) whom she brought out of Poland, as well as Jews from Hungary and Roumania, who felt that they could not remain in those countries. Czechoslovakia became a major transit center, through which the great migration of the survivors from Eastern Europe to the West took place. From Czechoslovakia, the Jews who left Poland, Hungary and Roumania crossed the border into Germany and Austria where some settled for a while in the many D.P. camps, and others traveled directly to France, or tried to get to *Eretz Yisrael* via Italy.

RABBI VICTOR VORHAND, the former Chief Rabbi of Prague, one of the great rescue figures of the postwar period and now Rabbi of Congregation Heichal Moshe in New York, related:

The Prague Testimony

I do not recall how many times Recha

Letter from the Chevra Kadisha in Bratislava [Pressburg] thanking the Sternbuchs for their help in reestablishing the Jewish hospital in that city

Sternbuch visited Prague. But I do clearly remember that from January 1946, through the end of 1947, she arrived unexpectedly every few months, and sometimes she stayed with us for a few days or a few weeks. But the word 'stay' would not be correct; because, in reality, she was always on the move. She came from Poland with a transport of Jews or Jewish children and saw to it that they were established for a while. Or, she might move them further to the West — or she might send them via Italy (illegally) to Palestine. Prague in those days was full of Jews from all parts of Eastern Europe who could not remain in their countries and needed all kinds of help. Mrs. Sternbuch was involved in every aspect of help to these refugees. Some people came without identity papers, and such papers had to be obtained. Some of them had to be sent to France and French visas had to be obtained from the French Consul. Here and there were individuals with some possibilities of obtaining immigration or visitor's visas to countries overseas. I went with Mrs. Sternbuch to the consular offices of many countries. All of us admired her, not only for her devotion to every Jew — which was well-known — but also for her persistence, which enabled her to accomplish so much in helping many people.

Rabbi Eliezer Silver and Yitzchok Sternbuch with rescue activists in Czechoslovakia. Recognizeable, right to left: Herman Landau, Israel Goldstein, Joseph Goodman, Eliezer Gips, Rabbi Silver, Mr. Sternbuch and Meir Shenkolewski

Chapter 17: HELP FOR THE TRANSITION CENTERS

ANOTHER KEEN AND ADMIRING observer of her rescue work is Mrs. Faiga Feldman, who now resides in Brooklyn, the former wife of Mr. Zalman Brunner, one of the Orthodox rescue activists. After the war she lived with her husband in Stetin, Czechoslovakia. Mrs. Feldman recalls:

The Stetin Cross-over

> I remember Recha Sternbuch's first visit to our home. Stetin was the border town between Poland and Czechoslovakia, one of the easier crossing points between the two countries. When, in 1945, Recha Sternbuch started her work of taking Jews out of Poland, she came to Stetin to look around for connections. She did not know anybody in town but was searching for some Jews who could assist her. And so she came to our house. She overwhelmed us so that my husband, who was engaged in a profitable business, left everything and became one of her main lieutenants. For about two years we were engaged in smuggling Jews out of Poland, especially children, putting them up in the special transit camp in Diablitz near Prague, and then sending them to Germany, France, or to Italy for their voyage to *Eretz Yisrael*. I recall those years as one of the most glorious chapters of our life.

Prague remained an important transit center for Jewish migration for quite a while. At the request of Mrs. Sternbuch, Prague was visited by almost all Orthodox rescue leaders who came to Europe to take part in this work: Rabbis Silver, Herzog, Mishkowsky, Lewin, Wohlgelernter, Wasserman, etc. Besides, Prague was fortunate to have Rabbi Vorhand in its midst to oversee the relief work. Nonetheless, Mrs. Sternbuch herself remained in close touch with all that was going on in Czechoslovakia until it became a full member of the Communist empire and ceased its role in the resettlement of Jewish survivors.

WE HAVE NO RECORDS as to whether Mrs. Sternbuch ever visited Austria for any appreciable period of time, but we can assume that she was there for a short stopover during her visit to Germany. It is clear from the correspondence between her Montreux office and Vienna that she personally knew a number of community leaders in Vienna who, as early as August 1945, formed a local Vaad Hatzalah committee to equitably distribute the help they received from Mrs. Sternbuch's HIJEFS office in Switzerland.

Her Net Spread to Austria

THE JEWS IN AUSTRIA immediately after the conclusion of the war — numbering about 6,000 — were mainly former inmates of concentration camps located in Austria, or Jews whom the Germans had transported from concentration camps in Germany during the very last days before their capitulation. Many of them were freed by American Army units while still on trains or in the midst of their march on open roads in the Austrian Alps. The situation of the latter group was even more precarious than those who were freed in the concentration camps. The former at least had a roof over their heads, while those on the march, although free from the fear of being killed, were totally without shelter. The American Army authorities, for their part, were involved in organizing their occupation administration, while the Austrians had no sympathy for the liberated Jews. Thousands of the survivors — hungry, sick and almost naked — were left on their own, without care.

Free ... and Stranded

From the documents of HIJEFS, we see that the Sternbuchs had a deep concern for those Jews stranded in Austria immediately after the liberation. Since Austria borders on Switzerland, the Sternbuchs were promptly informed about the refugees' plight. They promptly enjoined the American representatives in Switzerland to instruct the army commanders in Austria to give the necessary attention to the needs of these liberated Jews. Thanks to these interventions, the U.S. military government in Austria placed groups of Jews who were stranded in the Austrian Alps into various empty hotels in such resorts as Bad-Gastein, Ebbensee, and Seefeld. In addition, the Americans ordered the local Austrian authorities to provide some food for these survivors.

Although it was extremely difficult, Mrs. Sternbuch also managed to send some immediate help to these places, especially kosher food and religious articles.

MR. MANNES ZYTNICKI, a rescued Orthodox leader from Kalisz, Poland, who later organized a number of Orthodox institutions in Austria and founded a Gerer yeshivah in Bnei Brak, told us of the importance of the seemingly small amount of help that they initially received from Recha Sternbuch:

Little Packages of Great Hope

It was not very much, since all the food was sent through

individual American officers or Jewish chaplains attached to the American or British troops in Austria, whose means of transportation were very limited. But it meant a lot. The few boxes of kosher meat, kosher cheese, etc. reminded many of the survivors that it was time to return to *kashrus* (laws of kosher food). The few *siddurim* (prayer books) and pairs of *tefillin* served as a reminder to observe *Yiddishkeit* (Judaism)

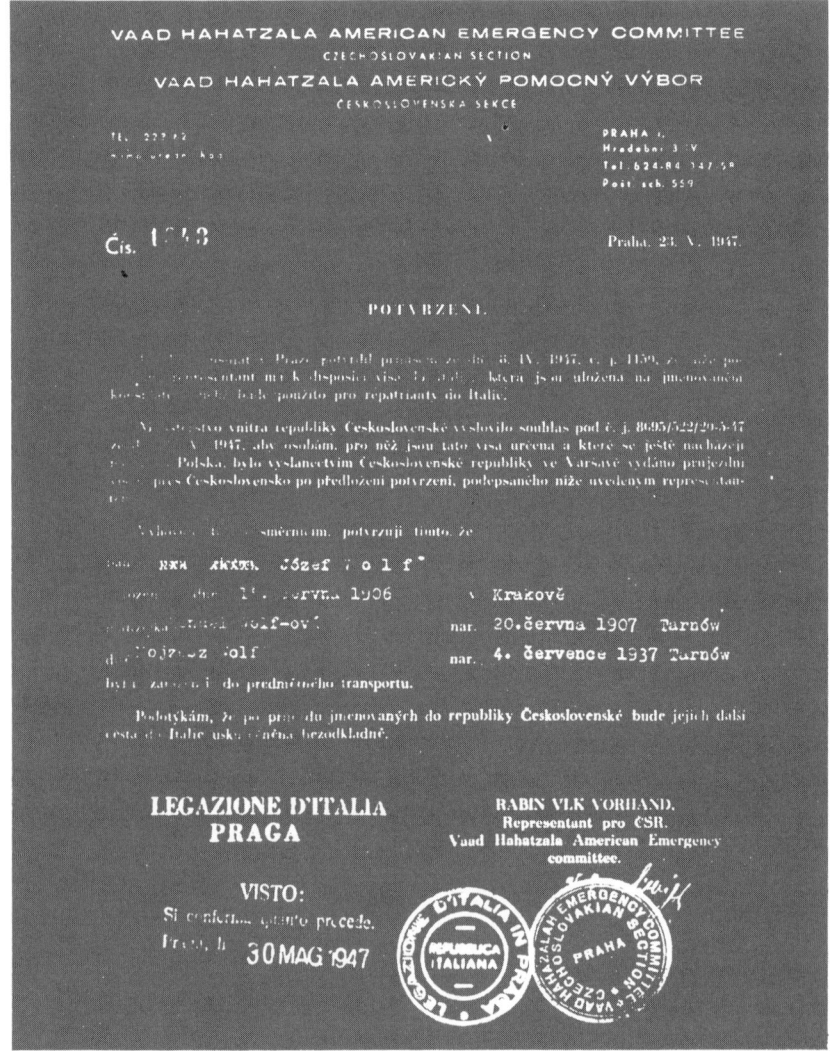

Photocopy of a so-called visa devised by Mrs. Sternbuch together with Rabbi Victor Vorhand from Bratislava to enable Jewish refugees from Poland and Eastern Europe to proceed to Italy

in general, and affected an immediate change in the way of life of many of us. *Minyanim* (prayer quora) were formed and some stopped eating anything that was not absolutely kosher. It meant the resumption of a fuller Jewish life, which some seemed to have totally forgotten. It is impossible for someone who did not live through these experiences to fully understand how devoid of any hope or spiritual content our lives had become and what these packages meant.

Later, when the situation stabilized and D.P. camps were formed, Mrs. Sternbuch took the initiative to contact the few Orthodox leaders among the survivors in Vienna and in Salzburg, who supervised the religious life in the D.P. camps. The records of HIJEFS show that she sent food as well as religious articles through Jewish chaplains and the International Red Cross. For Passover 1946, for instance, we find that HIJEFS provided the Vienna office of Vaad Hatzalah with 4,400 pounds of *matzah*, as well as with other Passover food. Copies of letters from after Passover report the dispatch of hundreds of cartons of condensed milk, butter, chocolate, sardines and kosher meat. The accompanying letters instructed the leaders that, when distributing the food, they should give preference to the activists of *Bricha* who had been engaged in bringing over Jews and Jewish children from Poland and Czechoslovakia. Besides its own value, all of this help enabled the Orthodox rabbis and lay leaders to organize an active religious life in the various D.P. camps.

Radical Increase in D.P. Population

IN THE MONTHS that followed — at the end of 1945 and beginning of 1946 — the Jewish D.P. population in Austria increased substantially. Since Austria borders Italy, where a great illegal emigration to *Eretz Yisrael* was being organized by *Bricha*, many Jews who had left Poland, Czechoslovakia, Hungary, and Roumania were directed to Austria, some with the help of Recha Sternbuch. The planned illegal emigration to Palestine, however, dragged on because of many difficulties. In fact, it almost came to a complete stand-still when Great Britain intercepted the illegal ships and sent many of them to Cyprus. In the meantime, the Jews in Austria had to be settled in various D.P. camps, which were established throughout Austria. By the end of the summer of 1946, there were about 50,000 Jews in about fifteen D.P. centers, including 6,000 to 8,000 Orthodox Jews who needed much more than the food and shelter provided by the UNRRA and the minimal help from the Joint Distribution Committee.

The main concern of the Sternbuchs now shifted in another direction. They saw it as their obligation to enable the Orthodox leaders to keep up the religious spirit in the D.P. camps by providing proper religious education for the youth. UNRRA had no interest in this and even the Joint was not always ready to help on an appreciable scale.

At the initiative of the Sternbuchs, these D.P. camps were visited by representatives of the Vaad Hatzalah from the United States including Rabbi Eliezer Silver, Dr. Isaac Lewin, Dr. Jacob Griffel, Rabbi S.P. Wohlgelernter, among others. With their help and encouragement, a large number of homes and institutions were founded. These institutions contributed substantially to maintaining and strengthening the religious life of the survivors. Mrs. Sternbuch was in constant contact with the above-mentioned emissaries to acquaint herself with how she could best direct further help for the religious life in D.P. camps.

Meeting D.P. Deficiencies

TO UNDERSTAND THE IMPORTANCE of these visits and the help which the Sternbuchs continued to extend to the religious survivors, it is useful to quote here Mr. Isser Salzberg, a leading activist in Salzburg who, together with Mr. Mannes Zytnicki, was a member of the Presidium of the Agudath Israel central office in Salzburg:

> In each of the D.P. camps there were a few hundred Orthodox Jews who had many problems and difficulties in maintaining their religious way of life. The UNRRA people, mostly non-Jews, could not comprehend their needs, and some representatives of the Joint Distribution Committee, who were secular in their outlook, did not sympathize with the requirements of these D.P.'s. Kosher food was inadequate and there were difficulties with establishing a prayer house, a *mikvah* (ritual bathhouse), and so on. We required all kinds of help which could only be provided by those who understood the importance of these needs. It was only thanks to the help of HIJEFS that we could provide them.
>
> Our greatest concern was our youth who, after the war

and life in concentration camps, were estranged from their *Yiddishkeit*, or had completely forgotten it. In addition, they were now surrounded by all kinds of temptations. Without parental supervision, they were being lured by secular groups — secular Zionists, Socialists and others — who maintained clubs and entertainment centers, movie houses and many other types of amusement facilities. Moreover, the secular groups had many emissaries, or *shlichim*, from the Jewish Agency, equipped with money and influence with UNRRA, and they offered a wide assortment of inducements. All of them openly tried to corrupt our youth, who after years without proper education and living in demoralizing conditions could not easily resist their enticements.

The only way to keep these youngsters within our fold was to maintain proper religious homes, institutions, and cultural centers. And here, the financial help, food parcels, clothing, etc. that we received from Montreux were invaluable aids in the spiritual rescue of these youths. With these funds we founded and later maintained the homes, paid the instructors, organized lectures and many other events that helped to inculcate the youngsters with a religious spirit. Later, when many families arrived from Russia with little children, we also founded Talmud Torah and Beth Jacob schools.

Vaad Hatzalah HIJEFS Conference in Montreux 1946. From left to right: Dr. Shaul Weingort, Hugo Donnenbaum, Herman Landau, Yitzchok Sternbuch, Recha Sternbuch

There is no question that without this help many youngsters would have left us to join secular groups, where they would have been totally lost to *Yiddishkeit*. With the help that we received, not only did we prevent many youngsters from leaving our religious camps, but we were also successful in attracting some young people who had already joined left-wing *kibbutzim* and who had completely abandoned *Yiddishkeit*. With these funds we also founded and maintained three yeshivos for boys and Beth Jacob schools for girls of high school age. It is no exaggeration to state that thousands of Orthodox Jews who later succeeded in raising blessed families of Orthodox children and grandchildren all over the world are now indebted to the efforts of Recha Sternbuch in those years after the war.

Stranded in Italy

THERE WERE NOT MANY Jews in Italy who were in need of extensive help immediately after the war. Yet the Sternbuchs also kept in mind that the small Jewish communities were eager to restore their religious life. As early as May 1945, Mrs. Sternbuch delegated Mr. Donati to go to Italy to form a committee of rabbis to help in this task. From communications with New York, we see that the Sternbuchs were in contact with Rabbi Castabelognesi in Milan and Rabbi Friedenthal of Verona and that they assigned 20,000 Swiss francs as an initial sum for helping them. It seems that Italy, like France, had a problem with some Jewish children in Christian homes, since Mr. Donati took along a special letter of recommendation from the Papal Nuncio Bernardini to the Vatican.

Later, Italy had its share of Jewish refugee problems similar to those of all other countries in Europe. Starting in the autumn of 1945, we find many thousands of Jews were in D.P. camps in various parts of that country.

The Jews in Italy mainly came from Austria, or via Austria from Roumania, Hungary and Czechoslovakia, with the hope of proceeding from there to *Eretz Yisrael*. But the planned illegal immigration to *Eretz Yisrael* proceeded at a much slower pace than envisioned. In time, the stronger vigilance of the British fleet around Palestine brought the illegal immigration almost to a halt. In 1946, about 10,000 Jews were stranded in Italy, among them many hundreds of Orthodox Jews in need of special assistance to carry on their religious lifestyle.

In addition to the many Orthodox Jews in various D.P. centers, there was also a yeshivah in Rome, *Sridei Esh*, established by Rabbi Ephraim Oshry, Rabbi of Kaunas (Kovno), Lithuania. Most of its students also wanted to go to *Eretz Yisrael*, but because of their love for Torah they joined the yeshivah in the meantime.

Since the Orthodox rescue work in Italy was directed by the highly capable and indefatigable Dr. Jacob Griffel, Recha Sternbuch did not visit Italy, but the records of HIJEFS show that the Jews in Italy were very much on her mind, as is evident in an excerpt from a memo of December 15, 1945, to the Vaad Hatzalah:

> Dr. Griffel reports from Italy that the Orthodox groups are in desperate need of help. There are by now about 1400 Jews who want kosher food, among them two yeshivah groups in Ostia and Cesarea. Even if the Joint takes proper care of their needs, we still need about 40 additional liras a day. About 500 Orthodox people need clothing. We put 5000 francs at the disposal of Dr. Griffel. Mr. Donnenbaum and Dr. Shaul Weingort will travel shortly to Italy in order to acquaint themselves with the situation.

Mrs. Sternbuch continued to send similar memos to the United States. She was in constant touch with Dr. Griffel and he often visited Montreux on behalf of the Orthodox refugees in Italy. She continuously pleaded with the leadership of the Vaad Hatzalah to support their temporary institutions, so as to maintain the religious standards of the refugees.

CHAPTER EIGHTEEN
Roumania and Hungary — Rehabilitation and Emigration

EXAMINING A MAP of postwar Europe, one cannot find a single Jewish center where the Sternbuchs were not involved in the rehabilitation of the surviving Jews. HIJEFS documents reveal fascinating details about their work in Roumania and Hungary in particular.

As in Poland and Czechoslovakia, some Jews believed in the possibility of renewing their shattered lives in Roumania and Hungary. Others quickly realized the impossibility of ever again living with their former neighbors, especially under the new regimes that arose there, and promptly began to plan their departure. Some, with the help of *Bricha*, immediately smuggled themselves into Czechoslovakia, and continued on to Germany, Austria or Italy, with the hope of emigrating from there to *Eretz Yisrael* or the West.

Others still lingered on in Roumania since the gates of Palestine and the Western countries remained closed anyway. Meanwhile they were in great need of assistance, both in terms of organizing illegal emigration into other lands and even more so in terms of simply living their day-to-day lives. Most Jews in Roumania had little or nothing left after the war. Those who had not been deported were impoverished and those who returned from the camps had nothing at all. In addition, there were many boys and girls in their teens, and even children, who urgently needed homes. They had yet to recover physically and spiritually from their horrible experiences during the war. They also needed a proper education. Orthodox Jews had other needs of their own, since the general public assistance did not fill their special requirements.

BRINGING FOOD AND OTHER KINDS of assistance into Roumania was far more complex than it was in Poland and Czechoslovakia. After the area had been liberated by Soviet forces, the new regime that arose was quite unstable. As a result, contact with the West was extremely difficult. For a short period of time, beginning in the spring of 1945, there was not even a telegraphic connection between Roumania and Switzerland. The Sternbuchs were forced to cable their inquiries through Sweden to learn what was happening in Bucharest and elsewhere and generally received only sketchy information in return.

Roumanian Barriers

The Sternbuchs were not discouraged by this state of affairs. From the very first day of the liberation, they made great efforts to communicate with Orthodox rabbinic and lay leaders in Roumania. Finally a link was set up with the help of a few leading rabbis in Slovakia, who used the services of some Jews who, for one reason or another, would steal across the border to Roumania. Upon their return, they would bring back information concerning the lives and needs of the Roumanian Jews. The details would then be relayed to the anxiously awaiting Sternbuchs in Switzerland. Matters were complicated, though. Much of the information was vague, and finding the best channels through which to send assistance to Roumania was difficult. Although the Sternbuchs were eager to act as swiftly as possible, they could only guess which need should take priority.

DESPITE CONFLICTING INFORMATION, the Sternbuchs decided not to wait to send aid. On September 11, 1945, with the help of Rabbi Sholom Ungar of Nitra, the Sternbuchs succeeded in getting $20,000 into the hands of the rabbinic leadership of Roumania. Before receiving acknowledgment of that first sum, they sent another $15,000 the following month. From HIJEFS documents, it is clear that at the

Aid Now, Ask Later

same time, the Sternbuchs requested of their close confidant Mr. Link in Bucharest (with whom they had lost contact for a while) to forward some funds. Link then provided between $75,000 and $90,000 for the needs of Oradea (Grosswardein) where the Vizhnitzer Rebbe, Rav Chaim Meir Hager, had established a yeshiva.

For quite a while, Roumania remained a sealed country to the Sternbuchs. In order to learn more about the needs there, in October 1945, they asked their collaborater Dr. Reuben Hecht to travel to Czechoslovakia, and from there to make contact with Roumania. Hecht spent several weeks in Prague and Bratislava before he sent the Sternbuchs a lengthy report on the dire circumstances in Roumania. (Meanwhile, he also gathered important information about Slovakia's Jews and about the *Bricha* movement in which he was very active.)

ONLY AT THE END of 1945, (with the aid of illegal couriers) did the Sternbuchs succeed in establishing written contact with Roumania's Orthodox leadership. Evidence of this is a letter from Roumania's Orthodox Central Council, located in Cluj, at the head of which were the esteemed Rabbi Yosef Adler, Rabbi of Turda (later a prominent member of the *Moetzes Gedolei HaTorah* in Israel) and Rabbi Avrohom Shlomo Katz, Rabbi of Riskov. The letter, dated November 1945 (third day of *Vayetzeh*, 5706) reads in part:

Breakthrough

> We have tried many methods of contacting you directly in order to make you aware of the latest state of affairs of survivors in Roumania, who number more than fifty thousand Orthodox Jews. We did not succeed due to the lack of postal and telephone connections between our countries. Presently, Rabbi Y. M. Teitelbaum of Kirlohozo and previously of Satu Mare (i.e. Satmar) is traveling as emissary of our Rabbinical Council in order to inform you of our great needs. He is authorized to represent our Central Council and the more than fifty rabbis who are leading our communities here.

There was little delay in answering this call. On January 21, 1946 (again through Rabbi Ungar of Nitra, since legal and official transfer of funds was as yet impossible) the Sternbuchs provided another $10,500. From that point on, having an authoritative body with whom to deal, the Sternbuchs undertook to extensively support the Orthodox council and its institutions. In the HIJEFS archives one can find records of steady correspondence during 1946 and part of 1947 between the Sternbuchs and the Turda Rabbi and other communal leaders throughout Roumania. Among the HIJEFS documents is also correspondence with many of the other rabbinic personalities in Roumania, including the renowned Rabbi David Sperber of Brasov, as well as with leaders of Agudath Israel.

The greatest efforts in Roumania were directed at restoring religious life. Talmud Torahs, Beth Jacob schools and yeshivos were founded, as well as orphanages, kosher kitchens and *kibbutzim* for those preparing for life in *Eretz Yisrael*. Substantial help was also extended to Jews who wished to leave Roumania immediately.

Special Delivery Problems

AT FIRST, THE STERNBUCHS made use of the services of the Red Cross, just as they had done earlier in Germany and Austria. When the Red Cross did not appear to be cooperative, the Sternbuchs arranged for transports of food to be shipped directly from the United States. Finally, in June 1946, the Sternbuchs succeeded in arranging a series of transports of clothing and foodstuffs through the Red Cross.

In time, the Sternbuchs established a special Roumanian Vaad Hatzalah committee, to oversee the organization and distribution of various types of aid for the entire land. This was no simple task, for conflicts arose among the various groups involved in religious, social and institutional life in Roumania. Mrs. Sternbuch feared these conflicts would interfere with the objectives which were for the common good. As Mrs. Sternbuch could not obtain a visitor's visa to enter Roumania, she resolved to settle the distant dispute by "remote control." To a great measure she succeeded.

Difficult as it was to get the aid to Roumania, the Sternbuchs also had to see to it that all aid was delivered into the proper hands. Frequently the food or clothing meant for the Orthodox institutions in Roumania were misdirected away from the Vaad Hatzalah into the hands of others. More than once this was due to interference by Jewish Communist officials. The Sternbuchs were forced to appeal to the Roumanian authorities to ensure that their shipments from the United States or Switzerland were properly delivered.

The Sternbuchs also endeavored to gain official recognition for the Vaad Hatzalah in Bucharest. Eventually, the Vaad Hatzalah was also recognized by the Red Cross, giving it status and winning a share of the general aid provided by the Red Cross to Roumania.

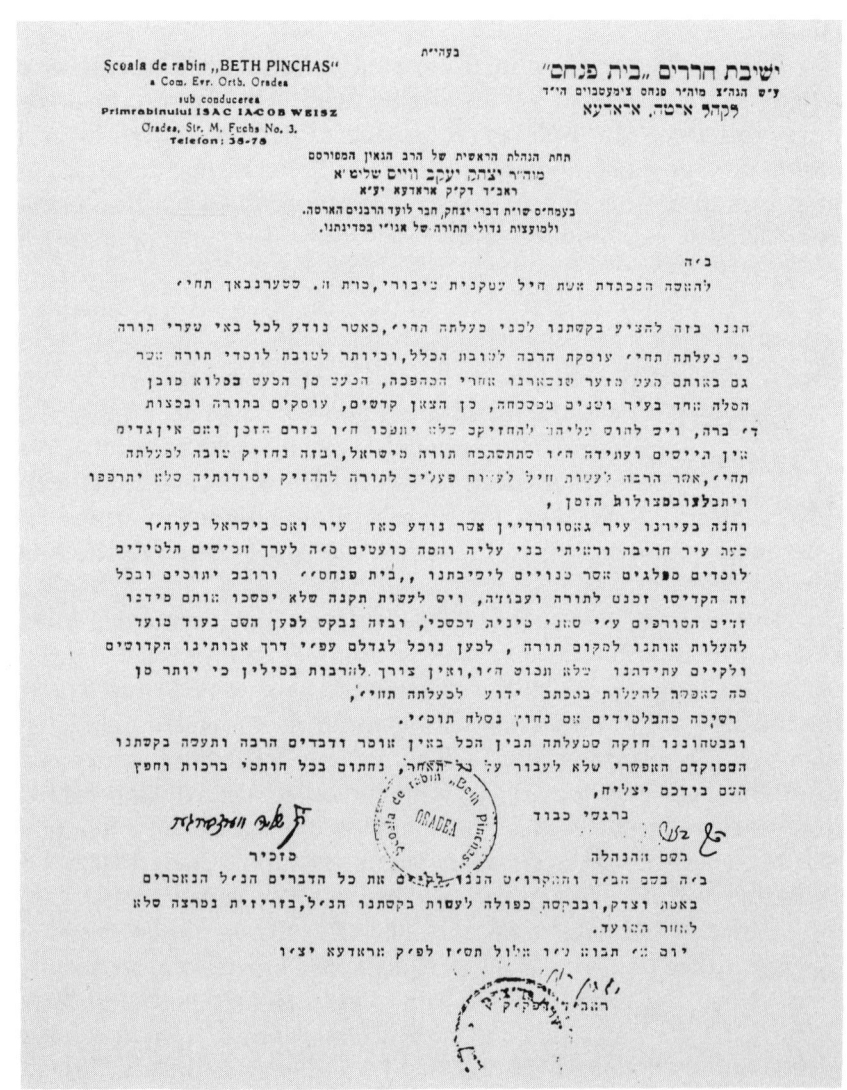

Letter from the Yeshivah Beth Pinchas in Oradea Rumania to Mrs. Recha Sternbuch concerning efforts to rescue their students to safer havens

MANY JEWS WHO WERE IN BUKOVINA and Bessarabia, which were officially annexed by the Soviet Union at the end of the war, were eager to leave. With the help of the Sternbuchs, the Bucharest office of the Vaad Hatzalah and Agudath Israel smuggled many thousands out of Soviet territory into Roumania. When the Sekulener Rebbe, Rabbi Eliezer Zusia Portugal, arrived in Roumania, this illegal work was intensified. It was carried out in great secrecy, as is illustrated by the abundance of ambiguities in the telegraphic messages between the Sternbuchs and the Orthodox leaders in Roumania — this action was referred to as "help for Alexander Zushe."

Escape from Soviet Control

Another major breakthrough for the Sternbuchs came when they obtained 250 immigrants' visas from the Belgian government for Jewish youths from Roumania. This meant safe passage for a large number of adults out of Roumania as well, because they posed as the counselors or guardians of these children on their journey into Belgium.

Aside from the work done by the Sternbuchs through the Rabbinical Council in Cluj and the Vaad Hatzalah committee in Bucharest, HIJEFS documents reveal that they indirectly arranged for financial assistance for some individual institutions in Roumania, by connecting them with friends and supporters living in the United States and England. Special mention must be made of Yeshivas Beis Pinchas in Arad and Oradea (Grosswardein) which was headed by Rabbi Yitzchok Yaakov Weiss, later *dayan* (religious judge) in Manchester, England, and presently the spiritual leader of the *Eidah Hacharedis* in Jerusalem.

TO APPRECIATE THE STERNBUCHS' efforts for Roumanian Jewry one must take into account that the funds allocated by the Vaad Hatzalah in America for use by the Sternbuchs were quite limited. In time, less and less money was provided. Furthermore, the needs of Roumania's Jews were not top priority on the Vaad Hatzalah budget. More pressing to them, apparently, were the needs of Jews in the D.P. camps and the thousands of others wandering aimlessly through Europe. Providing for the Orthodox institutions in Roumania thus became a frustrating task, but the Sternbuchs continued doing all

Increasing Needs, Diminishing Funds

that was possible. When funds were redirected by the Vaad Hatzalah, the Sternbuchs sought other sources of funding in the U.S., England, Switzerland, and elsewhere.

The Sternbuchs indirectly prodded the more affluent American Jewish Joint Distribution Committee to increase the support for the projects spearheaded by the Orthodox communities in Roumania. In the HIJEFS archives, one can find numerous complaints by Orthodox groups about discrimination suffered at the hands of the Joint's representatives in Roumania. One such petition reached the Sternbuchs at the end of the summer of 1947 from the *Agudas Harabonim Umachzikei Torah* in Bucharest, signed by well-known Bucharest rabbis, charging that the rabbis and scholars in Bucharest they were supporting had not "received any financial support at all from the Joint ..."

The Sternbuchs were familiar with some Joint officials in Europe who deemed all religious bodies to be "parasitical nuisances." This feeling was shared by professional social workers who lacked authentic Jewish feelings. In all such cases, the Sternbuchs would immediately ask the Orthodox leadership in the U.S.A. to intervene with the central office of the Joint in America. In the end, a positive modification in the Joint policy was effected. Countless petitions sent to the Joint regarding aid for Roumanian Jews can be found in the HIJEFS archives. Worthy of mention is the fact that the Sternbuchs were also instrumental in obtaining some Joint support for the projects of the Sekulener Rebbe.

Roumania Emigration

IN ROUMANIA THE STERNBUCHS apparently relied on *Bricha* agents from Palestine, which included several Orthodox emissaries, notably Dr. Jacob Griffel. However, when the situation became desperate in Roumania, in the spring of 1947, and most Orthodox Jews were struggling to leave the country, Recha Sternbuch renewed her efforts to secure a visa to Roumania for herself. She was finally successful in July of that year.

In Bucharest, Mrs. Sternbuch involved herself especially with the one hundred orphans cared for by the Sekulener Rebbe. (See the chapter on the Sekulener Rebbe.) She visited several yeshivos and even had a hand in the restoration of *mikvaos*. In addition, she assisted as much as possible in the emigration of countless individuals out of Roumania, an endeavor which was becoming increasingly difficult.

As HIJEFS records show, Recha Sternbuch did not return home from Bucharest, but rather flew directly to Paris and then to London, to arrange the transport from Roumania for the orphaned children cared for by the Sekulener Rebbe. The following is an excerpt of a letter dated October 27, 1947, from Mr. Yitzchok Sternbuch to Mrs. Gross-Hamburger at the Bucharest bureau of the Vaad Hatzalah:

> My wife, in making arrangements for the Roumanian matters, was detained for a certain length of time in England. She hasn't returned home even for the High Holidays. Her desire was to return to Roumania, when an urgent call came in from Warsaw, where she is presently found. Hopefully she will bring back with her the orphaned children from a children's home near Katowice. We expect her back next week. We estimate that, following a short stopover in Paris, she will continue straight away to Roumania once again.

HOWEVER, RECHA STERNBUCH never returned to Roumania. Apparently some Roumanian officials did not want her visa renewed because of her assistance to the Sekulener Rebbe. But her ties with Roumania were not severed. Our documents indicate that she continued to correspond with Roumania until the middle of 1948, in order to aid the emigration of the Sekulener Rebbe's children and youngsters of several other yeshivos.

Recha Sternbuch "Not Wanted"

Following the establishment of the State of Israel in April 1948, large-scale emigration from Roumania to Israel began. Among those who headed for *Eretz Yisrael* were the majority of those Jews who had been previously helped by the Vaad Hatzalah — including nearly all of the children from the Orthodox *kibbutzim* and orphanages.

In general (with the exception of ongoing assistance given to specific individuals and projects connected with the Sekulener Rebbe) this brings to a close the chapter of the enormous rescue efforts of Recha Sternbuch on behalf of the Orthodox Jews of Roumania, efforts which are gratefully remembered to this day by countless rabbis and Orthodox lay leaders all over the world.

Hungarian Lapse

THERE ARE FEW documents available on the work of Recha Sternbuch for Hungary after the war. It is quite possible that this work was not as extensive as her work for the Jews in other East European countries, simply because most religious Hungarian Jews who survived the war were from the regions which were immediately incorporated into Roumania. There is also a possibility that some HIJEFS files on Hungary after the war were still missing when the research for this book was done.

Available documents, however, do indicate that Hungary was not excluded from Recha Sternbuch's postwar agenda. Immediately after the liberation of Budapest, the Sternbuchs succeeded in overcoming many obstacles and contacted the leaders of the Orthodox *Centralkanzlei* (central office), under the chairmanship of Mr. Kahan-Frankel, to whom they sent a substantial amount of money for the needs of the community.

The following items show part of the Sternbuchs' steady interest in the needs of Hungarian Jewry:

- A memorandum dated November 11, 1945, to the Vaad Hatzalah tells about three yeshivos reestablished in Budapest, for which they requested additional funds after the previous allocations had been exhausted.
- A memorandum dated November 24, 1945, tells about 200 cartons of food sent to Budapest.
- A cable sent to New York on January 24, 1946, requests a special allocation for five wagons of potatoes for the approaching Passover holiday.
- A memorandum dated January 1946, reports an allocation of 29,000 Swiss francs for the Orthodox institutions in Budapest.
- In a telegram from Montreux to New York, dated March 3, 1946, the Sternbuchs ask for help for 1200 children under the protection of their organization in Budapest. This meant that the Sternbuchs were helping a number of children's homes in Hungary.

In the above cable the Sternbuchs also mentioned the need for help in the emigration from Hungary to Belgium and Italy, indicating that the Sternbuchs must have gained a number of visas for Jews in Budapest at the same time that they succeeded in obtaining the 250 visas for children in Roumania.

The few documents available indicate that Mrs. Sternbuch visited Budapest three times in 1947. In fact, the visa to Roumania in July 1947 (for which she struggled two years) was issued to Mrs. Sternbuch while she was visiting Budapest. The numerous trips to Budapest indicate some extensive activities for the Jews in Hungary.

Although the lack of further documents prevents us from telling the story of Hungary in detail, we may assume that there too Recha Sternbuch wrote one of her glorious chapters of self-sacrifice in service of her brothers and sisters in distress.

CHAPTER NINETEEN
Recha Sternbuch's Work in Western Europe — Saving the Jewish Children

AFTER THE WAR, France remained a rescue and relief center for the Sternbuchs for a longer period of time than any other European country. In retrospect, the Sternbuchs not only saved thousands of Jews — mainly Jewish children — and established France as a temporary haven for many thousands of survivors; at the same time they strengthened the foundations of a renewed traditional Jewish life in France. It is not an exaggeration to state that the Orthodox Jewish community which exists today in France is due in great measure to the seeds planted by the Sternbuchs at the conclusion of the war.

Preparing France as a Haven

As mentioned before, in October 1944, after the German retreat from parts of France, Recha Sternbuch dispatched Dr. Julius Kuhl and her brother-in-law Eli Sternbuch to investigate the situation of the surviving French Jews. France was not yet entirely free, and her cities and roads were still considered a war zone. In addition, Recha Sternbuch was then almost totally immersed in various projects to rescue the remaining Jews in Nazi hands. Nevertheless, she felt the pressing need to work on plans for the physical and spiritual rehabilitation of the Jews who would survive all over Europe. France, the closest country, was uppermost on her mind.

AS DR. KUHL HAD REPORTED, he and Eli Sternbuch stumbled upon a small institution for Jewish children in Aix-Les-Bains, on the first stop of their journey. This children's institution had been organized by Rabbi S. Seil and Rabbi Moshe Lebel, a former student of the Lubliner Rav, Rabbi Meir Shapiro. During the German occupation of France, both of them were in hiding. After the liberation they began to gather together the children of deported Jews who were left in the custody of gentile neighbors. They were given some assistance by OZE, a French-Jewish self-help organization. The leaders of OZE, however, had no sympathy for the religious education of these children and refused to finance any such effort.

The Initial Twenty in Aix-Les-Bains

Rabbis Seil and Lebel had only twenty children in their home at that time. But they told Dr. Kuhl and Mr. Sternbuch that they were sure that there were many more Jewish children in the care of numerous non-Jewish French families and institutions. Those children would have to be rescued immediately, or they certainly would be lost.

The report of Dr. Kuhl and Eli Sternbuch from France alarmed Recha Sternbuch. Although she was still occupied with her many projects for the Jews in Nazi hands, she decided not to wait and promptly placed Aix-Les-Bains under her wings. With her keen insight, she sensed that this small institution could become the cornerstone for her later efforts to rescue the many thousands of Jewish children in non-Jewish homes.

ONE MONTH LATER other areas of France were liberated from the Germans and the news reached the Sternbuchs about more children discovered in the custody of non-Jews. Mrs. Sternbuch immediately embarked on a large project for the rescue of these children. Since Mrs. Sternbuch still could not obtain a visa to France and Rabbi Lebel could not get a visa to Switzerland, a hasty meeting was arranged at the French-Swiss border. They worked out a plan to enlarge the children's home in Aix-Les-Bains to accommodate more children. And, although it was a bit premature, they also discussed plans to establish a yeshiva in Aix-Les-Bains.

Meeting at the Border

Aix-Les-Bains later became the main center for rescued children from France as well as from all over Europe. A few children's homes were founded in Aix-Les-Bains and the yeshiva, established a while later, was the first yeshiva in Europe where boys liberated from concentration camps renewed their study of Torah.

THE PRESENCE OF JEWISH children in non-Jewish homes weighed so heavily on Recha Sternbuch that one day after the liberation of France, she attempted to enter the country to save them. On the very same day that she received the visa, she went to France, in May 1945, to start her rescue mission.

"They Are Not Your Children"

Her mission was not as simple as she had thought. It was one thing to prepare proper homes, but it was much more difficult to remove the Jewish children from the non-Jewish homes. Neither private people nor institutions were willing to release the children to Recha Sternbuch nor any other Jewish group. For many reasons, emotional as well as legal, they refused to part with these children whom they considered their own — or their responsibility.

Recha Sternbuch was adamant. She saw it as her obligation to get these children out, and as soon as possible. She felt compelled to impress upon all French authorities and the public in general that these children, entrusted to the French gentiles by their Jewish parents before being deported to be killed, belonged to the Jewish people, and no one had the moral or legal right to adopt them.

Recha Sternbuch started knocking on many doors. She went from one children's home to another, and received the same answer: These children were given to us, put into our custody; we cannot release them to anyone but their parents. Many Frenchmen would not even open their door to a "strange intruder" who asked for children to whom she was not even related.

FORTUNATELY, MANY CHILDREN in the French children's institutions were under the jurisdiction of an organization created by the French resistance movement named COSOR (Comite des Oeuvres Sociales de la Resistance). It was headed by a kind-hearted priest, Pierre Chaillet. In contrast to many others in the church hierarchy who would have had the Jewish children brought up as Christians, he did listen to Mrs. Sternbuch's plea. The warm letter of recommendation from the Papal Nuncio Philippe Bernardini,

Breaking the Resistance

which praised Mrs. Sternbuch's humanitarian work during the war on behalf of all war victims, was of great help.

Yet it was not easy. Msgr. Chaillet did not have full authority and it took more than a month of hard negotiations to convince all the committee members of COSOR to agree with Mrs. Sternbuch that the Jewish people had a moral claim to these children. The fact that HIJEFS — whom Mrs. Sternbuch represented — was not a French but an American-Swiss organization with no legal status in France, presented a problem.

Mrs. Sternbuch was faced with the difficult task of explaining to COSOR why the Jewish organizations in France were not involved in these efforts with her. She could not reveal that they had little or no interest in this cause. Instead, she explained that the French-Jewish groups were overburdened with the physical rehabilitation of the Jewish war victims.

Finally, Recha Sternbuch won her case, and on June 19, 1945, an agreement was signed in which COSOR recognized the right of HIJEFS to care for the spiritual needs of all the Jewish children in all the children's homes under the supervision of COSOR, and to provide for their Jewish education. In the legal aspects of this work Mrs. Sternbuch was generously assisted by the Paris lawyer Mr. Maitre Soifer.

The victory was not complete, since according to the agreement all the children legally still remained under the authority of COSOR. But COSOR did recognize that these orphans — who by some Christians were not considered to be Jewish anymore — were members of the Jewish community, that the Jewish children had a right to Jewish education, and that COSOR had some moral obligation to enable these children to obtain this education.

In reality, it meant much more. Since the agreement authorized HIJEFS to provide religious education to the Jewish children in all the children's institutions, it enabled Recha Sternbuch to negotiate with all the homes' managers individually. Some of them did not want to be burdened with the complexities involved in providing religious education for the Jewish children and willingly released the children to Mrs. Sternbuch or her people.

The agreement between Mrs. Sternbuch and Msgr. Pierre Chaillet also had a psychological impact on many private French people who had Jewish children in their custody. And so the two

```
C. O. S. O. R.                                    PARIS, le 19 JUIN 1945
COMITÉ DES OEUVRES SOCIALES
DE LA RÉSISTANCE
                                Entre les soussignés,
63, Boulevard Haussmann
PARIS (9e)                      - 1°) le C.O.S.O.R. dont le siège est à PARIS, 93 Boulevard
                                       Haussmann, représenté aux fins des présentes par son
                                       Président, le R.P. CHAILLET,

                                - 2°) Vaad Hatzala American Emergency Committee -Union of
                                       orthodox Rabbis of the United States of America and Canada-représen-
                                       té par Madame Recha STERNBUCH, membre de l'Oeuvre de Secours pour
                                       les Enfants Juifs en Europe, et mandataire en vertu d'une procura-
                                       tion du 20 Juin 1945.
                                       Il a été exposé ce qui suit :

                                L'OEUVRE DE SECOURS POUR LES ENFANTS JUIFS EN EUROPE,
                                soucieuse d'aider au regroupement, à l'éducation matérielle,
                                morale et religieuse des enfants de confession israélite en
                                France, victimes de la persécution, a offert au C.O.S.O.R.
                                qui l'accepte, de lui apporter son concours matériel en vue de
                                l'organisation de maisons destinées à l'hébergement et à
                                l'éducation desdits enfants, dans le cadre de leurs traditions
                                et de la communauté française.

                                A cet effet, il a été convenu ce qui suit :

                        - I.     Le C.O.S.O.R. s'engage, avec le concours de l'OEUVRE DE SECOURS
                                POUR LES ENFANTS JUIFS EN EUROPE, à administrer les établissements
                                destinés à ces enfants.

                        - II.    L'OEUVRE DE SECOURS POUR LES ENFANTS JUIFS EN EUROPE s'engage,
                                aussi longtemps que fonctionneront les établissements prévus à
                                ladite convention, à verser au C.O.S.O.R. les dépenses de toute
                                nature afférentes au bon fonctionnement de ces établissements.
                                Le budget sera arrêté tous les trois mois par la commission d'admi-
                                nistration ci-dessous prévue. L'Oeuvre versera une provision tri-
                                mestrielle calculée pour les trois mois à venir, à concurrence
                                de Soixante Quinze Francs par jour et par enfant. Cette somme
                                sera réajustée à la fin du trimestre, sur la base des dépenses offi-
                                ciellement réalisées. Une nouvelle provision sera versée chaque
                                trimestre, sur les mêmes bases.

                                L'administration des établissements sera assurée
                                sous la haute direction du C.O.S.O.R. par une Commission d'Adminis-
                                tration composée de deux représentants du C.O.S.O.R. et de deux
                                représentants de l'Oeuvre. Cette commission devra se réunir autant
                                de fois qu'il sera nécessaire et, au minimum, une fois par mois.
                                Elle assurera d'une manière générale le fonctionnement des établis-
                                sements, sanctionnera le recrutement du personnel, procédera à des
                                inspections régulières de chaque établissement, suggèrera les modi-
                                fications à apporter dans chaque cas particulier et s'assurera
                                d'une manière plus spéciale de l'éducation générale donnée aux
                                enfants.

                        III. -  La présente convention portera ses effets entre les parties
                                aussi longtemps que par leur âge, les enfants devront être
                                hébergés dans les établissements ci-dessus prévus. Sans autre
                                préavis de la part de l'OEUVRE DE SECOURS POUR LES ENFANTS JUIFS
                                EN EUROPE, le présent accord se renouvellera automatiquement,
                                d'année en année, par tacite reconduction.

                        IV. -   En cas de difficulté quelconque entre les parties sur l'ap-
                                plication des présentes, les parties s'engagent à recourir
                                à l'arbitrage amiable ou compositeur. Chaque partie nommera un
                                arbitre et les arbitres s'entendront entre eux pour choisir un
                                super arbitre, s'il y a lieu.

                                Fait à Paris, le dix neuf juin mil neuf cent quarante cinq.

                                                        LE PRESIDENT DU C.O.S.O.R.,

                                                                P. Chaillet

VAAD HATZALA
AMERICAN EMERGENCY COMMITTEE                            Recha Sternbuch
```

Copies of the agreement between Recha Sternbuch and the C.O.S.O.R. [the French social authority] about the religious care of Jewish war orphans in France

homes that Mrs. Sternbuch had prepared in Aix-Les-Bains were filled in a very short time.

THE ACCOMPLISHMENTS of these institutions are captured in an article by Dr. Isaac Lewin, which appeared in the New York *Jewish Morning Journal* on August 28, 1945, written while he was visiting Europe:

The Miracle of Aix-Les-Bains

> What is happening today in Aix-Les-Bains, the little French city near the Swiss Alps, is simply a miracle. When I crossed the Swiss-French border by car to visit two orphanages which had just been opened, I wondered: 'Who knows what Judaism is left in these children who were hiding among non-Jews? They certainly must be completely assimilated.' I was, however, pleasantly surprised. First there was the Villa Raphael, where three weeks ago the Vaad Hatzalah established a children's home. I saw the children in the huge dining hall at a meal, where I sat with Mr. and Mrs. Sternbuch ... The children radiated with happiness and pride as they recited a *Hamotzi* blessing over the bread and later said the Grace After Meals. They are again within the fold, again members of the society of their parents.
>
> You sit here and think: Many of these children saying their Hebrew prayers had already been baptized and converted. Legally they are still Christian, for it is too complex to change their identity papers. But in reality, they once again belong to their own people, their own faith. Their parents had left them in Christian hands, but this is certainly what their parents prayed for on their way to Auschwitz. They surely wanted their children to remain Jewish. Now their wish has been fulfilled in this home at the Villa Raphael in Aix-Les-Bains. You can see and feel the Jewishness in these children. Not far from Villa Raphael is another home, housing 45 children, also being brought up in the Jewish tradition.

In the same article, Dr. Lewin described the preparations for the yeshiva which the Sternbuchs and Rabbi Moshe Lebel were about to establish:

> The Yeshivas Chachmei Tzorfas is already a reality — not just a handsome building, but a palace. About a hundred youngsters will find their place here. By now many boys from Buchenwald and Dachau are registered. The yeshiva only awaits their arrival. The first Rosh Hayeshiva (dean) is already

here: Rabbi Chaikin, a former student of the Radiner Yeshiva. He too has just returned from [German] imprisonment.

More to Follow

THE TWO HOMES founded by the Sternbuchs and Rabbi Lebel in Aix-Les-Bains were merely the beginning. Later, when Recha Sternbuch brought out hundreds of other Jewish children from non-Jewish auspices in Poland, she established another much larger children's home in Aix-Les-Bains, at the huge five-story Hotel Bensite, which housed about 250 children.

Mrs. Shifra Yudasin, the educational director of the Hotel Bensite, and now a lecturer at the Beth Jacob Teachers Seminary in Brooklyn, related:

> There were many amazing things about Recha Sternbuch. Not only did she establish the home and continue to care for its efficient functioning and the well-being of the children, she was also deeply concerned about the educational standards of the institution. After all, she had saved these children so they would grow up Jewish in the full sense of the word. Between

Mrs. Sternbuch with a group of children saved from non-Jewish homes in France after the agreement with C.O.S.O.R. The children were placed at a home in Ville Juif. This picture was taken at the ceremony of putting up a mezuzah, performed by Dr. Isaac Lewin. At the right: the lawyer, Mr. Maitre Soifer.

trips to Poland and Czechoslovakia [from where she invariably brought more children], she would visit our home and attend to many details concerning the operation of the home. She enjoyed all aspects of the growth of the children immensely, but her greatest joy was to see their inner Jewish development — the growth of their Jewish personality, their Jewish knowledge and religious behavior.

Towards this goal, Recha Sternbuch was anxious to engage the best teachers and educators to instill into their young hearts a love for Torah and *mitzvos* ...and she urged our educators to attend the lectures of the great Torah authority, Rabbi Mordechai Pogramansky, whom she herself brought to Aix-Les-Bains. She also advised us to consult Rabbi Pogramansky about all our educational problems.

One day we were visited by a prominent Jewish-French personality who generously helped Recha Sternbuch with her homes in Aix-Les-Bains. He wanted to know why we were stressing religion so strongly in our home. I told him: "This is a home for children. They need a father, and since they don't have one, we try to instill in them that they do have a father — *our Heavenly Father!*" Recha Sternbuch was overjoyed when I told her this answer.

Mr. and Mrs. Sternbuch and Dr. Isaac Lewin with rescued children at the Villa Raphael in Aix-Le-Bains

Yeshiva at St. Germain

Recha Sternbuch helped in the development of the yeshiva and home for teenage boys with the same energy she invested in the children's homes. Whenever she returned from her trips to Poland and Czechoslovakia, she always brought along some boys, whom she placed in these institutions. Incidentally, she established a similar institution for homeless children in Versailles, near Paris, to which she was similarly devoted.

In 1949-50, after the State of Israel was established, most of the children left France, and the homes in Aix-Les-Bains were closed down. But Aix-Les-Bains is still famous for its yeshiva and the Beth Jacob Seminary in Aix-Les-Bains is a direct outgrowth of the institutions which Recha Sternbuch founded there after the war.

RECHA STERNBUCH'S ACTIVITIES in France involved much more than the rescue of Jewish children and guiding the few institutions.

More than Children In time it encompassed many other aspects of Jewish rescue and postwar relief efforts.

Soon after her first visits to France on behalf of Jewish children, Recha Sternbuch realized that France could serve as a temporary haven for Jews from other parts of Europe, who could not wait where they were until the doors of Palestine or other countries in the free world would open. For some Jewish survivors in Germany it was a psychological necessity to get

Elementary yeshiva at Bailly, France

out of Germany as soon as possible. In some D.P. camps, life, although free of any danger, was miserable. Only a change to a free country could relieve their psychological depression. It was more urgent for many Jews, especially Jewish children, to leave Poland, Czechoslovakia, Roumania and Hungary.

From the first moment Recha Sternbuch appeared in France on her missions, she won the admiration and respect of many French government officials who were sympathetic to the plight of the Jewish war survivors. Some were so overwhelmed by her dedication that they would not refuse any of her requests.

In September 1945, Mrs. Sternbuch, together with Dr. Isaac Lewin, was granted a blank visa for 500 children to be brought to France from D.P. camps in Germany. For some reason, this visa was never used, but it opened the door for similar efforts which followed.

Concern Across the Border

IN 1946 AND 1947, Mrs. Sternbuch succeeded in obtaining several hundred French visas for Jews whom she brought out of Poland, Czechoslovakia, Hungary and Roumania. Her concern for them did not stop at the French border. She also cared for them after their arrival and was instrumental in the establishment of two large Orthodox refugee centers in St. Germain and Bailly, near Paris. The latter served as the home for yeshiva scholars who

Mr. and Mrs. Sternbuch at a conference about Jewish children in non-Jewish homes, with Dr. Isaac Lewin and Rabbi Rubinstein in Paris

survived the war, either in the U.S.S.R. or in concentration camps. For a while, the center in Bailly became a large yeshiva with many renowned Torah scholars from various yeshivos. Mrs. Sternbuch, with her great love for Torah and respect for Torah scholars, accorded this refugee center her unlimited attention. Even when she was on her missions, and certainly when she visited Paris, she made great efforts to obtain visas to the United States for these scholars and to provide for their many other needs. Many Torah scholars who lived in Paris after the war recall her numerous deeds with great appreciation to this very day.

IN CONCLUSION, Yitzchok and Recha Sternbuch may be credited with another important achievement immediately after the **Lasting Imprint** liberation of France. They were the first to bring vital help to the few Orthodox Jewish communities in France, to revive their activities after the war. French Jews who came out of hiding or who returned from camps, although better off than the Jews in Eastern Europe, needed help to restore their various communal institutions.

At the end of 1944 and beginning of 1945, the Sternbuchs were instrumental in connecting the French rabbis and their communities with Vaad Hatzalah and other U.S. groups. In the years that followed, they were in steady contact on matters of rescue and relief with the rabbis of Paris: Rabbi Eli Munk, Rabbi Shmuel Yaakov Rubinstein, Rabbi Weil, and others. Indeed, they developed a lasting personal friendship with some of these rabbis, who remembered all their efforts with deep gratitude.

CHAPTER TWENTY
Survived, but Not Spared: Switzerland, Belgium and Holland

THE CONDITION OF THE JEWS who survived the Second World War was not the same everywhere. In liberated Western Europe, their situation was not as bleak as it was in Germany, Austria, Czechoslovakia, Hungary and Roumania, for they soon ceased to suffer from hunger and were not exposed anew to danger, as were the Jews in Eastern Europe. The surviving Jews in Western Europe had other problems and serious needs, however; here too, wherever a need existed, Recha and Yitzchok Sternbuch extended their helping hand. France was dealt with in the previous chapter. Now we will dwell on Switzerland, Belgium and Holland.

THE SWISS JEWS, as we know, escaped the horrors of the war and the Holocaust. Because of this — and in a large measure, due to the rescue work of the Sternbuchs — Switzerland became an important center of Jewish refugees and survivors during and after the war. Although the Sternbuchs' main preoccupation was with the emergencies of the Jews outside Switzerland, their imprint was also quite evident on the situation of the Jews who were saved in Switzerland.

Switzerland: A Battleground for Souls

Since a number of very effective relief organizations operated in Switzerland, among them Orthodox ones, not all the problems of the Jewish refugees came to the Sternbuchs. But whenever there was a serious problem, the Sternbuch address remained a dependable source of help. Wherever there was a seemingly insoluble situation, it became a case for Recha Sternbuch. When all doors were closed, their door remained open.

One such serious dilemma was the case of Jewish children who had been placed in non-Jewish homes and institutions in Switzerland. Shortly before the end of the war, the International Red Cross brought a few thousand Jews — among them several hundred Jewish children — to Switzerland. They were placed by Swiss government officials in non-Jewish private institutions, supported by various philanthropic agencies, a minority of which were Jewish. This disturbed the Sternbuchs greatly. They pleaded with the influential Jewish organizations to intervene to have these children placed in Jewish homes where they would receive a Jewish upbringing, but to no avail. The Jewish organizations were not interested.

The Sternbuchs then offered their own services: they would provide for the children themselves. But for this they needed the cooperation of the entire Jewish community. Only a united demand by all influential Jewish organizations could persuade the Swiss authorities to release the Jewish children. This help, however, was not forthcoming. In fact, some influential Jews even warned the government not to entrust the children to the Sternbuchs, who would bring them up in the spirit of Orthodox Judaism.

DR. ISAAC LEWIN, who visited Switzerland in August 1945, two months after the war, depicted this situation in his book *After the Holocaust*, a collection of his articles:

"Sternbuch Agitated, Moves Heaven and Earth"

Several hundred Jewish children are under non-Jewish auspices. Mr. Yitzchok Sternbuch cannot rest. The Vaad Hatzalah and HIJEFS are ready to place all monies at their disposal to ransom the children and to support them in Jewish homes, but to no avail. Sternbuch becomes extremely agitated. He confers, he negotiates, he moves heaven and earth.

I had the occasion, together with Mrs. Sternbuch, to visit the Chief of the Swiss Police several times regarding this matter. The Police Chief was aware of the sufferings of the Jewish people, who had endured such terrible losses. He agreed with the Sternbuchs that these children belong to the Jewish people. This was clear to many others in the government circles. But the children still remained in non-Jewish homes. Why?

The Jewish upbringing that HIJEFS and the Sternbuchs desired to give them was a religious one ... and, the Police Chief explained to me, official Jewish circles in Switzerland did not wish the Jewish orphans to obtain a religious education of the intensity represented by Mrs. Sternbuch.

The Sternbuchs carried on this battle for the Jewish children over a long period. Finally they achieved a partial victory. They persuaded Dr. Kopetzky, the Czechoslovakian ambassador, and Alexander Lados, the Polish ambassador, to approach the International Red Cross. The ambassadors demanded that the Red Cross turn over to them those Jewish children who had come from Poland and Czechoslovakia, and the Red Cross acquiesced to this request. They, in turn, entrusted those children to the Sternbuchs, who placed the children in Jewish homes where they received a religious upbringing. Thus, several hundred children in Switzerland were saved by the Sternbuchs.

The Belgian Struggles

THE JEWS OF BELGIUM, whether saved by hiding, or returning from the concentration camps, did not have too many difficulties in returning to a normal life. It was not easy, but slowly they regained their homes, reestablished some businesses and started life anew.

However, the revival of religious life was much more difficult. They lacked funds to rebuild their *shuls*, schools, or *mikvaos*. Again, the Sternbuchs provided the seed money for all these important initiatives, enabling them to rebuild Jewish religious life.

As in France, the most disturbing problem in Belgium was the orphaned Jewish children housed in non-Jewish homes. Some children were in private homes, others in general orphanages or church institutions, none of which were eager to return these children. Even Jewish parents often had difficulties in regaining custody of their own children who had been saved by Christian neighbors. The leaders of general institutions were reluctant to hand Jewish children over to the Jewish communities that were ill prepared to provide for them. And some church leaders refused to release children who had already been baptized and were considered by the churchmen to be Christians.

As in Switzerland, a bitter struggle to save the children developed; it succeeded, in great measure, thanks to the efforts of the Sternbuchs who founded a beautiful children's home in Marraburg, near Antwerp, in August 1945. The institutions' leaders could no longer refuse to release the Jewish children on the grounds that the Jewish community (not yet fully organized) could not provide properly for them. Some of them understood the claim of the Jewish community on these children, but others had to be morally pressured. In time, the home in Marraburg was filled.

Dr. Isaac Lewin describes his visit to that home in his book *After the Holocaust:*

> I met Jewish children there who were saved from death during the war — and from loss of their Judaism after their survival. It is the first such home in Belgium, and I spent several hours there. It was a moving experience to hear the children laugh again. They are again among Jews and in a Jewish atmosphere — and they are happy ... When I saw them I imagined how happy their perished parents in Heaven must be, knowing that their children were not lost to the Jewish people.

Even after this home was established, the struggle for many Jewish children did not cease. In some cases, the whereabouts of the children had to be discovered, since their foster parents attempted to hide their Jewish identity. In other cases, the Sternbuch agents were forced to put up a struggle. Inspired by Recha Sternbuch, who did similar work herself in France and in Poland, her people did not flag in their efforts. Prominent in this work were her brother, Josef Rottenberg of Antwerp, and two American emissaries, Herman Treisser, Vice President of the American Zeirei Agudath Israel, and Moshe Swerdloff, who was accompanied by his young wife. In the course of the next two years they rescued many Jewish children from being lost as Jews.

THE SURVIVING JEWS in Holland — where beautiful Orthodox communities had thrived before the war — were less secure than those in France and Belgium. The war in Holland ended much later than in its neighboring countries, and return to normal conditions took much longer.

The Precarious Dutch Terrain

The Orthodox Jews in Holland, who were a minority in the surviving community, were in the most precarious situation. The community leaders did not care much for their specific needs. As elsewhere, the Sternbuchs, from afar, were the first to alarm the religious Jewish world about their plight.

A cable that the Sternbuchs sent to the Vaad Hatzalah in the U.S. on June 6, 1945, urged:

> After we were informed of an alarming situation in Holland, we held an emergency meeting with Chief Rabbi [Tovia] Levenstein [who was the Orthodox Chief Rabbi of Holland during World War I and later the Chief Rabbi of the Orthodox Jewish community in Zurich] and decided to inform you about this catastrophic situation. There are 3,000 Jewish children in non-Jewish homes ... The Jewish Committee is non-religious and does not care ... It does not want to help the religious Jews ... Many families are forced to eat *treifa* ... We took the liberty of assigning 1500 gulden as initial help, but we need immediately 4000 dollars more as first aid. Rabbi Levenstein is ready to go to Holland and take over the rabbinate of the Hague. Please assign help and alarm Jews from Holland who reside in the free world to help the Orthodox communities.

From the documents of HIJEFS we see that the situation in Holland occupied the attention of the Sternbuchs for many months. Although travel to Holland was complicated — all bridges to Belgium were totally destroyed — they managed to send kosher food and mobilized financial aid to the Orthodox community, which recuperated much faster than expected.

But the situation of the Jewish children remained a nagging problem for quite a long time. The children's agencies in Holland adamantly refused to return the children to the Jewish organizations. At the initiative of the Sternbuchs, Chief Rabbi Herzog paid a special visit to Holland to plead with Queen Wilhelmina, and a few months later Rabbi Eliezer Silver took up this problem with the Queen.

All of these interventions finally bore some fruits. Many children were later taken over by the Jewish organizations, but many never returned. Until the end of her life, Recha Sternbuch mourned these lost Jewish souls.

CHAPTER TWENTY-ONE
Sweden: Unravaged but on the Sternbuch Map

SWEDEN WAS ONE of the few countries in Europe that did not suffer German occupation, and so the small Jewish community in Sweden was not affected by the ravages of the war. On the contrary, a few thousand Jews from Denmark were saved from the Nazis by escaping to Sweden, as is well known. In addition, during the last months of the war and immediately following, Sweden generously opened its doors for several thousand Jewish survivors from concentration camps. Yet Sweden too was on the map of Recha Sternbuch and her HIJEFS organization in Montreux for some important relief and rescue work.

AMONG THE JEWS who found their way to Sweden at the close of the war were a large number of Jewish women and girls from Hungary and Poland who were saved from various concentration camps. While all their physical and material needs were taken care of by the Swedish government and welfare agencies, a serious spiritual problem immediately arose. First, many of the refugees were Orthodox and they refused to eat non-kosher food. They were also eager to renew their religious life and they could hardly depend on the official Jewish leadership in Sweden. The general Jewish community in Sweden, headed by Dr. Marcus Ehrenpreiz, a Reform rabbi, did not show any interest or sympathy whatsoever

Physical Haven, Spiritual Swampland

212 / HEROINE OF RESCUE

Rabbi Shlomo Wolbe   *Rabbi Wolf Jacobson*

for the specific needs of the religiously observant survivors. As a matter of fact, they refused to intervene with the Swedish authorities for kosher food.

In addition, an acute spiritual problem threatened many Jewish survivors. This problem manifested itself when, only two months after their arrival in Sweden, a number of the Jewish refugee girls married non-Jewish men. Since there were so few Jewish men among them, many others were on the verge of following their example. After they had suffered so much pain and isolation, they were overwhelmed by the Swedish population's warm reception and their eagerness to integrate them into their society. Thus the danger of widespread, swift assimilation was all the more imminent. Indeed, many survivors abandoned their previous Jewish way of life, enrolled in non-Jewish schools, accepted jobs that required them to work on Sabbath, and were only too happy to join the new friendly Swedish society.

To meet this dangerous situation, Rabbi Wolf Jacobson (the former rabbi of the Orthodox community of Copenhagen) and Rabbi Shlomo Wolbe (now one of the outstanding *Mussar* personalities in Israel) led a few Orthodox Jewish activists in Sweden in taking action. Notable among them were Rabbi Abraham Israel Jacobson and Rabbi Jacob Israel Zuber. They immediately contacted the survivors, especially the women and girls, and started caring for their various needs, thus encouraging them to renew a religious life style. After obtaining permission from the Swedish government, they established kosher kitchens and synagogues in some of the centers, and also provided kosher food for religious survivors who had been placed in convalescent homes and hospitals.

Since a substantial number of the survivors came from religious homes, the efforts of Rabbi Jacobson and Rabbi Wolbe were met with a warm response. As a matter of fact, they themselves were highly impressed with the religious fervor of many of the youngsters who, after all their suffering, had not lost their faith and were more than eager to cling to their traditional way of life.

Although Rabbis Jacobson and Wolbe had made direct contact with the Vaad Hatzalah in the United States, here too Recha Sternbuch immediately stepped in and became active in these efforts in Sweden. Later the Sternbuchs were instrumental in helping to establish a number of important institutions in Sweden, which kept Judaism alive in the hearts of hundreds of young men and women. Somehow, they seemed to understand the special needs that prevailed in certain countries.

THE RECORDS OF HIJEFS show that from the time the Sternbuchs received news of the arrival of the first group of Jewish survivors in Sweden, they placed great emphasis on obtaining complete lists of their names. In the following months, when they learned more of the threat of assimilation and intermarriage, they were even more determined to obtain such lists, much more so than from other places. In numerous cables they strongly implored Rabbi Jacobson and Rabbi Wolbe to compile such lists; they were not satisfied until they were sure that these lists were complete. Mr. Herman Landau, the secretary of HIJEFS, explained the ardent efforts of the Sternbuchs:

"Send Us All the Names"

> From the very first moment of the liberation, the Sternbuchs were keen to have lists of all survivors. During the war they constantly received many thousands of inquiries from Jews all over the world asking about the location and fate of their relatives. Now that it seemed possible to obtain such

information, they tried to get these lists very quickly in order to be able to inform the relatives abroad of the survival of family and friends. They also realized that the availability of such lists would help to bring together many couples and families who had been separated during the war. However, Sweden was a special case. The Sternbuchs understood that speedy contact between the few thousand Jews in Sweden and their relatives abroad would also be helpful in combating all temptations of assimilation and eventually intermarriage. In fact, ... those Jewish women and girls who succeeded in contacting their relatives were more immune to the perils of assimilation so prevalent among the survivors in Sweden. This explains a telegram which the Sternbuchs sent to Rabbi Jacobson and Rabbi Wolbe on January 6, 1945, in which they ask for a list of *all* refugees — including non-Orthodox Jews who came to Sweden.

OF MUCH GREATER IMPORTANCE was the practical assistance which the Sternbuchs gave to the work of Rabbis Jacobson and Wolbe in Sweden. Their great contribution is clearly seen from the vast correspondence between the Sternbuchs and Rabbis Jacobson and Wolbe that took place in the months of May through August of 1945, not long after the arrival of the Jewish refugees in Sweden. Although the liberated Jews in Sweden were in no great need physically, the Sternbuchs at once grasped their spiritual plight and provided Rabbis Jacobson and Wolbe with the necessary funds for their activities. In their messages to the Vaad Hatzalah in the U.S., they continued to stress the importance of helping the survivors in Sweden.

"Help All the Children!"

A letter from Recha Sternbuch to Rabbis Jacobson and Wolbe, dated June 4, 1945, points out the importance of establishing special homes, to be run in the Orthodox spirit, and schools for the religious youth. Yet, as befitted Recha Sternbuch, her interest extended to *all* Jewish youngsters in Sweden. She wrote:

> It is our opinion that you not limit yourselves only to Orthodox children but rather make an effort to save all children for Judaism. We are afraid that if the children will fall into other hands, they will become entirely lost to the Jewish people.

In the same letter, the Sternbuchs address the future of these children in Sweden. At that time, some Jews still lived under the illusion of being able to rebuild a Jewish life in Europe. But the Sternbuchs already understood that there was no future for Jews in most of the European countries. Recha Sternbuch wrote:

> We beg of you to make all efforts that the children should not return to Poland, Czechoslovakia or Germany, whether they or their parents are so inclined. Please appeal to the Jewish leaders in America, England and *Eretz Yisrael* that the children be given the opportunity to emigrate to America or *Eretz Yisrael*.

Thanks to the encouragement and active support of the Sternbuchs, a number of wonderful institutions were established in Sweden for the Holocaust survivors. Among them were a religious high school for girls with a dormitory in Lidinge; a home for 300 girls in Lavey; a yeshivah; a religious camp for refugees in Robertsheid; as well as two *kibbutzim*, Hachalutz Hacharedi (Agudath Israel), and *Bachad* (Hapoel Hamizrachi).

After the Sternbuchs received the list of Jews in Sweden, they discovered through different channels that many girls fom religious homes were housed with non-Jewish families somewhere in Sweden. They immediately informed the Orthodox leaders in Sweden of their whereabouts, so that they could place them in their religious homes and institutions.

Inspiration Stays in the Camps

THE INTENSIVE RELIGIOUS spirit that permeated these camps and institutions, the inspiring Sabbaths and Jewish festivals, and the thirst to study Torah on the part of these youngsters who had suffered so much, is vividly described by Rabbi Wolf Jacobson in his book *Eso De'i Lemeirachok*:

> A girl stepped out of one of the buses, looked around in great wonder and cried out, "Oh, so many trees and no barbed wire!" Tears streamed down her cheeks and suddenly she shouted the *Shehecheyanu* blessing. I was taken aback. After these six terrible years of hunger and pain, how did this girl still remember the blessing?

Rabbi Jacobson tells of over a hundred girls who upon their arrival in Sweden refused to eat non-kosher food. He describes how through the efforts of Rabbis Wolbe and Zuber, they were brought to the Helshin camp where they had a kosher kitchen. He then describes his first Sabbath with them.

> It was a Sabbath such as I never witnessed before. A holy and awesome sight: thirty young widows kindled the Sabbath light, made *kiddush*, washed and made the blessing over bread and later said the Grace ... all the others followed suit, most of them orphans. I reminded myself of the Yom Kippur prayer: "My soul quivers over hearing this tiding ... Fortunate is the eye that sees this all."
>
> In the beginning someone tried to sing the Sabbath *Zemiros*, but without success. After Grace, however, three sisters started singing and others followed. Yes, genuine Sabbath *Zemiros* with all its charm and grace. Later some of them told us that they were surprised that they still remembered all these hallowed tunes ... This was the beginning of their new lives.

All the above-mentioned institutions, which functioned in Sweden for two or three years, had an enormous impact on their hundreds of charges. Almost all of the religious youngsters sheltered in Sweden successfully withstood the religious alienation and assimilation that threatened the survivors.

MR. CHAIM HERTZ, currently an Orthodox community leader in Brooklyn, is a survivor who came to Sweden to be reunited with his wife shortly after his liberation from Buchenwald. He recalled that the Vaad Hatzalah-HIJEFS institutions also had an impact on many young Jewish women and girls outside their walls:

Long Reaching Impact

> I remember one young Jewish girl — let's call her Esther — whom I know to be living in Tel Aviv. She came from a Chassidic family in Warsaw, but after being alone for many years in a number of concentration camps she became completely estranged from Judaism. After arriving in Sweden, she lived with a non-Jewish family in Upsala. A girl friend who met her in Stockholm invited her for a Sabbath to Lidinge, and when she saw the other girls singing *Shalom Aleichem* at the *Shabbos* table she broke out in uncontrollable weeping. She did not even know that there were Jews left who kept the Sabbath, ate kosher and led a Jewish life. Esther never returned to Upsala. She just wrote them a letter that she found a "few sisters" in Lidinge. A few months later she immigrated

to *Eretz Yisrael*, where she now is the grandmother of 15 Chassidic grandchildren.

She is not the only one. My friend and I, who were in Sweden after the war, know many such women who were brought back to the fold, thanks to the institutions founded by Rabbi Jacobson and Rabbi Wolbe with the help of Vaad Hatzalah and HIJEFS.

The Sternbuchs can also be credited with the efforts made both in America and in *Eretz Yisrael* to remove these young men and women from Sweden very promptly. The Sternbuchs constantly appealed to the Orthodox leaders in the free world to focus their attention on the Jews in Sweden, where the risk of assimilation was greater than anywhere else. The Vaad Hatzalah was especially responsive to this plea and as a result the surviving Jewish youth of Sweden were among the first to emigrate to the U.S. and *Eretz Yisrael*.

CHAPTER TWENTY-TWO
Recha Sternbuch and Her Individual Beneficiaries

A UNIQUE ASPECT of Recha Sternbuch's rescue and relief efforts was her deep interest and compassion for individuals in distress. It is common knowledge that people at the head of great relief agencies may develop a tendency to overlook the individual, who becomes a small and insignificant part of their task (and with whom they cannot be bothered). This was never the case with Recha Sternbuch. As busy as she was, with rescue projects for thousands, she never lost sight of the fact that her rescue efforts were aimed at people. She was not just out to protect the burning forest, she wanted to save the trees.

While the majority of letters and telegrams of the HIJEFS archives deals with rescue and aid projects for groups and communities or the establishment of institutions, a significant portion of this correspondence deals with the needs of individuals.

This was certainly the case when Recha Sternbuch started her rescue work after the Nazis occupied Austria in 1938. At that time her work was mainly concerned with saving individual lives. But it also continued throughout the war, when the Sternbuchs sought to locate many people in response to inquiries from abroad, and also transmitted messages about others whom they heard were in captivity and danger.

A CODED MESSAGE the Sternbuchs received from Mr. Jacob Rosenheim and Dr. Isaac Lewin of the World Agudah via the Polish Embassy in Bern in July 1944, illustrates this concern for individuals. After inquiring about contacts with Rabbi Weissmandel in Bratislava, the message read:

"Save the Bobover Rebbe"

> From Sweden we heard that Piasechner Rebbe, Rabbi [Klonymos] Kalman Shapiro, born 1889, has been in a concentration camp in Opola, near Lublin, with his son-in-law Chaskel Rabinowitz and his daughter Rochel, born 1915. Save them. The Bobover [Rebbe] Shlomo Halberstam is still in Nagyvarad. Mother and brother arrested. Rest of family in Bucharest. Save them. In December 1943, we sent you $3,000 to save Rabbi Chaskel Halberstam of Czeshanow. Let us know if this money was spent or is still at disposal.
>
> Contact Rabbi Aaron Rokeach of Belz, Tel Aviv about saving Rabbi Pinkas Twersky (of Ustila). If necessary put 20,000 Fr. at his disposal to save same.
>
> London asks for help to Rosenbaum, packages to Theresienstadt ... How about Abraham and Simcha Klein ... Ilone Lichtig ...

This is only part of one of many messages the Sternbuchs were receiving daily during 1943 and 1944 from the United States, Britain, Palestine and other countries of the free world. The ongoing annihilation of European Jewry was already well known. Thus, many desperately tried to save their relatives by requesting help from the Sternbuchs who constantly managed to maintain some contacts with the Nazi-occupied territories.

INTERESTINGLY, THE STERNBUCHS already had initiated some efforts in regard to some of those listed in the above message. For instance, the Sternbuchs were already informed of the whereabouts of the Bobover Rebbe, Rabbi Shlomo Halberstam, who was in hiding in Nagyvarad on the border between Roumania and Hungary. The Bobover Rebbe and his family escaped from Budapest in April of 1944, after the Germans occupied the city. They tried to reach Roumania where Jews were not in immediate danger of deportation to Auschwitz, even though the country had been allied with Germany. On the way to Roumania the Bobover Rebbe's mother and sisters were arrested, but the Bobover Rebbe

"The Only Address We Knew"

Bobover Rebbe, Rabbi Shlomo Halberstam

himself managed to hide at Nagyvarad (Grossvardein) from where he tried to save his family. He contacted the Sternbuchs with whom he had communicated since he left Poland. A while later, when he clandestinely reached Bucharest, he again appealed to the Sternbuchs. On January 2, 1945, he cabled them:

> Mother Rivtcha Rutcha children still irhabiru [meaning Budapest] we worry to bring them here stop my wife children mother-in-law till now without information ...

Why did the Bobover Rebbe cable the Sternbuchs? He later explained: "It was the only address we knew which we could rely upon to deliver our messages to our relatives in the U.S. and Britain and through whom we also hoped to get, and in fact did receive, very necessary assistance."

IMMEDIATELY AFTER THE WAR the Sternbuch's concern for individuals grew immensely and thousands upon thousands of

"Where is Buna Blacher?"

individuals became their affair.

When Recha Sternbuch came to Germany in July and August of 1945 to help the liberated Jews with their many problems, she brought along lists of names of people for whom she was asked to provide special care, from relatives in Switzerland and overseas. While conferring with groups of rabbis or activist laymen about the establishment of kosher kitchens, schools or children's homes, she always kept those lists before her, in order to find the people and to extend some help to them. Rabbi Abraham Ziemba, quoted above in Chapter 15, related:

> When Mrs. Sternbuch came to Feldafing she immediately inquired about a number of individuals, and especially about a Buna Blacher, the daughter of the Rosh Hayeshiva of the Mezritcher Beth Joseph Yeshiva in Poland, Rabbi David Blacher. She had heard that Buna Blacher was gravely ill in the Feldafing Hospital. It so happened that we all knew Buna Blacher and were aware of her illness, but when we tried to visit her together with Mrs. Sternbuch we discovered that she had been relocated to another hospital in northern Germany. Her file was misplaced, however, and nobody knew anything of her whereabouts.
>
> It was not so simple at this time to find someone in Germany. Our offices had no telephones yet, and the mail was not functioning. After trying many hospitals without locating her, we gave up our search. But Recha Sternbuch could not and did not rest. She finally discovered that Buna Blacher was in a hospital near Frankfurt, and although she had already visited Frankfurt and its D.P. camps and made plans for her return to Switzerland, she again undertook a special trip from Munich to Frankfurt to visit her personally. Miss Blacher had tuberculosis, but this did not deter Recha Sternbuch from sitting at her bedside, holding her hand and comforting her for many hours. Later she brought her to a sanatorium in Davos, Switzerland, where she was partially cured and lived for a number of years.

Buna Blacher is only one of many such cases. There were many more ailing Jews among those liberated from camps whom she brought to Switzerland. Mrs. Sternbuch was also instrumental in getting other relief organizations in Switzerland to take care of many such people, by placing them in sanatoriums in Switzerland. As busy as she was with all her communal projects, she took a personal interest in the well-being of many of these individuals even after she had placed them in trustworthy caring hands.

IN POLAND, TOO, she took a personal interest in every lonely, sick, or helpless individual she met. She tried to expedite their emigration from Poland, and later continued inquiring about their welfare.

The Polish Vigil

Moreover, from 1945 through 1951, the HIJEFS office in Montreux cared for many thousands of individuals, especially in matters of emigration from Europe to countries overseas. Recha Sternbuch took a special interest in helping people searching for missing spouses — and there were many thousands of them. In such cases, she never tired of cabling and writing to all corners of Europe and engaging people in such searches. She was personally overjoyed whenever a search ended in the reuniting of a family.

The Sternbuch archives contain copies of hundreds of cables and letters to Jewish chaplains of the American, British, and French armies who served in Germany, who had turned to the Sternbuchs to help many individuals.

Rabbi Leib Cywiak, a well-known Orthodox community leader and the former executive director of Beth Medrash Govoha in Lakewood, recounted another incident. Rabbi Cywiak was repatriated from Russia to Poland in the spring of 1946. After arriving there with his small children and his elderly father-in-law, he was sent to Czechoslovakia on an illegal transport organized by Recha Sternbuch. When they arrived in Prague, however, they could not proceed any further. Recha Sternbuch had blank French visas ready for this group of 500 people, but there were no carriages available on the Prague-to-Paris train. Rabbi Cywiak recalled:

> We were told that we would have to wait for about three weeks. When Mrs. Sternbuch heard this she was terribly upset. Among the 500 people whom she brought out from Poland were a few families with little children and a few elderly rabbis. She had planned to go back to Switzerland for that Sabbath after having been away from home, in Poland, Czechoslovakia and France, for about seven weeks. But she decided to remain in Prague over Sabbath. She just could not bring herself to leave these families with children and elderly

members. On Sunday she succeeded in hiring a bus for those families, but even then she did not return home. New emergencies arose which to my knowledge kept her in Prague and Warsaw for another few weeks.

SINCE BANKS AND POSTAL services were not functioning during the first year after the war, Jews in the U.S. and other countries **Messenger to the Missing** who wanted to provide their relatives with funds had no way to do so. Recha Sternbuch volunteered to become a "messenger" for delivering such funds. She did all this although it was forbidden in some countries because of severe monetary restrictions. Furthermore, it was quite a complicated task, because of the intricate bookkeeping it involved.

The following is a sample of a few of the tens (sometimes even hundreds) of cables which the Sternbuchs received daily from many corners of the globe.

From Chief Rabbi Herzog in Jerusalem:

Jerusalem, 13.3.45.
HIJEFS, MONTREUX
WARMEST BLESSINGS SACRED WORK PRAYING SUCCESS STOP PLEASE INTEREST YOURSELVES ... MARTHA POSNER AND FAMILY AT PRESENT BERGEN BELSEN ARRIVED THERE HOLLAND FEBRUARY 1944 ... CABLE ANY NEWS ... GREETINGS ISAAC HERZOG CHIEF RABBI

From the Vaad Hatzalah office in New York:

4/5/45
STERNBUCH
HIJEFS, MONTREUX
BRONISLAWA BORN WYGODNA WITH MOTHER BLUMA AND HUSBAND MOJZESZ PORHUCZEWSKI CHILD JERZY ADDRESS REPATRICANI TABOR PRAHA HLBOUBETI CZECHOSLOVAKIA STOP PLEASE ENDEAVOR SECURE ENTRY SWITZERLAND FORWARDED YOU AFFIDAVIT FROM THEM.

Vaad Hatzalah

From the Agudath Israel Youth Council in New York:

NEW YORK, 26.11.45
STERNBUCH, HIJEFS,
MONTREUX
URGENT ... BRING TO SWITZERLAND ALTE LIPOVAN 19 YEARS CECILA LIPOVAN 15 YEARS NOW PODMOKLY

> CZECHOSLOVAKIA TEPLICKA 72-371 STOP NONQUOTA VISA APPROVED ... STATE DEPARTMENT WASHINGTON TO AMERICAN CONSUL ZURICH ... FATHER AMERICAN CITIZEN ...
>
> AGUDAH YOUTH NEW YORK

Another from the Agudath Israel Youth Council in New York:

> NEW YORK, 1.6.45.
> ISAAC STERNBUCH,
> HIJEFS, MONTREUX
> URGENT DOING EVERYTHING POSSIBLE EITHER KEEP LEAH WEINSTOCK FROM BEING SENT BACK TO HUNGARY OR BRING TO SWITZERLAND STOP ... LIBERATED FROM CAMP OF JEWISH GIRLS FROM HUNGARY STOP EXPECT AMERICA VISA
>
> AGUDATH ISRAEL
> YOUTH COUNCIL

On the same day a cable from the Agudah office in Jerusalem:

> 1.6.45
> STERNBUCH C/O HIJEFS
> MONTREUX, SWITZERLAND
> CHAYA COHEN FREED LADSBERG VERY SICK STOP PLEASE ASSIST HER STOP ALSO MOSHE BERGER FROM LODZ PLEASE FIND HIM HAS CHILDREN HERE STOP MOTHER IN JERUSALEM MIRIAM BRECHER HEARD DAUGHTER MIRYAM FREED NEAR DACHAU PLEASE FIND HER
>
> I. M. LEVIN

Recha Sternbuch did not file away these thousands of cables for the secretaries, but took a personal interest in each of them. Recognizing these cases as matters of life and death, she did not rest until she was able to find these people, immediately take some action, and promptly report to the inquirers.

It was not easy to locate all these individuals among the thousands of survivors. It meant cables and letters at a time when the mail and even telegraph hardly functioned. It also meant constantly asking others for help. Nevertheless she did not tire.

CHAPTER TWENTY-THREE
"K'vod HaTorah" — Special Deference to Scholars

MRS. STERNBUCH SEEMED to harbor a boundless interest in the welfare of rabbis and other Jewish scholars, an attitude she developed in her parents' home. Whenever she met a rabbi or Torah scholar on her trips, she immediately did whatever possible to help him, and she continued to send him help after she returned home.

Rabbi Victor Vorhand, the Chief Rabbi of Prague, who was also the head of Vaad Hatzalah in Prague, recalled the following incident:

> I remember a day when Mrs. Sternbuch came to my office. Knowing how important her missions were, I was ready to see her immediately. But she noticed that there were a few rabbis in the waiting room and she insisted that I receive the rabbis first. As important as it was for her to see me, she could not bring herself to talk to me before I saw the rabbis. Later, when we met, she inquired about them and wanted to know who they were and if she too could be of some help to them.

R' Mordechai Pogramansky and the Sternbuchs

RECHA STERNBUCH'S DEEP admiration and reverence for Torah scholars, especially those who distinguished themselves with their *tzidkus* (piety), is reflected in the special care she extended to one of the few well-known survivors amongst the great Torah scholars of Lithuania, Rabbi Mordechai Pogramansky, known in the yeshivah world as "Reb Motel" of Telshe.

In his youth, Rabbi Pogramansky earned fame in the Lithuanian Torah world, both for his prodigal Torah scholarship and for his *tzidkus*. His vast knowledge in virtually all areas of Torah and his deep insights in *Mussar* (Jewish Ethics) and philosophy won him admiration and great esteem in all Torah circles. At a very young age he became a close friend of such great Torah personalities as the Ponevezer Rav, Rabbi Joseph Kahaneman; the Kovno Rav, Rabbi Avrohom Shapiro; the Telsher Rav, Rabbi Avrohom Yitzchok Bloch; and other Torah dignitaries.

Two years before World War II, Rabbi Pogramansky became one of the spiritual leaders of the yeshivah in Heide, Belgium, where he exerted great influence and simultaneously endeared himself to the Orthodox Jewish community in Belgium. Among his admirers were the Rav of Antwerp, Rabbi Mordechai Rottenberg, (father of Recha Sternbuch), and his entire family.

Shortly before the outbreak of the War, Rabbi Pogramansky returned to Lithuania for a visit, and spent the terrible war years in the Kovno ghetto. There he played an important role in keeping up the spirit of the ghetto inhabitants, especially young Torah scholars from the various Lithuanian yeshivos. In the clandestine Beis Hamidrash of the Kovno ghetto, he often delivered Torah lectures, helping to boost their morale. To this very day there are many legendary stories still circulating about how he miraculously survived the Germans' liquidation of the Kovno ghetto.

Smuggled to the West

AT THE END OF 1945, when Lithuania became a Soviet republic, part of the U.S.S.R., Rabbi Pogramansky smuggled himself into Poland. When Recha Sternbuch came to Poland and she heard that Rabbi Pogramansky was there, she immediately contacted him and made special efforts to spirit him out of Poland. Secrecy was of great importance, since Rabbi Pogramansky had no Polish identification papers. In fact, he was in great danger, because he was a fugitive from the U.S.S.R. With the help of Recha Sternbuch he was smuggled out of Poland to Czechoslovakia in a special car, then he was brought to France where he settled for a while at the yeshiva in Bailly. There he immediately became the unofficial spiritual mentor of all the refugee Torah scholars.

But the Sternbuchs did not satisfy themselves with merely bringing Rabbi Pogramansky to safety. Since he was in poor health, they did not cease to care for him, seeing to it that he received the proper medical attention. Whenever they visited him — which was quite frequently — they were overwhelmed by his Torah wisdom and his *tzidkus*. Rabbi Pogramansky soon became their chief advisor in all matters pertaining to their rescue activities.

MRS. STERNBUCH SOON BROUGHT Rabbi Pogramansky to Aix-Les-Bains, where she had established a number of children's homes and other institutions for which Rabbi Pogramansky served as spiritual leader. Rabbi Pogramansky later married and settled in Versailles, near Paris, where he led a yeshivah. However, he continued to be the main source of guidance for the further rescue activity of the Sternbuchs.

Spiritual Guide in Aix-Les-Bains

Shortly thereafter, Rabbi Pogramansky became severely ill. The Sternbuchs brought him to Switzerland and for more than a year, together with Mr. Wolf Rosengarten, made every effort to save his life. Recha Sternbuch brought him from one hospital to another, and mobilized Europe's greatest physicians. According to Rabbi Pogramansky's widow, "It is just impossible to describe their efforts, for over a year, in order to sustain him." When they did not succeed and Rabbi Pogramansky passed away in 1949, the Sternbuchs brought his remains to *Eretz Yisrael*, where he was put to rest in Bnei Brak, in the presence of many Torah leaders, led by the Chazon Ish. Rabbi Pogramansky's young widow stayed on as a guest in the Sternbuch house for more than a year.

ANOTHER EXAMPLE of Recha Sternbuch's deep respect and concern for rabbis and scholars is the great interest she took in one of Western Europe's great Jewish scholars, Rabbi Dr. Yechiel Weinberg, who was freed from German imprisonment in the spring of 1945.

Rabbi Dr. Yechiel Weinberg

Rabbi Yechiel Weinberg, who was of Lithuanian descent, had gained fame in his youth in the great yeshivos of Slobodka and Telshe. In the 1920's he became the Dean of the Hildesheimer Rabbinical Seminary in Berlin. Living in Germany, and as the educator of its future spiritual leaders, he enjoyed great prominence among Western European religious

Rabbi Mordechai Pogramansky   *Rabbi Dr. Yechiel Weinberg*

Jewry and was highly respected by its rabbis. After the Nazis came into power, the Hildesheimer Seminary declined in enrollment and importance, but nonetheless he tried to maintain the school throughout this difficult period. Even after a large number of the faculty members left Germany, he remained at his post. Since he was a Lithuanian citizen, however, he was abruptly deported from Germany after the infamous *Kristallnacht* in 1938.

When the war broke out, Rabbi Weinberg was in Warsaw. When the Ghetto was created, he was not required to live in it because the Germans respected his Lithuanian citizenship. Nonetheless, he chose to join his brethren in the Ghetto, where he worked on many relief projects with some of Warsaw's great rabbis. For a while he was allowed to move in and out of the Ghetto, which enabled him to be of great help to many Jews. Later, however, when the Germans started to liquidate the Warsaw Ghetto, Rabbi Weinberg was arrested and for more than two years was kept in a small German prison together with other foreign citizens. He was freed by the Americans after the German surrender in May 1945.

RABBI WEINBERG WAS SERIOUSLY ill after the liberation and, because of his illness, was isolated from the other liberated Jews.

"Send Papers, Avoid Repatriation to Russia"

Through their connections, the Sternbuchs learned of his survival and immediately took steps to help him. They were especially concerned about the possibility that he would be forced to return to Lithuania. On June 18, 1945, just five weeks after his liberation, the Sternbuchs sent the following telegram to the Agudath Israel in Palestine, to Chief Rabbi Herzog in Jerusalem, and to the office of Rabbi Israel Brodie, Chief Rabbi of Great Britain:

> JUST RECEIVED MESSAGE, DR. YECHIEL WEINBERG FORMER RECTOR OF RABBI HILDESHEIMER SEMINARY BERLIN LIBERATED CAMP WEISENBURG, BAVARIA STOP PROCURE IMMEDIATELY PALESTINE CERTIFICATE TO AVOID HIS REPATRIATION TO RUSSIA.

Their concern was not unfounded. At that time, some American government officials were inclined to give in to the Soviet demand that all East European citizens who were liberated

Rabbi Mordechai Shulman, Slobodka Rosh Hayeshiva, meeting with Rabbi Dr. Yechiel Weinberg at the Sternbuch home in Montreux

in Germany should be repatriated to the countries of their origin. The Sternbuchs feared that Rabbi Weinberg, who was ill, would not muster up the necessary resistance when faced with the traveling Soviet representative who confronted Soviet citizens and demanded that they return.

It is almost certain that Rabbi Herzog, Rabbi Brodie, and Agudath Israel pressured the British government to obtain an entry certificate to Palestine for Rabbi Weinberg. But communication with Germany was still extremely cumbersome, and Rabbi Weinberg remained in a German hospital in Nuerenberg. In the meantime, the Sternbuchs cared for him from their home and office in Montreux, Switzerland. In July 1945, when Recha Sternbuch visited Germany, she made a special trip to Nuerenberg to visit him. She made sure before her return that the Jews living around Nuerenberg and Furth would care for his needs, and that he be visited by Jewish American Army chaplains and by all Jewish dignitaries who came to Germany.

BY THEN THE FEAR that Rabbi Weinberg would be forcibly repatriated to the U.S.S.R. had subsided. After many protests to the American government, in which the Sternbuchs were very active, the military authorities in Germany decided not to cooperate with the Soviets in forcing anyone to return. Still, the Sternbuchs did not diminish their concern about Rabbi Weinberg and his deteriorating health, and decided to bring him to Switzerland for proper care and recuperation. A major role in this effort was assumed by a nephew of the Sternbuchs, Dr. Shaul Weingort, who was a former student of Rabbi Weinberg. Dr. Weingort made special guarantees to the Swiss government that he would be responsible for Rabbi Weinberg's maintenance for the duration of his stay in Switzerland.

Move to Montreux

With these efforts and the help of Rabbi Alexander Rosenberg of Yonkers, New York (the religious representative of the Joint Distribution Committee in Germany), Rabbi Weinberg arrived in Switzerland at the end of 1945. He was immediately brought to Montreux, where he enjoyed Dr. Weingort's close personal care as well as the frequent cordial hospitality of the Sternbuch home. The Sternbuchs went out of their way to make his stay in Montreux as pleasant and soothing as possible.

*The Viznitzer Rebbe
Rabbi Chaim Meir Hager*

*The Ponovezer Rav
Rabbi Yosef Kahaneman*

For about twenty years Rabbi Weinberg remained in Montreux, where he was surrounded with the great love and respect of the Sternbuch family. Although their family tradition was different from his ideology, and they even disagreed on some issues affecting Jewish life and Jewish problems, Rabbi Weinberg was a welcome guest on many Sabbaths and even presided at many family occasions at the Sternbuch home. In his honor they invited other guests to their house to create a cordial and interesting atmosphere for him.

In this environment of warm affection and reverence, Rabbi Weinberg, who was gravely ill at his liberation, recuperated fully and resumed many of his previous activities. He was constantly visited by famous rabbis, scholars and former students, and he kept up a wide correspondence with his admirers all over the world. He even published a number of volumes of his rabbinic responsa, *Seridei Esh*, which are recognized as some of the most important contributions to rabbinic literature in recent times.

THROUGH THE WAR YEARS and the years thereafter, leading Torah personalities stopped in at the Sternbuchs. Rabbi Yonasan

The Kopitchnitzer Rebbe
Rabbi Avraham Yehoshua Heschel

The Boyaner Rebbe
Rabbi Shlomo Friedman

Torah Leaders at the Sternbuch Home

Steif stayed for several weeks. The Satmar Rav visited for a brief period. The late Vizhnitzer Rebbe led a *tisch* in their home and they were also hosts to other Chassidic leaders, such as the Rebbes of Boyan and Kopitchnitz. The Sternbuchs were also hosts to numerous dignitaries and Torah leaders who were traveling through Europe on missions of *hatzalah* and rebuilding of Torah — men such as the Ponevezer Rav, the Lomzer Rav, Rabbi Chizkeyahu Mishkowsky, Rabbi Abraham Kalmanowitz, Rabbi Yechezkel Abramsky, Chief Rabbi Herzog, Rabbi Eliezer Silver, and Rabbi Mordechai Shulman. Another distinguished guest was Rabbi Moshe Soloveitchik, who came to Switzerland before the war and settled there, becoming a mentor to the Sternbuchs and guiding them in many of their activities.

Rabbi Simcha Elberg, editor of the rabbinical magazine *Hapardes* and Chairman of the Board of the Union of Orthodox Rabbis of the United States, who was often a guest of the Sternbuchs in Montreux, describes the warm yet reverential hospitality for Torah scholars at the Sternbuchs' home:

Visits of a great rabbi or Torah scholar at the Sternbuch house was not an extraordinary occurence. Almost all great Torah personalities who visited Switzerland were guests of the Sternbuchs at their house in Montreux. Nevertheless, for the Sternbuch family and especially for Mrs. Sternbuch, every visit turned into a festive occasion. The royal treatment had no limits. The visiting Torah scholar was always seated at the head of the table and was served first as if it were he who was the owner of the house and the Sternbuchs were his guests.

The reverence shown to Torah scholars was not limited to the great, the recognized and the famous. Mrs. Sternbuch extended similar treatment to unknown Torah scholars. It was enough for her to hear that someone was learned in Torah and immediately he was the object of all sorts of honors and hospitality.

Recha and Beth Jacob: a Member in Spirit

ANTWERP, WHERE RECHA STERNBUCH grew up, had no Beth Jacob school for girls. But the spirit of Beth Jacob was instilled in her by her father, who was one of the great Torah leaders of the World Agudath Israel. She always considered herself a part of this movement, whose activities and miraculous growth she followed from afar.

Recha Sternbuch also accorded intensive attention to a number of leading Orthodox women, especially the associates and students of the legendary founder of Beth Jacob, Sarah Schenirer, who were at the helm of the Beth Jacob movement in Poland, Czechoslovakia, and Roumania.

These women had played a major role in the education of Jewish womanhood in Eastern Europe prior to World War II. Through them emerged a generation of Jewish women — mothers and daughters — staunchly loyal to Torah tradition, proud of their Jewish heritage, imbued with a fiery zeal to preserve Judaism. For this achievement, Beth Jacob won the warm recognition and admiration of Jews from the broad spectrum of religious Jewry.

The Beth Jacob movement endeared itself to her even more during the trying years of the Holocaust. Fired with inspiration by the leadership of the Beth Jacob teachers, many Jewish girls in the ghettos and concentration camps distinguished themselves with exemplary behavior and a readiness to sacrifice themselves for others. This combination of virtues turned these girls into legends of heroism. Recha Sternbuch, who maintained a constant clandestine contact with Eastern Europe, was aware of the Beth Jacob activities in the ghettos, which filled her with a mixture of awe and pride.

It is no wonder, therefore, that when Recha Sternbuch started sending food packages to Poland during the war, a number of Beth Jacob leaders were on her list of recipients. After the war, when she visited the liberated camps, she searched for the survivors of Beth Jacob and gave them all her attention and consideration.

Her interest in the Beth Jacob movement was not only a matter of personal sentiment. Recha Sternbuch appreciated the important role these Orthodox women leaders would play in the restoration of religious life among those saved from the Holocaust.

Rebbitzen Cyla (Orlean) Sorotzkin of Jerusalem, a former lecturer at the Beth Jacob Seminary in Cracow and leader of the Beth Jacob movement in Poland, recalled:

> Not long after the liberation, when I was in Bendzin, I received a telegram from Switzerland with these words: "What kind of help do you need? (signed) Vaad Hatzalah HIJEFS Montreux, Switzerland." How Mrs. Sternbuch had my address just a few weeks after the liberation I do not know. But it was our first contact with the outside world. It really gave us a lot of strength to know that someone is thinking of us. Someone cares. We are not alone and forsaken anymore.

Mrs. Rivka Pinkusewich, quoted above in chapter 15, recounted:

> It was not easy to rebuild the Beth Jacob movement after the experiences of the war. Of course we were proud of the valor of our Beth Jacob girls in the concentration camps. But after the war, when we realized our huge losses and the magnitude of the Jewish destruction, we really needed a new injection of strength and courage to resume our work.
>
> Recha Sternbuch gave it to us when she came to the D.P. camp at Zeilsheim near Frankfurt, where a number of Beth Jacob teachers organized a *kibbutz* of Beth Jacob girls. The love she gave us, her respect and deep interest, her faith in each of us, gave us that fortitude for renewed work. It was after her visits that we mustered the courage to go out from camp to camp to assemble our girls and start Beth Jacob anew.

In reality, the rebirth of Jewish religious life after the Holocaust was in a great measure due to the hard work and the pioneering spirit of these Beth Jacob leaders. With the traditional Beth Jacob fervor they revived the religious spirit among the women survivors in the D.P. centers all over Europe. Later, when they settled in Israel, the United States — all over the world — they contributed immensely, everywhere, to the growth of the Beth Jacob movement, which is such a blessing in our generation. Recha Sternbuch had a share in this revival.

THE STERNBUCH'S overwhelming dedication for Torah study was best reflected in their personal lives. Instead of passing on their **Personal Footnote** business to their children, they brought them up to respect Torah study as the highest personal attainment. Indeed, their only son, Rabbi Avrohom Sternbuch, heads the Bobover Yeshiva in London; their older daughter, Netty is married to Rabbi Chaim Segal, principal of the Mesivta Rabbi Chaim Berlin, in Brooklyn; and their younger daughter, Esther, is married to Rabbi Yehudah Gutterman, *mashgiach* (dean) of the junior Yeshivas Ponevez in Bnei Brak. All of their grandchildren are also fully involved in Torah study, learning in yeshivos and kollelim.

Beth Jacob Girls' School in Hoff, Germany, established through the help of Recha Sternbuch

CHAPTER TWENTY-FOUR
The Sternbuchs and the Sekulener Rebbe — Partners in Postwar Rescue

THE GREAT TZADDIK, Rabbi Eliezer Zusia Portugal, better known as the Sekulener Rebbe, was one of the outstanding figures in the rescue of Jews in this century.

From the onset of the Second World War, the Sekulener Rebbe attained the reputation of a "Father of Orphans," a name that remained with him for the rest of his life. In addition, he was revered for a host of achievements on behalf of Torah, Judaism, and the needy.

His concern for orphans and homeless children began during the war years when Chernovtsy (Chernowitz), the capital of the Bukovina region in Roumania, changed hands many times between the Soviets and the Germans. The battles of the war resulted in a great number of homeless children in Chernowitz. The first one to care for them was the Sekulener Rebbe. His home became a center for these unfortunate children. It remained even more so after the war. While the Sekulener Rebbe maintained some children at home and placed others with friends, he personally supported them all.

AT THE END OF THE WAR, many more Jewish orphans were found in Chernowitz and the Soviet authorities placed them in general orphanages where they were indoctrinated with Communism. This shocked the Sekulener Rebbe, who rounded up these Jewish orphans and placed them with Jewish families. When the Soviets began to harrass him for these actions, he legally adopted a large number of these children. He took advantage of an adoption law that enabled him to remove many children from the Communist orphanages and raise these children in the Jewish spirit. He convinced a number of other Jews in Chernowitz to legally adopt children. The responsibility of raising the children and providing for them, however, remained on his shoulders. The total number of children under his care reached into the hundreds.

Father of Orphans

In time, the Soviets caught on to the Sekulener Rebbe's ruse and the whole project was endangered. Having no choice, the Rebbe smuggled the children out of Chernowitz into Bucharest, the capital of Roumania, at the end of 1946.

At that time, Roumania was governed by a pro-Soviet leftist regime, but there was still some freedom of religious activities. The Orthodox leaders in Bucharest were delighted with his arrival, and the Sekulener Rebbe immediately became the president of the regional Agudath Israel and started working on all fronts for Judaism and rescue. His work throughout the following years in Roumania is legendary. He became the father and mother for thousands of Jews in Roumania. He traveled from city to city to strengthen the Roumanian Jews in their faith, establishing religious schools and institutions, in addition to his providing for the physical needs of the survivors, particularly for the Jewish orphans.

AS DESCRIBED IN A previous chapter, the Sternbuchs were active on behalf of Roumanian Jewry from the time the War ended. The first documents about the link between the Sternbuchs and the Sekulener Rebbe consist of correspondence exchanged between the two during the spring and summer of 1947, when the Sternbuchs attempted to help the Sekulener Rebbe take Jewish children out of Roumania. From the intimacy evident in the correspondence, it is clear that this was not their first exchange but a continuation of previous contacts. It is evident that the Sternbuchs had previously provided assistance to the Sekulener Rebbe either for his children and institutions or his other relief work, from the day he had arrived in Bucharest from Chernowitz. Although Recha Sternbuch had not as yet personally met the Sekulener Rebbe she deeply respected him and admired his many self-sacrificing actions, and she invariably responded quickly to his calls for help.

The Sternbuchs' Contact with the Rebbe

THE CORRESPONDENCE during the spring and summer of 1947 mainly concerns a problem which confronted the Sekulener Rebbe soon after his arrival in Bucharest, namely his battle with the *Aliyat Hanoar* (the youth department of the Jewish Agency), which wanted to take away his children. The Sternbuchs assisted him in his struggle, for they were already in constant battle with *Aliyat Hanoar* over their general rescue activities in all other countries.

Battling Aliyat Hanoar

As is evident from correspondence to the Sternbuchs and Mr. Herman Landau, the secretary of HIJEFS, the *Aliyat Hanoar* offered "assistance" to the Sekulener Rebbe in transporting his children from Roumania to *Eretz Yisrael*. Since the *Aliyat Hanoar* had the support of the American Jewish Joint Distribution Committee and also the recommendation of the Vaad Hatzalah, the Rebbe, in his desperation to save the children, started to negotiate with their representatives in Roumania. Before long, however, he sensed that the representatives of *Aliyat Hanoar* were not simply concerned with saving these children from their homelessness, but intended to raise them as "new Jews" by placing them in left-wing *kibbutzim* in *Eretz Yisrael*. As desperate as the Sekulener Rebbe was to get these children out of Roumania, he quickly recognized the spiritual danger. The moment *Aliyat Hanoar* informed him that

Exchange of telegrams between the Sternbuchs and the Sekulener Rebbe, Rabbi Eliezer Zushe Portugal.

it planned to "take over" the children and that the educators appointed by the Sekulener Rebbe or the Agudath Israel of Roumania could not accompany the children, the Rebbe immediately stopped all negotiations.

Their correspondence records the Sternbuchs' encouragement to the Rebbe to resist *Aliyat Hanoar*. As an alternative, the Sternbuchs offered to evacuate 500 children to Paris, where they had a home ready to receive them. Simultaneously, they obtained a substantial number of visas for "war widows" — so-called "mothers" of these children — and educators, in accordance with the Sekulener Rebbe's request. These special visas were obtained by the Sternbuchs who used this opportunity to rescue others who wanted to get out of Roumania.

This plan was not to the liking of the leaders of the *Aliyat Hanoar* who wanted the children, and they tried to sabotage it in many ways. To execute his plan, the Rebbe asked Mrs. Sternbuch to personally come to Roumania, which she did in July of 1947.

Salvaging a Mission

DURING HER VISIT, Mrs. Sternbuch took steps to facilitate the evacuation of the children, but, unfortunately, the elaborate plan never materialized. There were many hindrances, as we learn from Mr. Jacob Rosenheim's correspondence with the Sternbuchs and with the Sekulener Rebbe.

It is evident from a letter of Mr. Rosenheim's to the Sternbuchs, as well as from letters from the Sternbuchs to Rabbi Abraham Kalmanowitz of Vaad Hatzalah in New York, that anti-religious circles in Bucharest undermined this project. Among other things, they notified the leaders of the American Jewish Joint Distribution Committee in New York and in Paris that it was entirely "unnecessary" to remove the children from Roumania. This caused much delay, and the Roumanian government soon decided not to allow any large groups of children to leave the country.

The Sekulener Rebbe and Recha Sternbuch were heartbroken, and had no choice but to handle the emigration of these children on an individual basis. This was, of course, much more complicated. But with their determination, they sent them out in small groups to Hungary and Czechoslovakia. From there they journeyed (like many other D.P. youngsters) via Paris, Austria and Germany to *Eretz Yisrael* and the United States.

Contacts, But No Documents

FROM FRIENDS OF THE SEKULENER Rebbe, we know that Recha Sternbuch's visit brought the Rebbe even closer to the Sternbuch family. After Mrs. Sternbuch's trip to Bucharest, there are no documents available showing any further contact between the Sternbuchs and the Sekulener Rebbe. It must be assumed that after Mrs. Sternbuch's visit further official and direct contact was not advisable and had to be terminated.

It is known from associates of the Sekulener Rebbe and the Sternbuchs that they did maintain a secret contact for a long time. This can also be seen from correspondence between the Sternbuchs and an official of the Roumanian Communist Party dated July 29, 1955, when the Communist regime already ruled Roumania with an iron hand, and the Sekulener Rebbe was in trouble with the regime.

From this letter it is apparent that the friends and admirers of the Sekulener Rebbe outside of Roumania considered it important to obtain permission for him to leave the country. The Sternbuch correspondence is addressed to Berko Feldman, one of the most prominent Jewish leaders of the Communist party in Roumania, with whom the Sternbuchs had previously been acquainted. In this letter, they strongly appealed to him to help the Sekulener Rebbe obtain an exit permit. It is not known whether Feldman did anything for the Sekulener Rebbe. After all, Berko Feldman was associated with those who hated the Sekulener Rebbe because of his Jewish activities. The possibility does exist, however, that the Sekulener Rebbe was not yet ready to leave Roumania, for he may have felt he could still accomplish something for the Roumanian Jews. There were many times in the early fifties when the Communists were eager to be "rid of him", but the Sekulener Rebbe refused to foresake his fellow Jews and his remaining children.

FURTHER CONTACT between the Sternbuchs and the Sekulener Rebbe is reflected in correspondence dated July 15, 1959, to

Arrest and Appeal another Communist leader in Roumania, a Mr. Bakal, with whom the Sternbuchs had struck up an acquaintance at an international congress in Montreux. At that time, in the spring of 1959, the Sekulener Rebbe had been imprisoned for a long period, which stirred up a storm in Jewish circles the world over.

Many groups were active on his behalf, especially the Agudath Israel World Organization, represented by Mr. Harry Goodman of London, Dr. Isaac Lewin in New York, and — as would be expected — Recha Sternbuch.

The Sternbuchs' letter to Mr. Bakal read:

> I believe you will remember me, since we met you at a congress in Montreux. Lately we were informed that Rav Portugal has been arrested. We are dealing here with a universally respected personality, a person who possesses qualities that are indeed rare in this world. He is religious but apolitical, and his arrest must therefore be an error.
>
> You will gain much stature from your friends throughout the world if you will attempt to clarify this to the authorities [in Bucharest] and prevail upon them to grant him his freedom.

Based on the energetic and self-sacrificing methods the Sternbuchs pursued in their wartime rescue activities, we can be sure that they were not satisfied with their personal intervention with Roumanian personalities. They surely mobilized many other influential people throughout Europe to intervene for the Sekulener Rebbe's freedom.

MORE DOCUMENTS about the Sternbuchs' efforts for the liberation of the Rebbe are not available to us. It is interesting to note, **With the "Family" in Antwerp** however, that as soon as the Sekulener Rebbe arrived with his family on April 19, 1960, in Antwerp as a free man (he left Bucharest via a Belgian Sabena airplane to Brussels), he was greeted by a warm invitation from the Sternbuchs to be their personal guest for Pesach in Switzerland. In fact, they were among the first to be informed about his freedom and his arrival in Belgium.

The Sekulener Rebbe remained in Antwerp for Passover due to some bureaucratic misunderstanding surrounding the entrance visa for the whole "family" of the Rebbe, which consisted of some ten adopted children. In a cable answering the Sternbuchs' invitation, the Rebbe told of difficulties in getting visas for his whole "family" and promised them an immediate visit as soon as the obstacles were removed.

As is appropriate for such a righteous man, the Rebbe did not forget the help of the Sternbuch family for his institutions and his children, as well as their efforts for his liberation. This is seen in the warm correspondence that the Rebbe maintained with the Sternbuchs in the ensuing years. Some of the correspondence deals with the Sekulener Rebbe's efforts to take out more Jews from Roumania. By then the Sternbuchs were officially retired from public activities but they took a great interest in these efforts and strongly assisted the Sekulener Rebbe, who actually succeeded in bringing out many Jews from Roumania even in the late sixties.

CHAPTER TWENTY-FIVE
A Holocaust Survivor Tells His Story — With Recha Sternbuch in Germany, Poland, Czechoslovakia, France, and Switzerland

Mr. Israel Yitzchok Cohn, a real-estate agent in Toronto, is well known as a volunteer activist for various religious and communal causes. He is the honorary secretary of the Toronto branch of the Friends of the Ger Institutions in Israel. He is active in Agudath Israel, as well as in many other religious undertakings. Before entering business, he was a teacher at the Yeshiva Etz Chaim in Toronto, and many young religious Jews in Toronto are his former students. Mr. Cohn is a survivor of Kaufering, a division of the infamous concentration camp of Dachau. The following report of his experiences with Recha Sternbuch after the war are typical of many.

THE FIRST TIME I met Recha Sternbuch was in the summer of 1945 at the D.P. camp of Landsberg, near Munich, Germany, a few months after my liberation from a camp near Dachau. A yeshivah was about to be organized for the young boys who had been liberated from the concentration camp, and I was to be one of its students. Mrs. Sternbuch was the first visitor from a foreign country to come to see us. She came together with Dr. Jacob Griffel, Rabbi Moshe Lebel and some

Landsberg: She Dispelled Our Despair

others. But she was certainly the most impressive of the delegation. She awakened memories of our lost mothers or older sisters who had perished. The deep personal interest she displayed towards each individual was overwhelming. She asked us for our names and if we had relatives somewhere overseas. She took some letters along with her to mail for us. She told us not to worry, since we would soon be able to leave Germany to go to *Eretz Yisrael* or America.

To some of us, shaken from the camp experiences — the hatred, hunger, beatings, and suffering we had endured — the meeting with her meant a new lease on life. After she left I never thought that I would meet her again, but I did.

Lodz: She Brought Us Hope — and Visas

THE NEXT TIME I met her was in Lodz, Poland, at the end of 1945 or the beginning of 1946. I had heard that my older sister was liberated and alive in Poland, so I left the Yeshiva in Landsberg to find her there. In Poland, however, I was told the bitter news that my sister had been killed by some Polish bandits not long after her liberation.

I was again alone and dejected, and I joined a *Kibbutz* of Poalei Agudath Israel, whose members prepared themselves for emigration to *Eretz Yisrael*. Every day we were told to be ready to leave Lodz, but the delays dragged on for weeks. The borders were closed, and Polish citizens could not leave without passports. With each day that passed, we became more desperate.

Finally, one day, Mrs. Sternbuch appeared at our *Kibbutz* and after a brief meeting with the leadership of the *Kibbutz*, we were told that we would leave that night. We were given some documents, and that evening we indeed boarded a train to Katowice. We were supposed to continue across the border to Czechoslovakia, but a hitch developed. Some police officers came on the train and started questioning our papers. A decision was made not to proceed but to stay in Katowice. Mrs. Sternbuch went to Warsaw and we were placed in a local Agudah *Kibbutz* in Katowice.

A few days later, Mrs. Sternbuch reappeared. She had worked out a "perfect" plan in Warsaw. Our group of about 50 Jewish youth was to join a big transport of Greek repatriates from Poland to Athens, supplied with some Greek documents which she brought with her from Warsaw. Of course, this was not without danger. We knew that these papers were fictitious. None of us knew a word of Greek. We were all frightened, but Recha Sternbuch told us that she was going along and that the border police had already been bribed. We were still not sure. Was she scared, too? I don't know. But her presence gave us a little strength and confidence.

At the border we were kept for a long time. Our hearts started beating faster, fearing a new hitch, which in fact was the case. The border police had a change of guards. She was conferring with the new officer in charge. There were telephone calls to Warsaw, to the consulate of Greece. Finally the officer came out with Mrs. Sternbuch, smiling, and he waved the conductor to move on. A few minutes later we were in Czechoslovakia and on our way to Prague.

BUT NOW, ON Czechoslovakian soil, a new problem developed. Because of the delay at the border it was now close to Sabbath and when the train stopped at a local station we did not want to ride any further. I don't know how, but somehow Recha Sternbuch found a way out of our dilemma. She went over to speak to the station manager. Our wagon was detached from the train and put on a side track. We stayed there over *Shabbos*, and on *Motzaei Shabbos* (Saturday night) a special locomotive took our wagon to Prague.

On the Way to Prague: A New Locomotive

In Prague we were placed in a transit camp with more Polish Jews, among them youngsters and even little children whom Recha Sternbuch had previously rescued from Christian monasteries. Also there were members of the leadership of the Lodz Agudah, who were working with Mrs. Sternbuch in Poland, Shimon Zucker, 'Chiel Granatstein, Moshe Binyomin Kleinman, and others. A few days later we were back on a train to France. We all had French visas, but we were still afraid of some new hitches. Suddenly Recha Sternbuch appeared. Since there were children among us, she was going to accompany us to France, Mrs. Sternbuch told us. With her present, all our fears disappeared.

Most of our group was brought to Paris and placed in the *Kibbutz* in Henoville near Paris. But a group of youngsters of yeshiva age, as well as young children, were accompanied by Recha Sternbuch to Aix-Les-Bains. We, the older ones, were placed at the yeshiva under the leadership of Rav Chaikin; the little boys and girls were placed at the children's home which had been established by Recha Sternbuch some time before.

WE ARRIVED AT AIX-LES-BAINS Yeshiva early in the morning of Erev Pesach. There we met a few friends, young Gerer Chassidim.

Aix-Les-Bains Shmurah Matzos for Recha Sternbuch

They were delighted by our arrival. They wanted to bake *Erev Pesach Shmurah Matzos* but they didn't have enough hands to do it. We joined them and went to work. We wanted to thank Recha Sternbuch and asked her to wait for our *matzos*, which she did. You cannot imagine how happy and proud she was when we presented her with our *Erev Pesach Matzos* which she could take home with her for her *Seder*. I cannot forget how warmly she thanked each of us for that beautiful *geschänk* (gift) ...

I later became a counselor for the children. Mrs. Sternbuch came quite often to visit the yeshiva and the children's home, and she was delighted to see how the children, who previously had known nothing about *Yiddishkeit*, learned to read the *Siddur* and observe *mitzvos*. Each time she came she brought a few more children to our home or a few boys to the yeshiva.

In Aix-Les-Bains we also met Guta Eisenzweig, who later became the wife of Eli Sternbuch, and her mother, Mrs. Sara Eisenzweig. These women were saved from Warsaw when the Sternbuch family sent them South American passports. Guta and her mother took a deep interest in our children's home, and Eli, too, visited our home quite often. Thus I had a chance to meet some more members of the Sternbuch family, all of them friendly, compassionate and eager to help and cheer us up.

WHILE STAYING IN Aix-Les-Bains it was discovered that I was very sick. In fact, I was not the only one. A severe illness was discovered among some other youngsters who had been freed from concentration camps. Again, Recha Sternbuch rushed in to help. Within a few weeks, a group of gravely ill boys and girls was brought to Davos, Switzerland, and placed in a sanatorium.

Davos: Recuperation from Ailment

Recha Sternbuch not only arranged the visas and payment for all of us, but kept caring for us all the way. When we were discharged, she arranged for us to be able to remain in Switzerland a little longer, and she helped some of us settle there.

Recha Sternbuch cared for us all the time we remained in Switzerland. Her private home in Montreux was literally open to us day and night. Many of us ate and slept there, and she even married off some of us. When I married, I was in Switzerland without parents and without a single relative; my *aufruf* was at the home of Eli and Guta Sternbuch, and I was led to the *chupa* by Nochum Sternbuch, another brother of Yitzchok, and his wife Renee. Yitzchok and Recha Sternbuch made a *Sheva Berachos* for us in a regal fashion, as if I was their child, or at least a nephew. And I was by no means their only "child." Many of my friends were treated in the same way — like children or very close relatives.

EPILOGUE
Recha Sternbuch — As I Knew Her

by Guta Sternbuch

BURNT OUT EMOTIONALLY, in desperate need of something to live for, I came to Switzerland, hoping for a miracle. Instead, I encountered a completely new world, populated by people who lived as if no war, no destruction, were taking place on the other side of the Alps. The contrast with what I left behind was traumatic. In my confusion, I could not see any meaning in my survival, any purpose in continuing to live.

Then I met Recha. This brought a complete turn-about in my thoughts and feelings. I had the good fortune to accompany her frequently, to stay close to her and to stay up many sleepless nights with her. So I was able not only to get to know her, but actually to live with her. I came to realize that as long as there are people like her — though they may be few — life is worthwhile.

I can picture her now — her majestic appearance: her impressive face with dark deep-set eyes, her head always crowned with a turban. I hear her voice, soft and dreamy — yet at times churning with passion when she was intent on inspiring others.

RECHA HAD A CHARISMA that was overwhelming, not previously apparent. The tragedy of the Jewish People must have awakened some dormant forces within her. The tortured cry of her hunted and persecuted people kindled a fire in her heart that never ceased to

**Charismatic
... and Silent**

Recha Sternbuch (right) with her sister-in-law, Mrs. Guta Sternbuch (left), and her mother, Mrs. Sara Eisenzweig who were saved from the Warsaw Ghetto through a South American passport provided by the Sternbuchs.

burn. She so identified with their suffering that self-denial became a part of her life. A thousand times she suffered their torment, and a thousand times she experienced their death. But she never despaired. She fought for every single human life with a frenzied desperation that made nothing impossible. She enlisted everyone's help: Swiss Border Police, the Chief of the Alien Police for the District of St. Gallen, the Papal Nuncio in Bern, and many others. None of them could avoid the rays of light she radiated. She sensed that every minute could mean a lost human life, so she pursued each case without fear of anyone. She demanded, requested, begged, shouted, pleaded until she stirred their conscience. If necessary, she was ready to resort to illegal means, even go to jail. The pressure did not crush her. On the contrary, she emerged ever stronger with each experience. The darker the situation became, the stronger she grew.

Yet, she was a silent, reserved person. Never did I hear her speak about herself, of her experiences and acts of bravery. She nagged herself constantly with feelings of inadequacy — perhaps this is what made it impossible for her to talk about herself. Only once did she break her silence; it happened when I, with my daughter, spent a night in her house. My daughter would not stop asking her to tell us one of her experiences. "Only one," she begged, until Recha finally gave in. Why I do not know ... perhaps to please my daughter. This is the story she told.

ON A QUIET, COLD WINTER NIGHT, like so many nights before, the telephone suddenly rang. It was her contact man informing her

On a Quiet, Cold Winter Night ... that a group of Jews — men, women and children — were sent back to Germany by the Swiss *Gendarmerie*, after trying to enter Switzerland, and they were now in the hands of the Gestapo: *Nothing can be done anymore. It would be senseless for her to come to the border since nobody dares come even close to the Gestapo.*

Within a quarter of an hour, Recha reached the border, by motorcycle. Her contact man was waiting for her on a side street near the border, and again he repeated his report, reiterating his warning to her not to attempt anything. She would be putting herself into tremendous danger. He too is powerless once they are in the Gestapo's hands. She must give up this time.

Recha continued toward the Swiss-German border, leaving him behind with his warning calls. She heard warning shots behind her, but nothing could stop her. She had entered no-man's-land, surrounded by pitch-black darkness. Suddenly she was flooded by dazzling light and before her three or four border guards in German uniform appeared — as though emerging from the ground.

"Halt! Halt!" they shouted. They were accompanied by gigantic barking dogs, which growled bloodthirstily and pulled at their leashes.

"Where are you going? What are you looking for here?" one of them shouted at her.

For a fraction of a second she could not answer, but then in a strong, clear voice, without a trace of fear, she said, "I want to talk to your chief. I have an important matter. Please announce me."

Taken aback by her firm attitude, they led her to the border house, where the unfortunate Jews were jailed. As soon as she entered, three soldiers surrounded her. She was so repelled by the sight of the middle-aged man sitting at the desk, his bloated face masked with a cold heartless expression, that for a moment she withdrew. On his chest rows of medals shone, while at his side sat a huge dog. "What do you want?" he asked curtly, in threatening tones.

She pulled herself together and answered: "I am Swiss. These Jews came upon my initiative. I am responsible for them. I would like to ask you to turn them over to me. I am taking them into Switzerland."

His eyes reddened with fury. He seemed as though he were ready to explode. But then he regained his composure, took several steps forward, planted himself directly in front of her, and hissed into her face, "What do you dare ask for? I'll send you away with these dirty Jews! You cursed Jewish woman! I'll rip up your Swiss passport if you don't disappear from here this minute! You, you ..." He was almost unable to breathe. The dog sniffed menacingly at her, and one gesture from his master was all he needed to tear her into pieces.

"I'll voluntarily join them if you don't turn them over to me. I am responsible for them," she said quietly even though her heart was quaking.

It became quiet. A fearful silence, and then the unbelievable happened. "Take your twelve Jews and be gone immediately," he shouted, "But at once! Otherwise I'll change my mind."

She disappeared with her twelve Jews into the darkness. She had succeeded in taking her twelve brethren with her.

This story should remain as a sample of many others stories which did not remain with us.

Once Again Recha Had Her Children

AFTER THE END OF THE WAR, Recha threw herself into a new task. Again she criss-crossed Europe: Poland, Roumania, Hungary, France, to take Jewish children out of convents, Catholic children's homes and farms.

It was not unusual for Poles to attack her with axes and set dogs against her. Sometimes they even threatened to kill her. But she did not shrink back. Wherever she could find a child, or thought a child might be, she went — despite all dangers.

Her task called for tremendous negotiation abilities. Even trickery and deceit were required to convince Communist countries to permit Jewish children to leave the country. Indeed, she stole them, she paid all sorts of legal fees and illegal bribes in these countries where a person can disappear for the slightest offense. She developed special tactics in her negotiations and succeeded in gaining the release of thousands of children. Again and again, she returned home — physically exhausted, but glowing with joy, because she had succeeded.

I was present when she arrived in Aix-Les-Bains, France, with a children's transport. As soon as we received news that the train had crossed the border into France, we all gathered at the station to meet them. There were several hundred children aboard. I do not remember the exact number. She came out of the train with wrinkled clothing, completely coated with a layer of coal dust, holding one child on her arm, grasping the hand of another one. Hundreds of children's faces peered out of the windows, curious and a little afraid.

Once again Recha had her children.

By the next day she had disappeared again — this time into another country behind the Iron Curtain.

Again she engaged in daring and dangerous manipulations, bribed, stole and abducted children, and brought them back to us. Danger lurked on all sides, but she was not aware of it. She would risk her life for even one single Jewish child.

AND THEN THE DAY CAME when her heart stopped. A mortal heart could not take anymore. It had crumbled — used up. It did not beat anymore ... Suddenly, somewhere on the road, on her way to another destination, she died precisely as she had lived. Her entire life had been a response of Hineni — "I am ready." And so she left us.

"Dear Recha, Please Forgive Me ..."

Only a few people were present to accompany her on her last trip. She was buried in Zurich next to her husband, Reb Yitzchok Sternbuch.

Dear Recha, please forgive me for breaking the silence about you. I know how you hated attention. But even with the richest flow of words we shall never be able to express the secret of your strength and the greatness of your soul.

But we can try to keep you alive in our minds so that we still gain from your greatness and our own lives will be worth living.

Appendix

> כל המקיים נפש אחת מישראל כאלו קיים עולם מלא

400 Bachurim, 26 Rabbinerfamilien
aus Mir, Telschi und Lublin

sind auf dem Wege nach Amerika in
Schanghai (China)
stecken geblieben und setzen dort ihr Studium fort.

Ihr letztes Telegramm lautet:

„Rettet uns vor dem Verhungern!"

Kein jüdisches Herz darf und wird sich da verschliessen.
Rettet unsere hungernden Brüder in Schanghai!

Jede Spende an der offenen Thora für diesen Zweck, ist ein
Beitrag zur Erhaltung edelsten jüd. Menschenlebens.

Hilfsverein für jüd. Flüchtlinge in Schanghai

Sekretariat: Recha Sternbuch, Montreux.

*First proclamation of the establishment of HIJEFS,
signed by Recha Sternbuch, Secretary.*

In 1979, after many years of silence, the Swiss press finally admitted, and condemned, the harsh policies of the Swiss authorities regarding Jewish refugees in the late thirties and early forties. In these pages from the Swiss magazine Blick, the arrests, persecutions and deportations of Jewish refugees are vividly described and deplored. It is against these inhuman policies that Recha Sternbuch successfully fought, and succeeded in bringing many hundreds of Jewish refugees into Switzerland.

Exchange of telegrams between the Sternbuchs and Mrs. Renee Reichman of Tangiers, who was very active in many rescue and aid projects on behalf of the Jews in Nazi-occupied Europe.

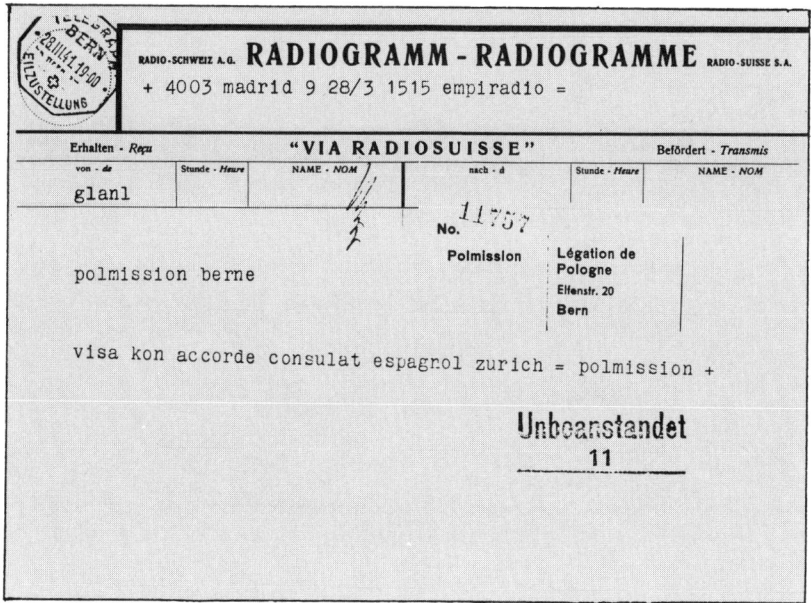

Telegram from the Polish mission in Bern requesting its legation in Madrid to facilitate transit visas for the Polish magnate Oscar Kohn. These transit visas and the Polish passport which was issued enabled him to proceed to safety in Mexico.

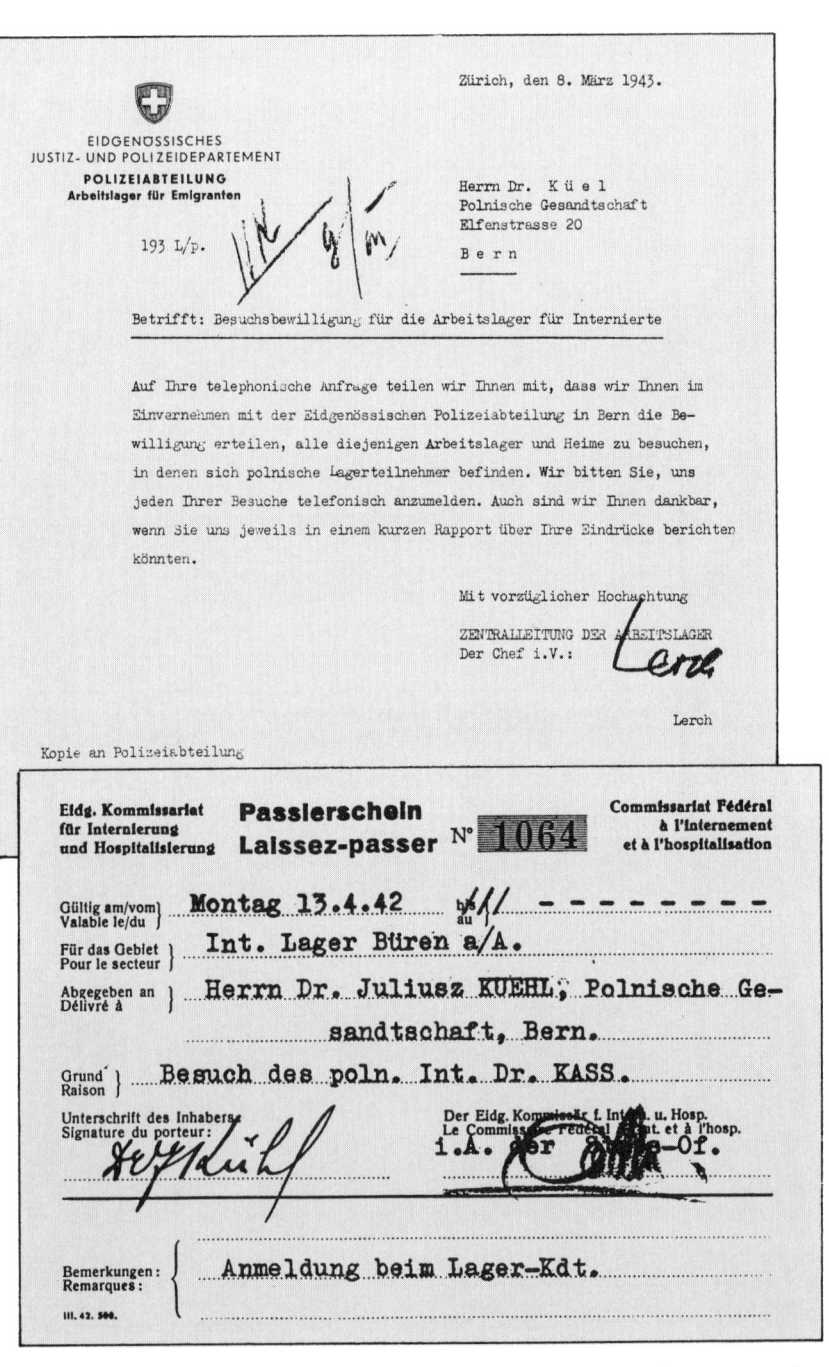

Permission granted to Dr. Kuhl of the Polish Consulate by the Swiss police allowing him to visit the refugee interment camp to assist Jewish refugees in need.

POSELSTWO
RZECZYPOSPOLITEJ POLSKIEJ
W BERNIE

LEGATION
DE LA RÉPUBLIQUE DE POLOGNE
A BERNE

Nr. 921/70 Bern, dnia 1 października 1941.

Do

Żołnierzy - Żydów 2 Dywizji
zgromadzonych na obchodzie Święta Dnia Sądnego

w **Burgdorfie**

    Cieszę się niezmiernie, że nadarza mi się sposobność zwrócić się do Was przy okazji jednego z największych Waszych świąt. Stan mego zdrowia nie pozwala mi obecnie nawiązać z Wami kontaktu osobistego. Przemówi do Was w moim imieniu Wasz współwyznawca, a mój gorliwy i rzetelny współpracownik, Dr. Juliusz Kühl.

    W szeregach wojskowych polskich, walczących o odrodzenie Polski, znaleźli się przedstawiciele wszystkich stanów, wszystkich zawodów, wszystkich wyznań. Nie zabrakło też i Żydów. Wiem, że niejednokrotnie spełniliście swój obowiązek żołnierski dzielnie i rozumnie, budząc uznanie swych przełożonych i kolegów innego niż Wy wyznania. Korzystam ze sposobności, by imieniem Rządu Rzeczypospolitej przyłączyć się do ich zdania i w dniu Waszego święta złożyć Wam serdeczne życzenia: oby ten rok przyniósł zakończenie wielkich zmagań narodów i spełnienie wspólnych naszych życzeń, nastania ery wolności i sprawiedliwości dla wszystkich. Wraz z resztą Dywizji powrócicie do oswobodzonej Polski. Jestem głęboko przekonany, że przyszła demokratyczna Polska da wszystkim swoim obywatelom równą szansę życiową wykazania dla wspólnego dobra swych zdolności i zalet. Nie wątpię też, że ze szczególną życzliwością zwróci się do tych, którzy - jak Wy - nie opuścili Jej w potrzebie.

    Ślę Wam moje najlepsze pozdrowienia

Aleksander Ładoś
Minister pełnomocny

Ambassador Lados' message to Jewish soldiers on the eve of the Jewish New Year in October of 1941. The ambassador often sent such friendly letters before Jewish holidays.

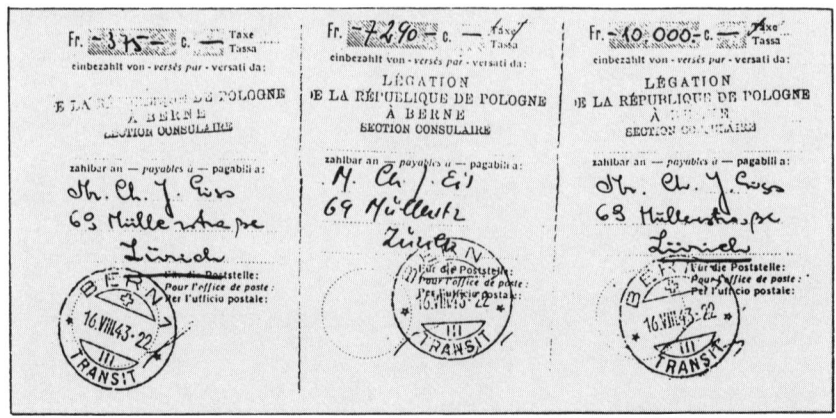

From November 1941 and later, the only way Jewish leaders in Switzerland could receive money from the United States was via the good offices of the Polish Legation in Bern. These are receipts for money received through the Polish Consulate by the rescue leader Mr. Chaim Yisroel Eiss in Zurich.

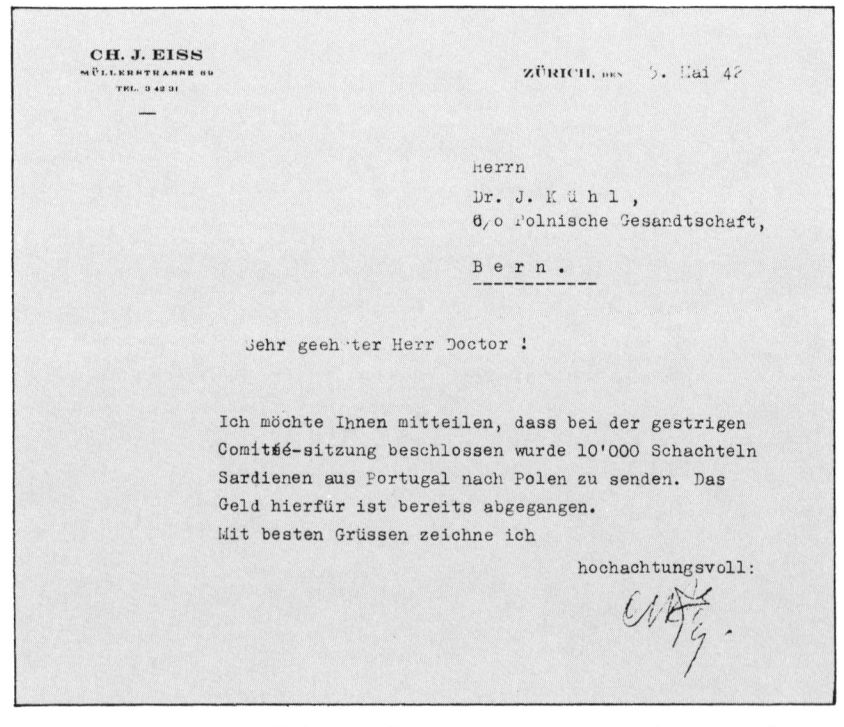

Dr. Kuhl at the Polish Consulate in Bern was constantly informed about all rescue and aid projects for Jews in Poland. In this letter, Mr. Chaim Yisroel Eiss informs Dr. Kuhl about 10,000 boxes of sardines ready to be sent to Jews in the ghettos of Poland.

D. A. SILBERSCHEIN

Télégmes : SILBADO-GENEVE
Télége : 2.73.32 2.81.25

GENEVE, le 10 stycznia 1942 r.
22, RUE DES PAQUIS

Drogi Panie!

Otrzymałem list Panski z dn.26.1.1941 r. i bardzo sie nim ucieszyłem. Bardzobym sobie zyczył,aby koresporencja nasza sie ozywiła i zacieśniła. Ignoruję zupełnie co sie dzieje w rszych kołach w Tel/ Awiwie i w Nowym Yorku.Biuletynu p.nie otrzymuje,czasmi jednak znajomi z Lizbony mnie go przysyłaja.Bede p.wdzieczny za przysłanie mnie p.biuletynu,oraz wszelkich wiadomości.Ja tez chetnie bede służł p. materjałami,ktorych tu jest sporo Mam tylko trudnosci co do przepisywania ich,gdyż nie ma, ani odpowiedniej ku temu siły,ani nawet polskiej maszyny do pisania.Praca ta jest jeszcze utrudniona z tego powodu,ze biuro nsze nastawione jest wyłacznie na akcje pomocową,oraz ze wzgledu na wady,twiwiące w zarodkach metod prac Kongresu.

Moze Pan tkx do mnie pisac otwarcie.Hamulce Panskie są nieuzasadnione. Bardo bde Panu wdzieczny,jezeli P. mnie napisze,albo zatelegrafuje co sie stało z Sommersteinem.Jego corka doytuje sie o niego i omatke.Z listu,jak od niej otrzymałem wynika,ze zona wraz z nim wywieziona została ze Lwowa. Co do Szora kraza tu rozne pogłoski.Mowią ze jest Vice-Prezesem Polskiego Komitetu Pomocy przy Ambasadzie.Czy wie Pan;cos o tem?Czy mogłby mnie Pan napisac o koncentracji naszych ludzi w Kazakstanie?B.mnie to interesuje.

Słyszałem,ze p.sie wystarał o pewną ilosc wiz dla Zydow Polskich do Jamajki.Czy to prawda?Mowią tu,ze w Lizbonie nie ma tylu ludzi,co wiz.Czy nie moznaby było uzyskac wizy dla naszych ludzi w Szwajcarji?Wprawdzie wyjazd jest stad utrudniony,ze wzgledu na trudnosci w zwiazku z otrzymaniem wiz tranzytowych do takiego kraju,lecz uważam,ze moznaby było i ta trudnos przezwyciezyc.Chodzi tu przedewszystkiem o ludzi,ktorzy są w obozach pracy w Szwajcarji,albo o takich,ktorym grozi dostanie sie do nich.

Bardzo mnie ciekawi sprawa nowej nominacji Pana i byłbym wdzieczny za szczegoły.

Mam do P.prosbe:w tut.Poselstwie pracuje ½ jedyny Zyd.Dr.J.Kühl z Sanoka gdzie jest b.powazany przez jego pilnosc,sumiennosc,pracowitosc,oraz jego orjentacje we wszystkich sprawach.W dodatku jest on tez dobrym Zydem.Figuruje on na etacie Poselstwa w Dziale Konsularnym.Jednak dotychczas nie dos tał on nominacji przez odpowiednie władze (Ministerstwo Spraw Zagranicznyc) Tut.Poselstwo sprawe popiera i byłoby dobrze,gdyby Pan mógł cos zrobic w tej sprawie.

Lichteheimowi i Kahanemu oddałem pozdrowienia.Zresztą Kahany dostał wprost od Pana list.

Zdaję sobie sprawę,ze list ten - nie systematyczny - ma być tylko odnowieniem naszego kontaktu.W chwili,kiedy Pan otrzyma ten list,dostanie Pan tez odemnie telegram.

Jestem bardzo zaniepokojony choroby Panskiej zony.Bardzobym sie ucieszył gdyby ten list zastał ja zupełnie zdrowa.

Serdecznie Pana i Panska zone pozdrawiam,panski

W.P.Dr.I.Schwartzbart,
45,Queens Court,
Quensway,W.2.
L O N D O N .

In order to get Dr. Kuhl a more prominent position at the Polish Consulate, Ambassador Lados needed the approval of the Polish government-in-exile in London. This was facilitated through the intervention of Dr. A. Silberschein who wrote to Dr. I. Schwartzbart, a Jewish member of the Polish Parliament-in-Exile. In his letter he describes the deep commitment of Dr. Kuhl to Jewish causes.

Odpis

POSELSTWO
RZECZYPOSPOLITEJ POLSKIEJ
W BERNIE

WYDZIAŁ KONSULARNY
Thunstrasse 21

LEGAT:

SECTI(
Thu₁

Nr. 788 A / Og / F 11.

Lista zasiłków
dla uchodźców polskich
po / franków na osobę.

Liste
pour les :
à / fran(

Miejsce - Lieu   Genewa
Miesiąc - Mois   od 1.4.1944 (

Nr. No.	Rej. Reg.	Nazwisko i imię Nom et prénom	Osób Pers.	Fr. Frs.	Pok(Pour
1.	1538	August Chana	1	1	145.-
2.	444	Brand Erna	1	1	145.-
3.	571	Brilantstein Basia	1	1	145.-
4.	1707	Cypel Chana	1		130.-
5.	1216	Gordon József	1		130.-
6.	1262	Ekstein Mizzi	1	1	145.-
7.	874	Bus Mendel	2	2	290.-
8.	1763	Klapman Ita	1		130.-
9.	58	Kurlandski Marek	2	2	175.-
10.	460	Laytman Zelda	1	1	145.-
		Do przeniesienia A reporter	12	9	1980.-

A page listing ten of the thousands of Polish Jewish refugees in Switzerland who received a monthly allocation from the Polish Legation in Bern, distributed under the supervision of Dr. Kuhl.

```
Telegramm – Télégramme – Telegramma
+ BURGDORF 24 51 2/4 18.26 =
```

Nº 888

MONSIEUR DOCTEUR KUHL
SULGENBACHSTR 20 BERN =

NOUS VOUS PRIONS TRANSMETTRE L EXPRESSION DE NOTRE PROFONDE
GRATITUDE A SON EXCELLENCE MONSIEUR LE MINISTRE POUR CES VOEUX
CHALEUREUX A L OCCASION DE NOTRE FETE DE PASSAH ACCEPTEZ AUSSI
NOS SINCERES REMERCIEMENTS POUR VOTRE NOBLE DON =
AU NOM DES INTERNES POLONAIS ISRAELITES = HIRSCHEL O

+ CT 20 +

Telegram to Dr. Kuhl from Polish-Jewish refugees in the Swiss internment camp in Burgdorf, asking him to transmit their thanks to the Polish ambassador for his help to the refugees for Passover.

```
RADIOGRAMM – RADIOGRAMME
koebenhavn 795 22 13/9 0710 = via rs =
ozt/wa   1946 SEP 13
```

lados c/o dr j kuehl
schosshaldenstr 206 berne =

prier telephoner copenhague treizieme vendredi apres 22 heur
numero central 3200 hotel norland =
                                    mikolajczyk +

A telegram regarding a secret meeting in Denmark at which Ambassador Lados and Dr. Kuhl met with Polish Prime Minister Mikolajczyk.

APPENDIX / 267

A letter from Saly Mayer, president of the Jewish communities in Switzerland and representative of the American Joint Distribution Committee, asking Dr. Kuhl to help contact Jewish leaders in Slovakia and Roumania through clandestine diplomatic channels, to discuss the situation of the Jews in those countries and the restricted means of helping them.

Dr. J. Kühl
--oOo--

Privat.

hargé/Express

Bern, den 12.Juli 1942.
Sulgenbachstrasse 20.

Herrn Saly Mayer,
Präsident des S.J.G.
S t. G a l l e n .

STRENG VERTRAULICH!

Sehr geehrter Herr Präsident,

A) Betr.: Polnische Juden.

a) Letzte Woche erschien in unserer Gesandtschaft ein junger Mann, der vor 14 Tagen Lemberg verlassen hat. Es handelt sich um einen Nichtjuden, namens Turski. Er überbrachte die Nachricht, dass in Lemberg allein in den letzten Tagen Pogrome gegen Juden stattfanden, bei denen 50.000 Juden ums Leben kamen. Es bestehe ein grosser Hass zwischen der polnischen und der jüdischen Bevölkerung.

Part of a lengthy report sent by Dr. Kuhl to Mr. Saly Mayer in July 1942, regarding the precarious situation of the Jews in Poland.

Through diplomatic couriers and underground channels some information, even newspapers, arrived at the Polish Legation in Switzerland, from which one could read between the lines about the martyrdom of the Jews under Nazi occupation. One of these newspapers was the Gazeta Zydowska (Jewish Gazette) published in Cracow. The front page of the Erev Yom Kippur issue of 1940 carried a lead article titled "Under the Charm of Kol Nidre" and a poetic translation in Polish of the prayer "Ki Hinei KaChomer". Both pieces relate the unbroken spirit of the Jews in the ghetto, who did not lose their faith, despite daily persecution, oppression and the constant threat of death. Their heroic spirit is also reflected in other news items in this issue which tell about varied religious, social and cultural activities carried on in the ghetto.

Other papers arriving at the Polish Legation included Nazi publications printed in Russia immediately after the invasion. Only two days after the occupation of Kovno, Lithuania, the Nazis began publishing the daily Kauener Zeitung, which served to spread hatred and venom against the Jews.

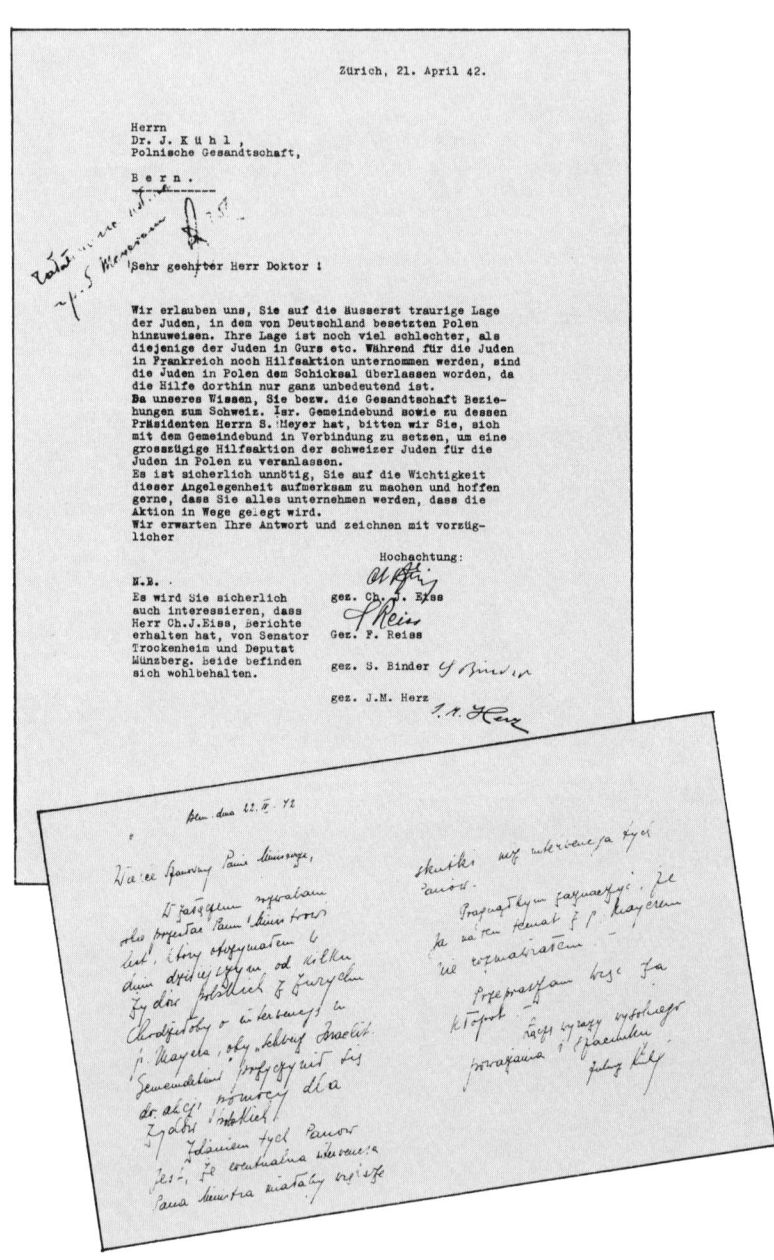

Some Jewish leaders in Zurich requested (via Dr. Kuhl) that Ambassador Lados meet with Saly Mayer and impress upon him the urgent need to extend more help to Jews in Poland. Dr. Kuhl submitted their request in a note to Mr. Lados.

> Dla Sternbucha.
>
> Wysłaliśmy ostatnio 100.000 dolarów, telegrafować jak zużytkowaliście i czy Joint bierze udział w akcji Neutrauera. Przez Szwecję dowiaduję się, że rabin z Piaseczna Kielman Szapiro, urodzony 1889, znajduje się w obozie koncentracyjnym Opole koło Lublina, z dziećmi Chaskelem Rabinowicz i córką Rachelą, urodzeni 1915, ratować.
>
> X) Rabin Bobowski Salomon Halberstan jest jeszcze Nagyvarad, matka i brat aresztowani, reszta rodziny w Bukareszcie, ratować.
>
> Kontaktować rabin Aron Rokach, Tel-Aviv, co do ratunku rabina Pinkasa Twerski jeśli trzeba dać do dyspozycji Rokacha 20.000 frs przekazane na ratunek
>
> X) W grudniu 1943, przekazaliśmy 3.000 dolarów na ratowanie rabina Chaskla Halberstana z Cieszanowa, telegrafować czy pieniądze zużyte lub są do dyspozycji.
>
> Lodyn prosi o pomoc dla Rosenbauma paczki do Theresienstadt, /? pokryć/ kwotę.
>
> Chcemy wiadomości o Saulu Becker, dla niego przesłaliśmy 2.500 dolarów. Czy macie wiadomości o rodzinach X) Abraham i Simcha Klein.
>
> Ilonie Lichtig wysłałem certyfikat palestyński Nr M/450/43/K/66 do agencji i konsulatu brytyjskiego Bazylea, kontaktować /? Ale/ x Tigerman, via Pessina 13, Lugano, telegrafować gdzie przebywa.
>
> /-/ ROSENHEIM
> /-/ LEWIN

X) rozminęło się z naszymi wiadomościami o tych właśnie osobach — Ele

> Proszę telegrafować przynajmniej ilość paszportów poszczególnych republik otrzymanych przez obywateli polskich.
>
> Brak danych /? o ile/ osób chodzi utrudnia interwencje nie możemy występować o wymianę niewiadomej ilości osób.
>
> /-/ POSNER

Mr. Jacob Rosenheim and Dr. Isaac Lewin of the Agudath Israel World Organization in New York sent many thousands of encoded messages to the Sternbuchs regarding rescue projects. This message, decoded at the Polish Legation in Bern by its code specialist Mr. Nachlik and then forwarded to the Sternbuchs, pertains to rescue efforts for the Chassidic rabbis of Piaseczna, Bobov, Belz and/or their families stranded somewhere in Poland and Roumania, as well as inquiries about other individuals in Nazi-occupied countries.

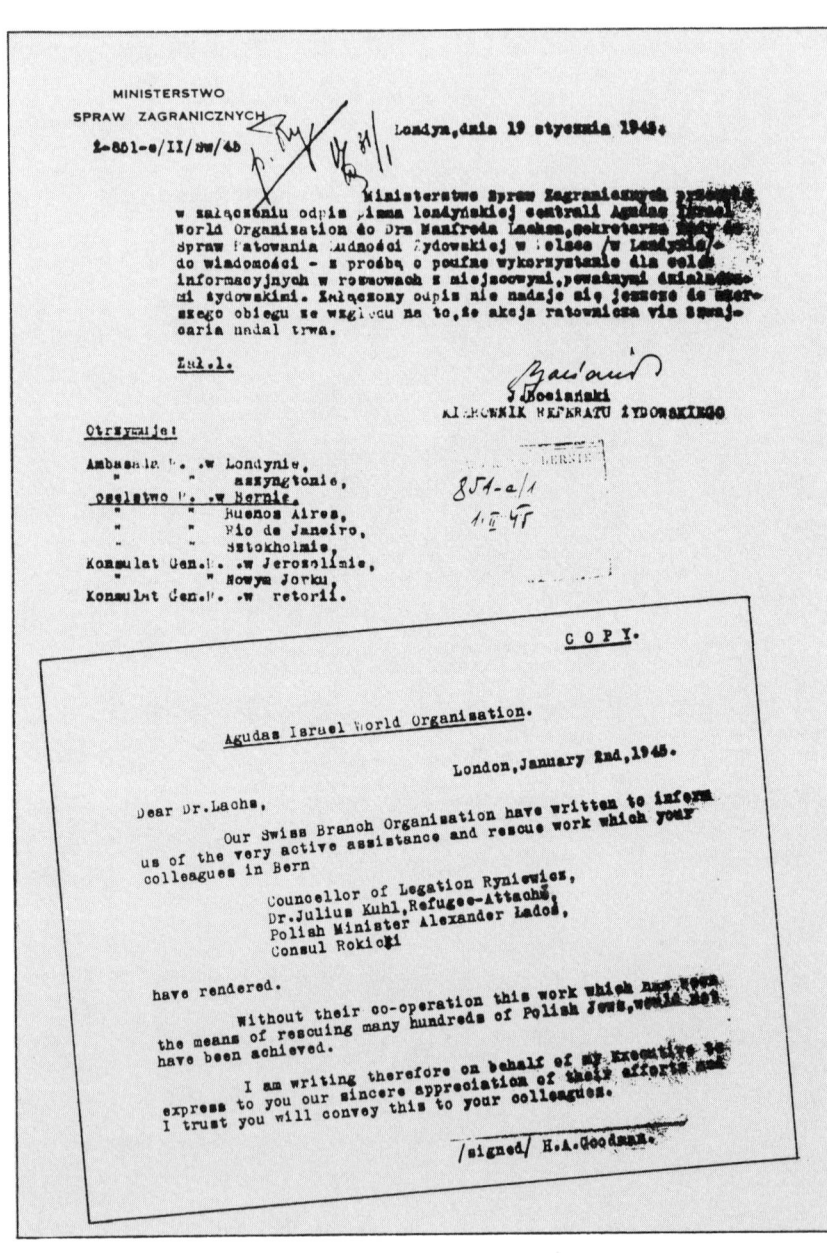

A letter, one of many, from Mr. H.A. Goodman, political secretary of Agudath Israel World's Organization expressing recognition for the help rendered by Polish Ambassador Alexander Lados and his assistants Mr. Rynewicz and Dr. Kuhl to the Sternbuch's in their rescue work. This letter was circulated by the Polish Foreign Ministry to its representatives in many parts of the world.

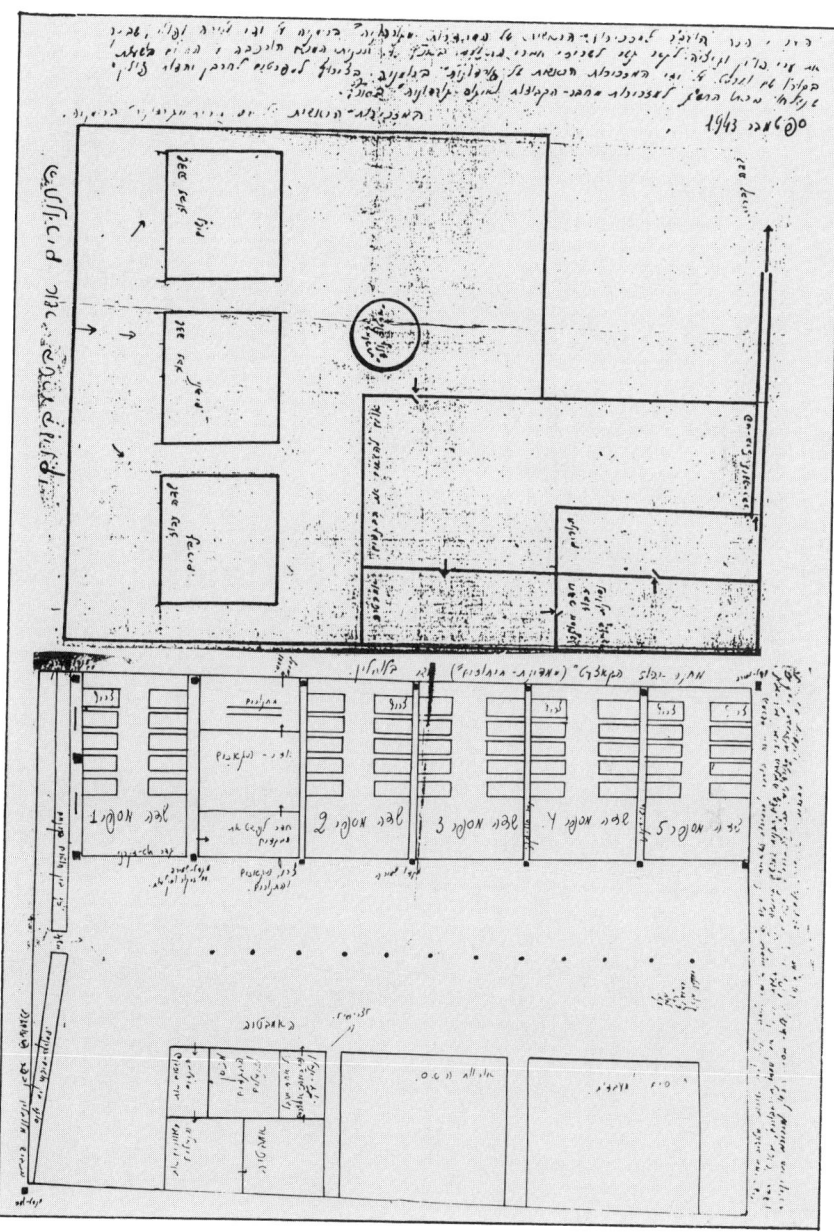

Through the diplomatic channels of the Polish Legation and the office of Papal Nuncio Phillipe Bernardini, the Sternbuchs and other leaders of the Swiss Jewish community were kept informed about the annihilation of the Jews in Eastern Europe. Drawings of the extermination camps at Treblinka and Maydanet were received from a Jewish underground organization in Poland.

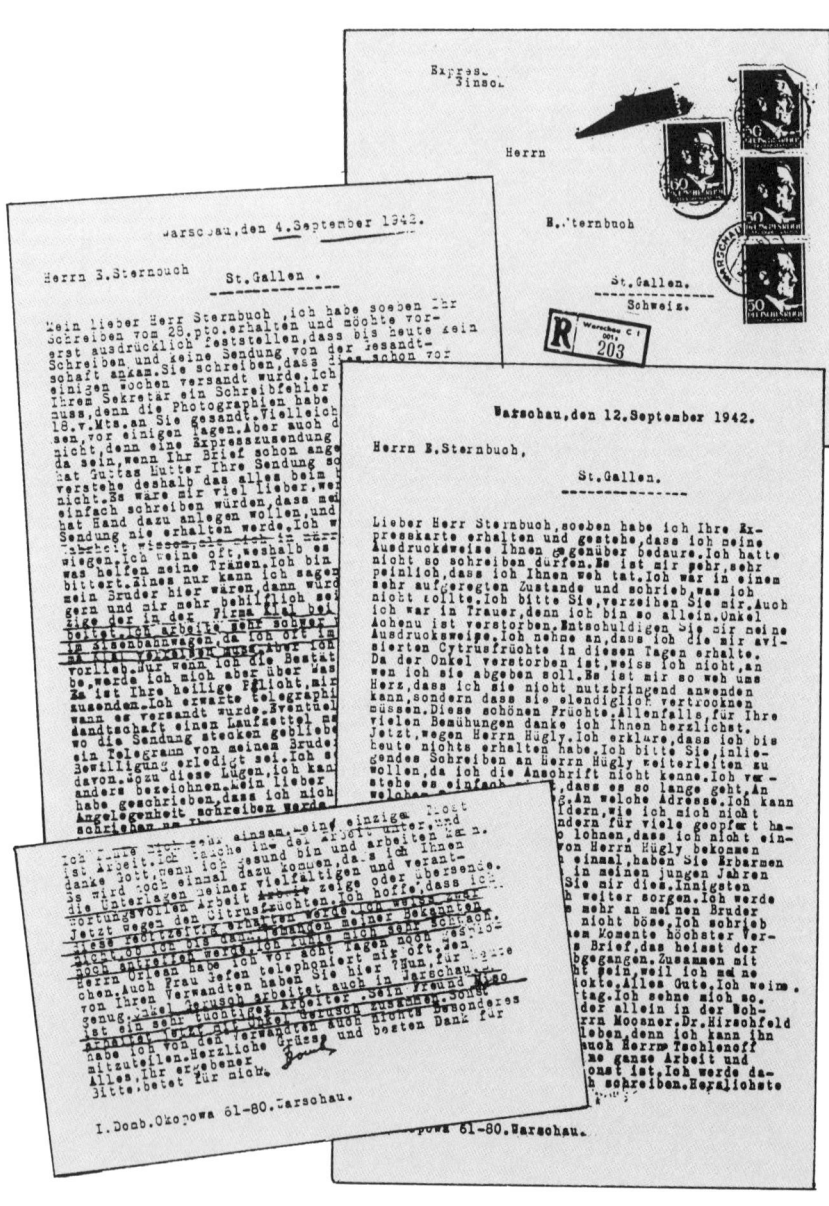

Parts of two of letters, sent from Warsaw in September 1942, by Mr. J. Domb (who lived in Warsaw with a forged Swiss document and could move in and out of the ghetto) in which he informs the Sternbuchs about the mass deportations from Warsaw, which began in the month of July. See chapter 8.

THE MILITARY ATTACHÉ
LEGATION OF THE
UNITED STATES OF AMERICA
BERN, SWITZERLAND

9 August 1945

Dr. Juliuz Kühl
Polish Legation
Bern.

Dear Dr. Kühl:

Upon leaving this post I wish to take the opportunity of thanking you for the wholehearted co-operation which you have given me in trying to do a workmanlike job here.

Our mutual relations have been most pleasant as well as profitable and I know that one day you will get full recognition for the way in which you have fulfilled your tasks.

With kindest wishes for the future,

Very sincerely,

Alfred R.W. de Jonge
Alfred R.W. de Jonge
Lieut. Colonel, GSC
Executive Officer

BRITISH LEGATION,
MILITARY ATTACHÉ'S OFFICE,
BERNE.

July 26th, 1945.

Dear Dr. Kühl,

I would like to take this opportunity of thanking you for the valuable help rendered and of acknowledging the many proofs you have given of your loyalty, sincerity and discretion ever since the year 1940.

I can assure you that it was always a pleasure to work with you and I hope that your activities will continue to be recognised at their true value.

Yours very sincerely

Robert Jellinek

Dr. Juliusz Kühl,
Polish Legation,
Berne.

After the war, the military attachés of the United States and Great Britain sent letters of appreciation to Dr. Kuhl. They were impressed by his work on behalf of the Jewish war victims who had been liberated by their armies.

APPENDIX / 277

8. Jan. 1960

S/B.

J. Sternbuch

Herrn Minister
Alexandre L a d o s
Château
L u m i g n y (S. et M) France.

Mein lieber und sehr verehrter Herr Minister,

Ich möchte es nicht unterlassen, Ihnen den Empfang Ihres lieben Schreibens vom 2. d. M. zu bestätigen.

Ich habe sicherlich keinen Dank nötig, es war mir ein Vergnügen, Ihnen behilflich zu sein. Ich kann mich gut erinnern, mit welcher Freundlichkeit Sie mich, lieber Herr Minister, während der kritischen Zeit im Verlaufe des Krieges immer empfangen haben und mit Rat und Tat zur Seite standen, ebenso auch meiner lieben Frau. Wir fühlen uns deshalb glücklich, von Ihnen zu hören, dass Sie wieder aufatmen können.

Nach dieser Transaktion werden Sie sicherlich keine Schwierigkeiten mehr in Frankreich haben und es ist Ihrem Ermessen überlassen, ob Sie ausreisen wollen oder nicht. Auf jeden Fall schonen Sie sich und trachten Sie darnach, sich gesund zu erhalten.

Ihre Mitteilung betreffend die Angelegenheit Pek habe ich nach New-York weitergegeben. Hoffen wir, dass die Leute noch einmal werden ausreisen können, es soll inzwischen viel schwieriger geworden sein.

Mit den besten Grüssen an Sie und Ihre liebe Schwester auch im Namen meiner Frau, die in letzter Zeit etwas kränklich ist, verbleibe ich

Ihr sehr ergebener

N.B. Vor den Feiertagen entboten wir Ihnen unsere Wünsche mit einer Schachtel Pralinés, die leider mit gewöhnlicher Post an Sie abging, statt eingeschrieben. Es besteht immer das Risiko, dass solche Päckchen um die Weihnachtszeit herum verloren gehen. Hoffen wir, dass Sie es trotzdem erhalten haben.

Almost twenty years later ... Here is a copy of a letter from the Sternbuchs to the retired Ambassador Lados, who lived in Paris, which shows the warm feelings of appreciation they felt toward him in recognition of his help.

Mons. Philippe Bernardini
Nonce Apostolique

présente ses compliments à Monsieur le Dr. Kuhl et Lui retourne, avec ses remerciements, le document ci-joint.

Berne, le 15 janvier 1945

Papal Nuncio Bernardini kept himself constantly informed about the rescue activities. In this note, he thanks Dr. Kuhl for certain documents he sent him.

le 9 octobre 1944.

Excellence,

Depuis que nous avons eu l'honneur de faire votre connaissance, nous avons pu apprécier l'esprit d'humanité, justice et sacrifice avec lequel vous avez défendu la cause des hommes en détresse, de nos malheureux correligionnaires en particulier.

Nous nous permettons de vous exprimer notre profonde gratitude et vous prions de daigner d'accepter ce qui nous est le plus cher, la raison même de notre existence à travers les siècles, un rouleau de parchemin sur lequel est inscrite notre "THORA".

Nous vous présentons, Excellence, l'assurance de notre considération respectueuse.

I. Sternbuch

Dr. J. Kühl

Son Excellence
Monseigneur Philippo BERNARDINI
Nonce Apostolique

B e r n e

Letter from Mr. Yitzchok Sternbuch and Dr. Kuhl, informing Monsignor Bernardini that a Torah scroll would be presented to him in recognition of his untiring efforts on behalf of Jewish war victims.

N° 29110

> Monseigneur Philippe B e r n a r d i n i ,
> Nonce Apostolique en Suisse, qui connaît fort bien
> Monsieur le Dr. Juliusz K U E H L
> avec lequel il a toujours eu d'excellents rapports
> empreints de la plus grande courtoisie, Le recommande
> vivement à la bienveillance des personnes avec lesquel-
> les il pourrait avoir affaire.
>
> Berne, le 4 septembre 1945

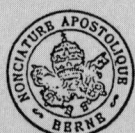

A letter of recommendation from Monsignor Bernardini for Dr. Kuhl recalling their collaboration on behalf of the war victims during the Holocaust years.

Telegramm – Télégramme – Telegramma

30868 newyork tw497 67 19/2 = wun rs = ctr =
[1945]

Bern

N° 2758

nlt = isaac sternbuch
3 teufener strasse stgallen =

we strongly affirm and make public that the vaad hanatzala,
emergency committee of 132 nassau street which includes all
religious jewish organizations comprising the majority of jews
america has since november 1943 recognized isaac
sternbuch and his committee as the official and only
representation of the vaad hahatzala emergency committee =
rabbis israel rosenberg el silver aron kotler abraham =
kalmanowitz +

Telegramm – Télégramme – Telegramma

+ 32434 SHANGHAI 50 58 20/9 1505

N° 1606

VIA RADIOSUISSE = NLT = STERNBUCH KOTLER GROSOVSKY
MONTREUX =

WORRYING YOUR SILENCE ABOUT OUR IMMIGRATION ANXIOUS KNOW WHAT
PROSPECTS OUR QUICKEST DEPARTURE STOP ENORMOUS INCREASE YAKRES
AND FRANC DEVALUATION REDUCED YOUR SUPPORT SENT TO 'ALF TRY MORE
PROFITABLE WAY OF REMITTANCE STOP TELL ABRAMYOFIN MICHOLABRAMCZYK
ENGAGED NEEDS MONEY FOR WEDDING RABBIS WOLMARK SZYMANOWICZ KRAWIEC
PANTOL ZYTMAN RAICZYK SOROCZKIN BOKOW KOPELOWICZ BREWDA SZNEIDER

Some of the many hundreds of telegrams that reached the Sternbuchs from the heads of the Yeshivos in Shanghai during and after the war years

Photocopy of a identification card issued by the authorities in Shanghai to Mr. Benjamin Fishoff, one of the refugee yeshiva students, who is now an important leader of the Orthodox Jewish community in New York.

The leaders and teachers of the Shanghai Talmud Torah, supported by the Sternbuchs. Seated from left to right are: Rabbi Shmuel David Warshavchik, today Rosh Yeshivah of Kfar Chassidim; Rabbi Jacob Nayman, now Rav of Congregation Adas Bnei Israel in Chicago; Mr. Hirsch Levin, head of the German refugee community; Mr. Leib Brailofsky, head of the Russian refugee community; Rabbi Meir Ashkenazi, the Rabbi of Shanghai; Rabbi Chaim Plotkin, the Shochet of Shanghai and Rabbi Eli Moshe Liss, one of the leaders of the Lubavitch refugee community. Rabbi Plotkin came to Toronto after the war and selflessly helped establish Torah life. His son-in-law, Rabbi Moshe Kaplan, became principal of the Etz Chaim school in Toronto.

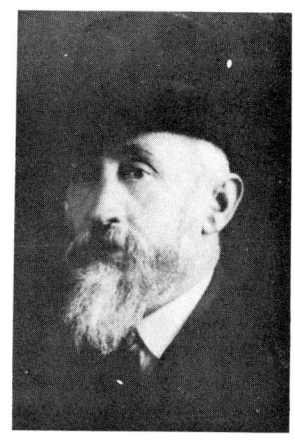

Mr. Chaim Yisroel Eiss, one of most active rescue leaders in Switzerland, passed away in the winter of 1943. Many of the projects that he initiated were continued by the Sternbuchs after his death.

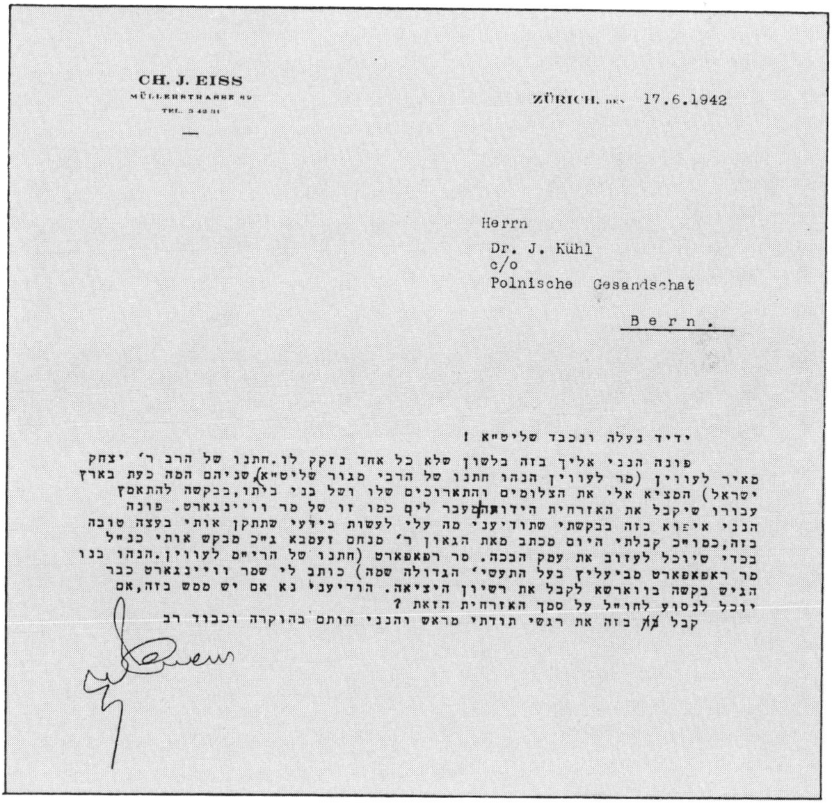

CH. J. EISS

ZÜRICH, den 17.6.1942

Herrn
Dr. J. Kühl
c/o
Polnische Gesandschat
Bern.

ידיד נעלה ונכבד שליט"א !

פונה הנני אליך בזה בלשון שלא כל אחד נזקק לו.חתנו של הרב ר' יצחק
מאיר לעווין (מר לעווין הנהו חתנו של הרבי מגור שליט"א),שניהם המה כעת בארץ
ישראל) המציא אלי את הצלומים והתארוכים שלו ושל בני ביתו,בבקשה להתאמץ
עבורו שיקבל את האזרחית הידועה מעבר לים כמו זו של מר וויינגארט. פונה
הנני איפוא בזה בבקשתי שתודיעני מה עלי לעשות בידעי שתתקן אותי בעצה טובה
בזה,כמו"כ קבלתי היום מכתב מאת הגאון ר' מנחם זעמבא ג"כ מבקש אותי כנ"ל
בכדי שיוכל לעזוב את עמק הבכה. מר ראפאפארט (חתנו של הרי"ם לעווין.הנהו בנו
מר ראפאפארט מביעליץ בעל התעשי' הגדולה שמה) כותב לי שמר וויינגארט כבר
הגיש בקשה בווארשא לקבל את רשיון היציאה. הודיעני נא אם יש ממש בזה,אם
יוכל לנסוע לחו"ל על סמך האזרחית הזאת ?
קבל נא בזה את רגשי תודתי מראש והנני חותם בהוקרה וכבוד רב

A letter by Mr. Chaim Yisroel Eiss, Agudath Israel leader in Zurich, asking Dr. Kuhl about the possibility of getting South American passports for the grandchildren of the Gerer Rebbe and for Rabbi Menachem Ziemba in the Warsaw Ghetto.

			Geller	Konrad	Paraguay
AJZENSTADT	Felix	Peru	"	Erna	"
"	Romano	"	"	Stella	"
"	Marcel	"	Goldberger	Henryk	"
BAUMINGER	Kalman	Paraguay	"	Malka	"
"	Martha	"	Gorlin	Eugenie	Chile
Bauminger	Joel	"	Goldstein	Nachmann	Peru
"	Bluma	"	"	Sara	"
BAUMINGER	Leon	"	"	Lea	"
"	Lea	"	"	Szyja	"
BERGER	Abraham	Haiti	Horenstein	Abraham	Honduras
"	Eugenie	"	"	Estera Sara	"
Berglas	Chaim Leib	Paraguay	Kacenelson	Izchok	"
"	Alta Hinda	"	"	Zwi	"
Blumenkopf	Aron	"	Kadysz	Icek	"
"	Riwka	"	"	Brucha	"
"	Rozia	"	"	Awiwa	"
BLUMENKOPF	Juda Leib	"	"	Rachmiel	"
"	Stella	"	Kaller	Frideryk	Paraguay
BULMENKOPF	Wolf	"	"	Halina	"
"	Helene	"	Kon	Felicja	Nicaragua
"	Christine	"	"	Jacek	"
BLUMENKOPF	Muchim	"	"	Peter	"
"	Chaje	"	"	Stefan	"
DUDELZAK	Schulem Mottek	Peru	Krystenfreund	David	Honduras
"	Tyszia	"	"	Ita	"
"	Jevzu	"	"	Szajndle	"
DUDELZAK	Rachmiel	"	"	Ruchla	"
"	Ita	"	"	Aron	"
"	Arcadius	"	Landau	Leib Alec	Paraguay
Beck	Nathan	Paraguay	"	Bronis Ester	"
"	Klara	"	"	Jevzy	"
"	Rosa	"	Lichtmann	Oscar	Costa Rica
EISENZWEIG	Szyja	"	"	Anna Rosalie	"
"	Gina	"	"	Regina	"
"	Gitla Miriam	"	Lindenbaum	Sonia	"
Fakler	Szywa	Costa Rica	Licber	Josef	Paraguay
"	Stefania	"	"	Friemeta	"
"	Henryk	"	"	Henryky	"
Frumkin	Anna	Chile	Lisewdder	Freidla	"
"	Hermina Rosa	"	"	Boris	Nicaragua
Fraenkel	Josef	Paraguay	"	Zypa	"
"	Cella	"	"	Alexander	"
"	Mathilde	"	"	Mirjam	"
"	Dorys	"	Malcowskjy	Schmul	Venezuela
"	Alexander	"	"	Sara	"
"	Jochwet	"	"	Moris	"
"	Pinkus	"	Mendelbaum	Sylvia	Costa Rica
"	Leib	"	Joskowicz	Moszek	Paraguay
"	Rutha	"	"	Chana Ita	"
"	Marta	"	"	Alina	"
Fraenkel	Mendel	"	Muszynski	Leon	Haiti
"	Rosa	"	"	Lili	"
Fleischer	Ester	Equador	Natanson	Ladislaw	Costa Rica
Garbinski	Henrico	Peru	"	Stefania	"
"	Helena	"	Osiek	Sara	Costa Rica
Gehorsam	Abraham	Paraguay	Poznaski	Jakob	Paraguay
"	Helena	"	"	Jenta	"
			RABIA	Marlan	"

Partial list of the Jews with South American passports interned by the Germans in Vittel.

284 / HEROINE OF RESCUE

Telegramm – Télégramme – Telegramma

Oskar Halpern Malomgasse 2

KOLOZSVAR Ungarn

Erfahret Aufenthaltsort von Dr. Davido Halpern und sendet ihm das Dokument nach

Konsulat von Paraguay

Bern, den 12. Oktober 1941.

Sehr geehrter Herr,

Hierdurch frage ich Sie an, wie es mit Ihrer Auswanderung nach Paraguay steht? Wann gedenken Sie zu verreisen und welche Route werden Sie einschlagen? Wollen Sie mir bitte umgehend antworten.

Mit vorzüglicher Hochachtung

Herrn Dr. Henryk Goldberger,
Potockiego 31/8,
L e m b e r g (Generalgouvernement).

Paraguayan Consul in Zurich corresponding with Jews in Poland and Hungary about their South American passports.

> **Telegramm – Télégramme – Telegramma**
>
> 12292 MANCHESTER W115 123 5/9
>
> Nº 524
>
> BOTH STATE DEPARTMENT AND BRITISH FOREIGN OFFICE INTERVENED
> THROUGH PROTECTING POWER WE SHALL TRY AGAIN STOP URGE SWISS
> GOVERNMENT ALSO PERHAPS WITH HELP OF AURCH AND OTHER PERSONALITIES
> AND NATIONAL ZEITUNG TO DEMAND PROTECTION AS LATIN AMERICAN HAVE
> ACKNOWLEDGED PAPER AND DECLARED FOR EXCHANGE OUR INFORMATION
> COMING ((12/50)) FROM BRITISH REPATRIATED ALSO HEARD THAT LETTER
> WAS RECEIVED IN CAMP FROM ONE DEPORTED WHO ESCAPED THAT DEPORTEES

> **Telegramm – Télégramme – Telegramma**
>
> SEND AUSCHWITZ BELIEVE NOT BASED ON ABSOLUTE ASSURANCE UNLESS
> YOU HAVE BETTER INTOFMATION WE PROCESS LIST OF ALL THE DEPORTEES
> SHALUS BROTHER SISTERS PROBABLY ESCAPED SHORTLY BEFORE
> DEPORTATION BELIEVED HIDDEN NEAR OLD ((3/23)) PLACE FOREIGN
> OFFICE JEWISH AGENCY ASSURED THAT CONFIRMATION CERTIFICATE
> ARRIVED BERNE BEFORE AND FEBRUARY HAVING HAD SUCH ACKNOWLEDGEMENT
> HOPE FOR BEST LOVE = ROTTENBERG ++

> **Telegramm – Télégramme – Telegramma**
>
> 12388 MANCHESTER W733 58 5/9 VIA RS
>
> = ELT = STERNBUCH MONTREUX =
>
> BRITISH GOVERNMENT INSTRUCTED SWISS AUTHORITIES THAT DEPORTEES
> BEING EXCHANGEABLE MUST BE RETURNED TO RED CROSS CAMP IN
> ACCORDANCE WITH GENEVA CONVENTION THEREFORE URGE EVERYTHING FROM
> THIS PART ALSO TRY THAT SWISS AUTHORITIES SEE THAT RED CROSS
> PROTEST AND GIVE IMMEDIATE ACTIVE HELP DERGENBELSEN TERESIENSTADT
> ORDINARY CAMPS WOULD BE GLAD IF DEPORTEES THERE BEST WISHES =
> = ROTTENBERG +

Telegram exchange between Recha Sternbuch and her brother, Dr. Menachem Rottenberg of Manchester, England, regarding the internees of Vittel. Dr. Rottenberg tried to get help from the British government for the endangered internees.

Bern, den 12. Oktober 1941.

Sehr geehrter Herr Minister,

Hierdurch gestatte ich mir Ihnen folgende Angelegenheit zu unterbreiten:

Nach der von den Russen erfolgten Besetzung Polens, ersuchte mich die Polnische Gesandtschaft in Bern, einigen polnischen Bürgern, die unter russischer Herrschaft weilen dadurch zu helfen, dass ich ihnen paraguayanische Identitätsausweise ausstelle. Durch die Russen wurden die betreffenden Personen sodann als Ausländer betrachtet und erhielten die Bewilligung zum freien Abzug nach Kobe (Japan). In Japan händigte ihnen die dort noch akkreditierte Polnische Gesandtschaft den normalen polnischen Pass aus. Diese Personen hatten jedoch niemals die Absicht wirklich nach Paraguay zu reisen.

Da ich mit der hiesigen Polnischen Gesandtschaft von jeher in guter Beziehung stehe, und es sich nur um wenige Fälle handelte, entschloss ich mich dieser Bitte Folge zu geben und dadurch einige Menschenleben zu retten. Ich sandte den mir genannten Personen die Ausweise mit dem Ersuchen, mir diese Dokumente sofort nach ihrem Eintreffen in Kobe zurückzusenden.

Inzwischen brach der deutsch-russische Krieg aus und der von den Russ besetztgehaltene Teil Polens wurde deutsch. Die Lage hat sich nun insofern geändert, als die Leute nicht mehr über Kobe, sondern über Deutschland nach Portugal reisen müssen. Die deutschen Okkupationsbehörden erteilen nur dann die Ausreiseerlaubnis und das Transitvisum, wenn die für dieses Gebiet zuständige Paraguayanische Gesandtschaft in Berlin, die von mir ausgestellten Identitätsausweise bestätigt.

Ich gelange daher an Sie mit der Bitte mir behilflich sein zu wollen, d.h. wenn sich einige Personen mit solchen Dokumenten an Sie wenden würden, dieselben bestätigen zu wollen. Ich wäre Ihnen zu Dank verpflichtet, wenn Sie mich sodann verständigten.

Ich sehe Ihrer geschätzten Antwort gerne entgegen, und begrüsse Sie, sehr geehrter Herr Minister, mit dem Ausdruck meiner vollkommensten Hochachtung

An die Gesandtschaft
der Republik von Paraguay,
B e r l i n /Deutschland.

Paraguayan diplomats in Zurich and Berlin correspond about the issuance of South American documents to Jews under German occupation.

**LEGATION OF THE
UNITED STATES OF AMERICA**

Bern, September 6, 1944.

Schweiz. Hilfsverein :
  jüd. Flüchtlinge
    Les Colonda[l]
      Montre[ux]

Sirs:

In answer to you[r]
September, I am please[d]
51 persons transferre[d]
Belsen on the 16th of

In answer to you[r]
ber regarding the ques[
Germany, I can state t[
Refugee Board on Augu[st]
the Spanish Governmen[t]
through its Embassy i[n]
Paraguayan passports i[
ment camps. The War [
that appropriate steps
Government in Asuncio[n]
Madrid.

Enclosure:
  List

**LEGATION OF THE
UNITED STATES OF AMERICA**

Bern, November 8th, 1944

Mr. Isaac Sternbuch
Villa "Les Colondalles"
MONTREUX (Vaud)

Dear Mr. Sternbuch:

I wish to acknowledge your letters of November 6th. and 7th. containing respectively lists (further) of holders of Latin American documents in Europe and a special list of Lithuanian Jews in whose names El Salvador Nationality Certificates were issued but who have in all probability not received these documents.

I shall take whatever useful action possible with the two lists in an effort, particularly, to locate the persons in question.

Any further information which you might receive concerning this special "camp" not far from St. Gallen, for Lithuanian Jews would be appreciated.

Sincerely yours,

Roswell D. McClelland
Special Assistant to
the American Minister.

Exchange of correspondence between the Sternbuchs and the American Legation in Bern concerning Jews with South American passports who were deported from Vittel and whom the Sternbuchs desperately tried to save.

**LEGATION OF THE
UNITED STATES OF AMERICA**

Bern, November 30, 1944.

Dear Mr. Sternbuch:

With reference to your letter of November 26 with you enclosed a letter from Mr. Naftali Amsel concerning the Honduran nationality of a certain Mr. Ephraim Packter, tho[se in the con]centration camp of A[...] happy to state that our Legation has pre[...] Department, Division [...] the Swiss authoritie[s...] at Berlin. The Swis[s...] inform the German Fo[reign Office...] considered a Hondura[n...] rights pertaining to [...] be accorded Mr. Pack[ter...] to his wife. In the [...] certainty, has reque[sted...] of Honduras, through [...] of the Honduran nati[onality...]

Mr. Isaac Sternbuch
Villa Les Colondalle[s]
Montreux.

**THE FOREIGN SERVICE
OF THE
UNITED STATES OF AMERICA**

AMERICAN ~~EMBASSY~~
LEGATION.

Bern, December 22, 1944.

Dear Sirs:

I wish to acknowledge your letter of December 14th, concerning the case of Dr. Leib HAGAR who is thought to be at the camp of Bergau bei Dresden.

As you know the American Legation has nothing to do with persons possessing Paraguayian documentation since the protecting power for Paraguay in Germany is Spain. In a large number of cases, however, we have drawn them to the attention of the War Refugee Board in Washington which has in turn signaled them to the American Embassy at Madrid. For there the intercession has presumably been made through the Spanish Embassy at Berlin. But, as you realize, very little if any practical results have been forthcoming, the moreso in the case of persons whose present whereabouts is unknown, it having never been confirmed that a camp of "Bergau" exists, as far as I know.

I shall draw this case to the attention of the WRB for whatever action they can undertake in favor of this man.

Sincerely yours,

Roswell D. McClelland
Roswell D. McClelland
Special Assistant to
the American Minister.

"HIJELFS"
Villa Les Colondalles,
Montreux.

```
LEGACIÓN DE CHILE
      TK:1149.-                    H.RN.den 14 DEZ 44

                 Sehr geehrte Herren!

                     Wir besitzen Ihr Zeichen: "HIJEFS" vom 12.
                 ds. Mts.,und haben Ihre Ausführungen,als Nach-
                 trag zu unseren früheren, der SCHUTZMACHT bekannt-
                 gegeben,mit der Bitte um Information über den
                 von Ih en berührten Gegenstand.

                     Sobald wir Nachricht haben,geben wir diese
                 an Sie weiter.

                     Inzwischen begrüssen wir Sie bestens als
                 Ihre Ihnen stets ergebenen .

                                    Carlos Morla Lynch.
                 AO GESANDTER UND BEVOLLM: MI-
                    NISTER CHILE'S IN DER SCHWEIZ.
```

An:"H I J E F S "
SCHWEIZER HILFSVEREIN FUER
JUEDISCHE FLUECHTLINGE IM
AULSNAD:

Montreux:Les Colondalles.

Chilean Ambassador to Switzerland acknowledges the Sternbuchs' inquiry about the Jews with Chilean passports in Vittel and promising intervention.

```
POSELSTWO R.P.
   w Bernie
Nr.727/1
   AM
```

odpis   Bern, dnia 17 kwietnia 1944.

Do Ministerstwa Spraw Zagranicznych
w L o n d y n i e

Stosownie do depeszy Ministerstwa Nr.136, Poselstwo R.P. w Bernie przesyła w załączeniu, nadesłaną przez Dr. A. Silberscheina w Genewie, listę osób, którym przesłane zostały paszporty republik południowo-amerykańskich.

ZA POSŁA R.P.:

/Stefan J. Ryniewicz/
Radca Poselstwa

Załącznik: 1.

Here is a letter from the Polish Legation in Bern to the Foreign Ministry of the Polish government-in-exile in London pertaining to the Jews with South American passports who were interned in Vittel.

```
Schweiz. Hilfsverein für
jüd. Flüchtlinge im Ausland
       «HIJEFS»                          Montreux, 1.Oktober 1944.
   Telephon 6 30 56 und 6 43 99            Les Colondalles
   Postcheck-Konto IIb 2107 Vevey
   Telegramm-Adresse: Hijefs Montreux
                                            Tit.
                                            Polnisches Konsulat
                                            Thunstr.
                                            B e r n e
                                            -.-.-.-.-.-.-.-.-.-
```

Sehr geehrter Herr Doktor,

    Wir nehmen höflich Bezug auf die Rücksprache mit Ihnen betreffend eine Reise nach Frankreich und Belgien. Wir wären Ihnen sehr zu Dank verpflichtet, wenn Sie sich der angeregten Sache alsbald widmen könnten. Die Reise scheint uns sehr dringend zu sein. Je früher abgeklärt werden kann, wohin versch. Deportierte verbracht wurden, desto eher können Hilfs- & Rettungsmassnahme abgeklärt werden.

    Selbstverständlich werden dem Consulat keinerlei Unkosten erwachsen, da wir alle Spesen auf uns übernehmen, ebenso würden wir ein Auto zur Verfügung stellen. Für diese wichtige Mission möchten wir von unserer Organisation aus auch E. Sternbuch delegieren, und wir zweifeln nicht daran, dass es Ihnen in gemeinsamer Arbeit mit G"ttes Hilfe gelingen wird, Material zu beschaffen, durch das noch viele Menschenleben gerettet werden kann.-

    Dürfen wir Sie um die Freundlichkeit bitten, diese Angelegenheit mit unserm sehr verehrten Herrn Minister zu besprechen und seinen gütigen Rat einzuholen. Empfangen Sie inzwischen unsere innigsten Grüsse & Dank für Ihre frdl. Bemühungen.-

                        Mit vorzüglicher Hochachtung:

HIJEFS (the Sternbuchs) officially request Dr. Kuhl to undertake his trip to parts of liberated France and Belgium.

Verband Schweizerischer
Jüdischer Flüchtlingshilfen

Zürich, den 9. Oktober 1944
Lavaterstrasse 57

Postcheck-Konto VIII 12711
Telephon 7 42 17
Telegramme: Israv

I/Schreiben:
I/Zeichen:

An das

Polnische Konsulat

B e r n

Thunstrasse

Bitte in Ihrer Antwort anführen:
Betrifft:

Sehr geehrter Herr Doctor Kühl,

    Wir bestätigen Ihnen mit bestem Dank den Empfang der uns
freundlichst zugestellten Zirkulare, die wir gerne zu unserer
Information benützen.-

    Mit grossem Intreese haben wir von Ihrer Mitteilung Kenntni
genommen, dass Sie sich nach dem Westen begeben und wir sind Ihnen
sehr dankbar dafür, dass Sie uns Gelegenheit gaben, unsere Wünsche
zu äussern.

    In erster Linie interessiert uns naturgemäss die Frage
der Rückwanderungsmöglichkeit nach Frankreich und Belgien der-
jenigen Peronen, die nicht Staatsbürger dieser beiden Länder sind,
aber dort ihren Wohnsitz hatten. Die Abklärung dieses Problems
wäre von ausserordentlicher Wichtigkeit.

    Sollten Sie Gelegenheit haben, mit informierten Kreisen in
Fühlung zu kommen, würde uns noch besonders interessieren, in
welchen Städten jüdische Hilfscomités bereits ihre Arbeit wieder
aufgenommen haben, damit wir Rückwanderer eventuell an sie ver-
weisen können.

    Wir danken Ihnen im Voraus für alle Informationen, die
Sie beschaffen können werden und wünschen Ihnen, sehr geehrter
Herr Doctor, eine gute und erfolgreiche Reise.

    Mit den freundlichsten Grüssen und
        vorzüglicher Hochachtung
           V.S.J.F.

Letter from the Swiss Association for Relief for Jewish Refugees expressing satisfaction with the planned mission of Dr. Kuhl to France.

CENTRALE

VOLKSVERWERING
Strijdbeweging ter beveiliging van Bloed en Bodem
Leiding: Mster René LAMBRICHTS ■ Gesticht in 1937
F.-DE-CHAMPAGNESTRAAT, 52, BRUSSEL, TEL. 12.59.07
POSTCH.: 43.45.88 (VOLKSCHE AANVAL - BRUSSEL)

Brussel, den 24 September 1942.
An die Sicherheitspolizei
Louisalaan, 510
BRUSSEL.

Geachte Heer Asche,

    Men meldt ons wat volgt: dat joden zich schuil houden in de volgende huizen: Koningslaan, 14
                              de Merodestraat, 323

    Men meldt ons dat honderden rijke joden zich schuil houden in Etablissements TITECA, rue de Lucerne, 11, zothuis, alsook in de twee bijhuizen van dit instituut, waarvan wij de adressen niet kennen. Zij betalen 5.000 fr. per maand en wandelen in den hof. Als er alarm is gaan zij allen in een cel en doen zich als zot doorgaan.
Het loont dus de moeite dit een goed na te pluizen.

                                        Met volkschen groet.

/L

                                    R. BOTTE

Betr.: *Versteckte Juden: Koningslaan 14*
                        rue de Merode 323
Hunderten von reichen Juden verstecken

IV.B.3.
                                     Brüssel, den 6.November 1943.

Betr.: Statistik : Juden nach Staatsangehörigkeit

    Beiliegende Statistik in 3 Ex., der 43.193 im Judenregister Eingetragenen erfasst, wurde auf Basis der selber Dokumentation der beiliegende Statistik "Altesaufbau" vom 31/7/1942 aufgestellt.

    Es geht also um die Juden worüber vor dem Arbeitseinsatz (4/8/1942) amtlichen Angaben zur Verfügung standen.

    Von diese Juden wurden bis heute bereits ungefähr 20.000 evacuiert.

                                     Brüssel, den 15.9.42

Fernschreiben :

a) An das
   Reichsicherheitshauptamt, Referat IV B 4
   z. Hdn. SS- O-stubaf. Eichmann o. V.i.A.
   B e r l i n .

b) An den
   Inspekteur der Konzentrationslager
   in O r a n i e n b u r g .

Am 15.9.42. , 8,35 Uhr, hat Transportzug Nr. D a 8oi den Abgangsbahnhof Mecheln in Richtung Auschwitz mit insgesamt tausendneunundvierzig Juden verlassen.
    Der erfasste Personenkreis entspricht den gegebenen Richtlinien.
Transportführer ist Ltn. d. Sch. .E.S.S.E.R...........
dem die namentlich Transportliste in zweifacher Ausfertigung mitgegeben wurde.

On his return from France, Dr. Kuhl brought a number of very interesting Nazi documents on persecution of Jews and of their deportations to the extermination camps.

Schweiz. Hilfsverein für
jüd. Flüchtlinge im Ausland
· HIJEFS ·

25. August 1944

Telephon 6 30 56 und 6 43 99
Postcheck-Konto IIb 2107 Vevey
Telegramm-Adresse: Hijefs Montreux

An das
Comite International de la
Croix Rouge.
Geneve.
- - - - - - - - - - - - - -

Sehr geehrte Herren,

wir haben soeben verschiedene Einzelheiten über das Lager B e r g e n - B e l s e n bei Celle (Hann.) erfahren und da wir wohl mit Recht annehmen, dass Sie hierfür Interesse haben, erlauben wir uns, Ihnen diese Nachrichten weiterzugeben.

Das Lager umfasst z.Zt. 6440 Juden aller Länder, wie z.B. ca. 2000 Holländer, Italiener, Portugiesen, Montenegriner, einige Franzosen usw. Zuletzt kam der Transport von 1690 ungarischen Juden, von welchen – wie Ihnen ja bekannt – 320 Menschen nach der Schweiz kamen.

Jede Landsmannschaft ist von der anderen getrennt und wir extra bewacht. Es existiert dort auch eine Gruppe von 258 polnischen Juden, die sämtlich Inhaber von südamerikanischen Papieren sind und etwas bevorzugt behandelt werden.

Die Holländer, für welche das Lager anscheinend als Deportationslager gbbtaachtet wird (der entsprechende Teil wird als Arbala-Lager Bergen-Belsen bezeichnet), arbeiten sehr schwer etwa 9-10 Stunden täglich.

Es scheint, dass die bisher bestandene Postsperre seit etwa 2 Wochen aufgehoben wurde, allerdings haben wir noch keine direkte Post erhalten.

Wir erfahren ferner, dass in den Städten Aspern und Hildesheim (Osterreich) Arbeitslager für ungar. Juden bestehen.

Es sind uns auch ferner Namen einzeler Lagerinsassen bekannt die wir Ihnen auf Wunsch gerne aufgeben.

Wir hoffen, Ihnen mit diesen Angaben gedient zu haben und begrüssen Sie

mit vorzüglicher Hochachtung

Letter dated August 25, 1944, from HIJEFS to the International Red Cross in Geneva, informing them about conditions in various concentration camps.

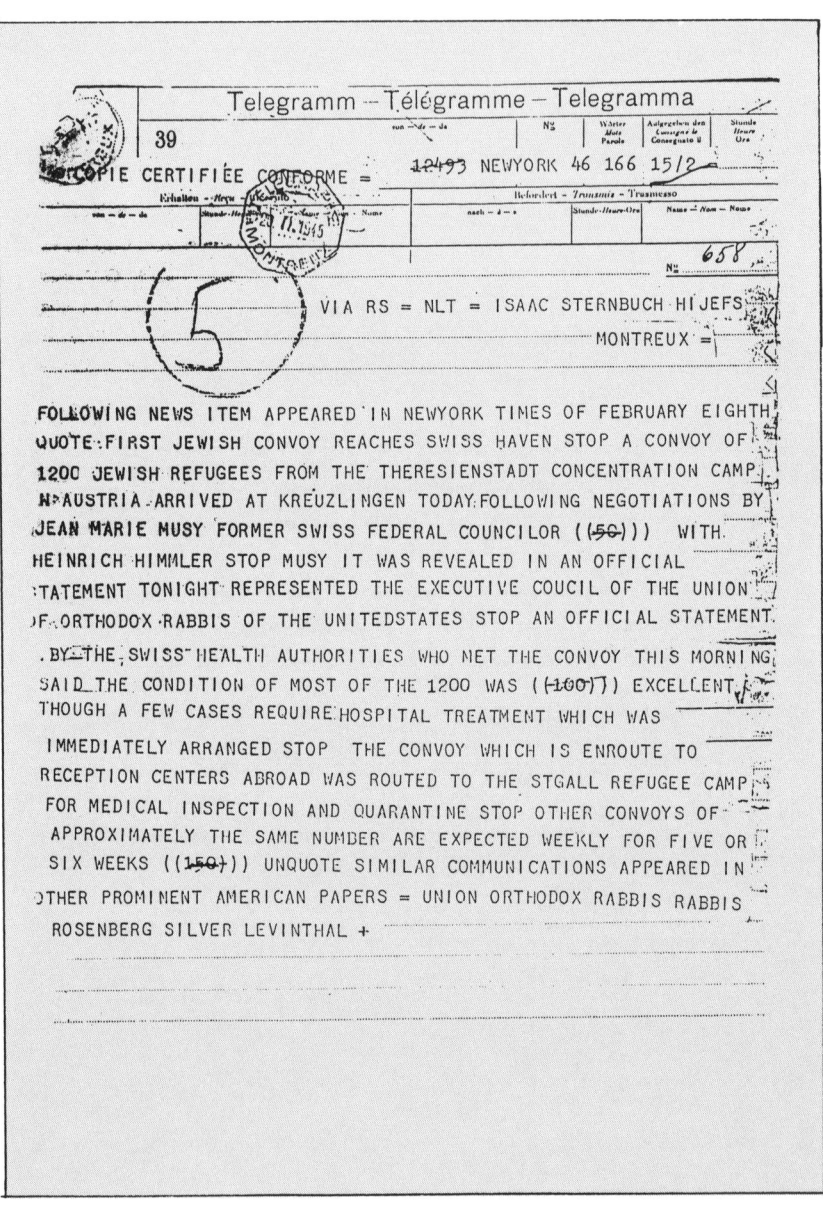

Telegram from the Rabbinic leaders in the U.S. to the Sternbuchs informing them that word of the Musy rescue team's arrival from Theresienstadt to Switzerland was published in the U.S. press. The Sternbuchs needed this information to impress Himmler thereby enabling them to arrange more releases of Jews from concentration camps.

Office Memorandum · UNITED STATES GOVERNMENT

TO : U - Mr. Grew
DATE: February 15, 1945
FROM : WRB - George L. Warren
SUBJECT: Release of further refugees into Switzerland from Germany.

On February 7, 1945, 1,200 refugees arrived in Switzerland from Germany. Their release was arranged by Musy, a former Federal Councilor of Switzerland, who had made a number of trips to Germany at the instigation of Sternbuch, the representative in Switzerland of the Vaad Hahatzala Emergency Committee of the Union of Orthodox Rabbis of the United States and Canada. Musy returned to Switzerland in advance of the refugees announcing that he had secured their release by direct negotiation with Himmler, whom he had seen on his previous trips to Germany. He stated that additional groups of refugees would arrive weekly in Switzerland dependent upon German transportation facilities. He advised Sternbuch that he would require a deposit of 5,000,000 Swiss francs in his (Musy's) name in the Swiss National Bank immediately after the arrival of the 1,200. This money he suggested might later be paid over by the Germans to the International Committee of the Red Cross as a further gesture of good faith.

The Rabbis are now pressing the War Refugee Board and the Treasury Department for a license to transmit 4,000,000 Swiss francs to Switzerland to be paid to Musy. They have on deposit in Switzerland 1,000,000 Swiss francs under a previous license. The Department has been asked by Brigadier General O'Dwyer, Executive Director of the War Refugee Board, if it will approve the transaction. He has advised the Rabbis that he will issue the license if the Department agrees.

In view of the unusual humanitarian considerations involved, FMA, EE and WT are willing to consider approval of the license provided the funds after payment to Musy can be blocked in Switzerland. Mr. Currie, on mission in Switzerland, has the item of "safe havens" on his agenda for discussion with the Swiss. British comment on the Dutch inquiry was to the effect that the negotiations should be continued as long as possible but that the payment envisaged would be inconsistent with current safe haven proposals.

Two suggestions have resulted from the discussions in the Department.
1. That Mr. Currie might induce the Swiss to agree to block Musy's account after the proposed payment is made, or
2. That the blocking might be accomplished by general safe haven arrangements still to be negotiated with the Swiss.

With respect to the latter, the time element is a consideration. The Rabbis fear that delay in payment may jeopardize the rescue of additional refugees.

Report from George C. Warren of the War Refugee Board to Joseph Gruen, Undersecretary of State, informing him of the Musy-Himmler negotiations which resulted in the arrival of 1200 inmates from Theresienstadt. Mr. Warren also informed Mr. Gruen of requests for a license from the U.S. government for additional funds in view of prospects for further releases.

```
Vertrauensausschuss                          Morgins, den 28. November 1944.
Flüchtlingsheim, Morgins.


                                    An die H I J E F S ,
                                    Villa Collondales,

                                    M O N T R E U X ;


        Sehr geehrter Herr Mandau !

            In der Anlage erlaube ich mir Ihnen einige Adresse einzusenden
        die zum Teil noch nicht bei Ihnen registriert sind, und wollen
        Sie bitte eine Möglichkeit suchen, dort Pakete hinzuschicken.

              Epediteur: I. Mond, Morgins.
Empfänger:    Helena, Sara Mond, geb. 9.7.1926 Anvers Polin Birkenau
              Nora Weiss                       Birkenau
              Tonia   "                           "
              Regine  "                           "
              ==========================================================
              Expediteur : Frau Jakubowicz, Morgins.
Empfänger:    Regine Lebensfeld, Stabsgebäude, Birkenau
              Jonas Seelnefreund  Arbeitslager Monowitz, Oberschlesien
              Mathilde Seelenfreund        "    Birkenau   "aus 7.
              Josef Sprung                 "        "       " 16.
              Topper, Samuel               "        "       " 17.
              ==========================================================
              Epediteur : Geschwister Heitner, Morgins.
Empfänger :   Isak, Loebel Heitner, Bergen - Belsen.
              ==========================================================
              Expediteur : A. Strossberg, Morgins.
Empfänger :   Isidore Bucheister, KZ. Weimar - Buchenwald 15, No.48953 Bl.52
              ==========================================================
              Expediteur : L. Teitelbaum, Morgins.
Empfänger :   Hirsch D o b r e s , Arbeitslager Monowitz, Haus 15.
              ==========================================================

            Ferner lege ich Dir bei, eine Etiquette für eine Kriegsge-
        fangenensendung. Ich hoffe, dass es Ihnen möglich sein wird
        an oben angegebene Adressen baldigst Paket zu senden, und
        danke ich Ihnen im Namen der Absender, wie auch der Empfänger.

            Wir verbleiben mit besten Grüssen und vorzüglicher

                                            Hochachtung
                                            Der Vertrauensausschuss


Am Donnerstag abend werde ich bei Ihnen sein, um wegen
weiteren Möglichkeiten mit Ihnen zu sprechen.
```

Requests from individuals in the concentration camps of Bergen-Belsen, Birkenau and Theresienstadt, asking HIJEFS to send food packages.

Letter from the Bobover Rebbe, Rabbi Shlomo Halberstam, written from Bucharest, Roumania, in which he thanks the Sternbuchs for funds which enabled him and his son to be rescued. He also asks for additional help to enable others to be saved.

Correspondence between the Sternbuchs and Captain Robert Monheit, Jewish chaplain of the French Army, through whom the Sternbuchs delivered many shipments of kosher food, clothing and religious articles to the Jews in the liberated camps in Austria.

Capitain
M o n h e i t
Hotel du Rhin
S t r a s b o u r g
- - - - - - - - - -

Sehr geehrter Herr Monheit,

wir erhielten Ihr Schreiben vom 5.ds. und sehen Ihrer telefonischen Mitteilung gerne entgegen, wann die Eroeffnung der Hachschara stattfindet.

Wir haben nochmals beim Roten Kreuz reklamiert, das erklaert, dass die Tefillaus etc. bereits an das Juedische Komitee in Konstanz abgegangen sind. Wir haben auch an das Juedische Komitee in Bregenz 1 Paket (enthaltend je 40 Siddurim, 5 Chumoschim und 5 Kizzur)
an das Juedische Komitee, Deutsches Museum, Muenchen 1 Paket
"   "   "   Rabb. Horowitz, Augsburg   2   "
"   "   "   Rabb. Halberstamm, Feldafing 10 "

gesandt und heute Auftrag gegeben, auch nach Innsbruck an Ihre Adresse 4 Pakete, an Ihre Adresse nach Konstanz 2 Pakete und an das Lager Jordanbad bei Biberach 1 Paket abzusenden.

Was nun die Frage der Koscher-Lebensmittel anbetrifft, so sind wir hier verschiedene Meinungsverschiedenheiten aufgetaucht. Der Vaad Hahatzala aus Amerika beabsichtigt uns etwa 100000 kg Koscher Lebensmittel (Fleisch, Konserven, Mazzoth, Kakao, Kaffee) etc. zuzusenden, jedoch wissen wir nicht, ob es nicht schade waere, dieses Geld ausgeben zu lassen. Man musste pruefen, ob die Unrra nicht evtl. bereit waere, koscher-Knech einzurichten, sodass man lediglich eine separate Kueche haben muesste. Schochtim wird es wohl xxxx ueberall geben und man die man dort nicht be
wissen, wieviele Mens
Frage kommen, da man
fuer nichtorthodoxe M
also bitte genau auf
usw. und ob es wirkli
Koscherkuechen einzuri

Wir nahmen an, dass S
mit Herrn Dr. Lewin i
Auch Herr Griffel hat

Wir bitten Sie noch u
zur Weiterleitung zuse
die Post in der franz
niert.

Wir begruessen Sie

---

17. Dezember 1945

Le/h.

M n ieur
Capitain
R. M o n h e i t
S t r a s b o u r g.
- - - - - - - - - -

Sehr geehrter Herr Monheit,

wir nehmen hoefl. Bezug auf unser Schreiben vom 5.ds. an Sie nach Konstanz und wiederholen Ihnen, dass wir an Ihre Adresse nach Konstanz folgende Waren abgeschickt haben:

```
1000 Kisten Feigen a brutto 11 kg
  25   "    Thonfisch brutto va. 40 kg
  30   "    Sardinen à je 100 Dosen à 200 gr
```

Die Waren gehen Ihnen durch Vermittlung des IRK zu und sind fuer folgende Lager bestimmt:

150 rituelle Insassen des Lagers Bregenz
160   "   "   des Lagers New-Palestine bei Salzberg
                     zu Haenden des Herrn Iser Salzberg
300   "   "   des Lagers Bad-Gastein zu Haenden des
                     Herrn Manes Zytnicki
500   "   "   des Lagers Linz (Bindermichel) --
                     Haenden des Herrn S. Romanowski

Sie wocoen die Waren bitte proportionell und gleichmaessig verteilen und keine Aenderung vorzunehmen.

Wir nahmen davon Notiz, dass Sie die Waren unter Ihrer persoenlichen Aufsicht mit Camions expedieren werden und wir waeren Ihnen dankbar, wenn Sie uns jeweils Quittungen der einzelnen Lager zusenden wuerden, da wir dieselben nach New-York weitersenden wollen (es handelt sich keinesfalls um irgend ein Misstrauen Ihnen gegenueber).

Nach Verteilung dieses Postens werden wir weitere Waren gerne zur Verfuegung stellen und wir bitten Sie uns mitzuteilen, ob noch andere Lager bestehen, in welchen sich rituelle Lagerinsassen befinden.

Wir danken fuer Ihre Bemuehungen und zeichnen

hochachtungsvoll

APPENDIX / 301

Schweiz. Hilfsverein für
jüd. Flüchtlinge im Ausland
•HIJEFS•

Telephon 6 30 56 und 6 43 99
Postcheck-Konto IIb 2107 Vevey
Telegramm-Adresse: Hijefs Montreux

Montreux,
Les Colondalles

29. Mai 1945

La/b

Mister
K a t z k y
c/o
American Legation
G e n e v e .
- - - - - - - - -

Sehr geehrter Herr Katzky,

wir erlauben uns, Ihnen anbei Auszug eines Briefes
aus Mauthausen vom 19. Mai zu übersenden, der soeben
bei uns eingegangen ist.

Es ist wirklich unbegreiflich, dass hier in der Schweiz
Lebensmittel versandbereit stehen und keine Möglichkeit gefunden wird, diesen unglücklichen Menschen Hilfe
zu leisten. Sollen diese wenigen Ueberlebenden einer
solch grossen Katastrophe sogar jetzt nach ihrer Befrei-
ung noch Hunger leiden müssen? Wir haben wiederholt
Versuche unternommen, um derartige Lebensmittel-
Transporte arrangieren zu können, jedoch behauptet das
IRK dass seitens der Militärbehörden noch keinerx Erlaubnis
zum Besuch und der Versorgung dieser verschiedenen Lager
erteilt wurde.

Wir wären Ihnen sehr verbunden, wenn Sie uns mitteilen
würden, was unternommen werden kann, damit diese Missstände
behoben werden können.

Wir sehen Ihrer Rückäusserung gerne entgegen und zeichnen

hochachtungsvoll

Sternbuch letter dated May 29, 1945 [just a month after the liberation of a few concentration camps] to Mr. Katzky of the American Legation in Bern in which the Sternbuchs complain about the difficulties they have in providing food and other help to the liberated Jews in Germany.

```
Telegramm – Télégramme – Telegramma
        von – de – da        N°   Wörter   Aufgegeben den   Stunde
                                  Mots     Consigné le      Heure
  38 ·  + 32038  NEWYORK  SZW6 351  41  3/10  1753
```

= VIA RS = NLT = RECHEL STERNBUCH HIJEFS
                    MONTREUX =

ENTIRE COMMITTEE EXPRESSES GRATEFULNESS YOUR REMARKABLE WORK
BEST WISHES NEW YEAR PLEAD YOUR RETURN TO POLAND SAVE
REMAINDER YESHIVA SCHOLARS RABBIS ANXIOUSLY WAIT YOU =
VAADHATZALA RABBIS ISRAEL ROSENBERG ARON KOTLER ABRAHAM
      LAMANOWITZ IVBING BUNIM STEPHEN KLEIN ++

Telegram to Recha Sternbuch from Vaad Hatzalah in New York thanking her for her successful work in Poland and asking her to return to Poland for further rescue work.

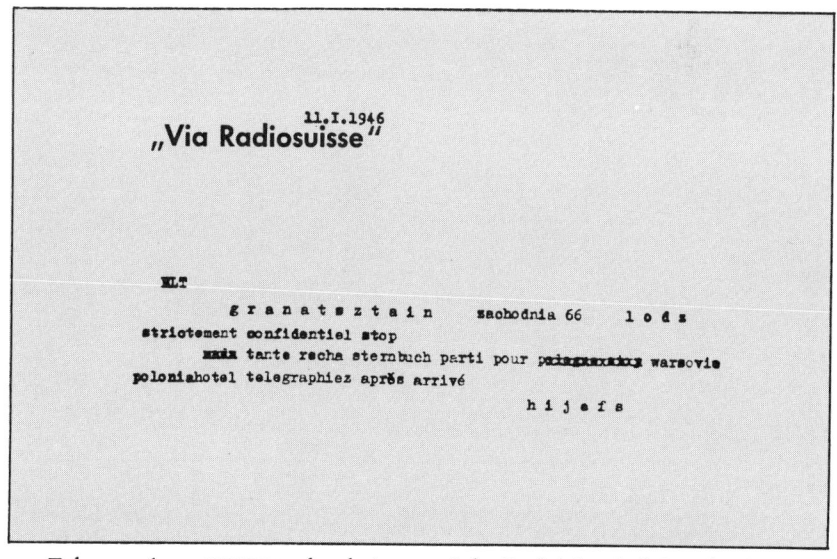

Telegram from HIJEFS to the chairman of the Poalei Agudath Israel office in Lodz, Mr. Granatsztain, informing him in confidence about the arrival of Recha Sternbuch in Poland.

Letter from a group of Orthodox young men and women, brought from Poland to France by Mrs. Sternbuch, in which they thank her and describe the assistance through which she enabled them to establish children's homes. They finish with an expression of gratitude for finally bringing them to a "land where no one is afraid of a bullet and where one can breathe freely."

ב"ה. לודז, כ"ב אייר תש"ו

לכבוד הגבדת מקת ר. שטערנבוך
סתמי'

שלו'וברכה!

"לישועתך קוה תהלה". מרגישים אנו בעצמנו לחוב נעים לכ'
את רגשי תודות אלפי היהודים הנדרים בפולני', שניצלו מבית ישראל
שרידי חרב ואבדון אשר גזלו במאמצי ה' ורחמיו המרובים מגזירת הכליון
אשר השבו שונאי ישראל לבצוע בערם בית ישראל, בעד עבודתה המסורה והנאמנה,
להצלתם, לרוחתם ולישועתם. אנו כעדי ראי' להמסירות נפש שלה – להצלת
ילדי ישראל מבתי המנזר ועכו"ם שנמסרו לטמא בין הגויים לבלי השאיר
זכר ושארית לקדושים והטהורים שנהרגו ונשחטו ונשרפו על קדושת השם יתברך,
בני ציון היקרים המסולאים מפז, עוללים ויונקים שלא טעמו טעם חטא, הוא זו
לחיק אמם-אומתם, להיות בנים – בוגרים למקום להתחנך על ברכי התורה ומסורת
אבות לבל תכבה גחלת ישראל ח"ו; להצלת עשרות בני-ישיבה, אודים מוצלים מאש,
יסד יחיד לנו, ה' לצלי'סא, להציל מחית חלילי בגרשה את כנפיה על שב יהדות
בהזרבן הכי גדול בתולדתנו; להצלת מאות בע"ב חרדים, חסידים ואנשי המעשה,
צעירי ישראל ובנות ישראל הכשרות, אשר שמרו על קדושתם וסמרו את נפשם
על דת תוה"ק בהיותם בצרה ובשבי' לבלי לחלל ש"ק ומבלי להתנאל במאכלות
אסורות וכדומה מהם יסד ופנה לבנין בית ישראל החדש, על יסודות הנצח של
אמנה בה'. ותודתי – אני רוצה את עדים להעריך את ערך ופרשת גדולה
עבודתה הגדולה בעד עמנו האומלל לעת כזאת ואת טמה הטוב אשר נשא נפו כל
"שם עולם לא יכרת".

יודעים גם אנו את אשר עם לבבה הטהור לעשות עם מאות בני הישיבות
ואלפי היהודים החרדים לדבר ה' הנמצאים בצר ומצוק ועיניהם כלות ומצפות
למרחף למטפי הקדושה, למזון ולבש אבניה ולמבוא מנוח לכף
רגלם, אחרי שנות הטפל והתלאה לעבוד את ה' בלי שום מעצור ומניעה.

ואנו חדרי בסחון לה', וברכתו במעשי ידיה, להתגבר על כל המכשולים
והמניעות, אשר על דרכה, עד אשר עוון ה' יצלח בידה, להצלת שארית ישראל
האומרים שמע ישראל.

תקבל נא איפוא את ברכותנו הלבביות, בשם אלפי ישראל רבנים וחסי... ודוי'
ה' ובאמני', בני' ובנותי' הכשרים ותינוקות של בית רבן, סיהי' נועם ה'
עליהא לכונן את מעשי ידי' להצליח בכל אשר תפנה ויחזק ה' את כוחותי'
לפעול גדולות ונצורות בעד אלק-נו ועמו, מתוך אושר ועו שר, לשם ולתפארת
למשפחתה בכלל כישראל.

בברכת

אברהם קרוויעץ
אבד"קק לודז

אלחנן

Letter to Recha Sternbuch from the Chief Rabbi of Lodz, Rabbi Abraham Kravietz [also signed by the then-president of Agudath Israel of Poland, Rabbi Elchonon Sorotzkin], expressing their deep appreciation for her work in Poland.

ב"ה

לשכת מרכזית אויט. ארטה. מטראנסילוואניא ובאנאט

קלוזש ־ רחוב סטראאספסקא נומ. 14   טלפון _____

נשיא ההנהלה: נשיא ועד הפועל:
הרה"ג יוסף אדלער מורדא   הרה"ג אברהם שלמה כ"ץ ריסקווע

קלוזש _____ ג' וירא תש"ו לפ"ק

"וכתו"ס לכבוד הרבנים הגדולים העומדים
לנס עמינו עושי צדקה וחסד היסקיב המפורסכים
ראשי ועד הצלה איש כפי מהללו יבורך מאת ה'

אחדשה"ס.

הנני בזה להודיעכם שעד'נו כל מיני פעולות שנוכל לבוא תסככ בהתקשרות כדי שתדעו מה שנשפע אצל שאירית פליטת היהודים החרידים המטה.סרובו בעת בראמענצא יותר מחמשים אלפים יהודי חרידים כ"י אבל לדאבונינו עד כעת לא קבלנו שום תשובה סכם מפני הדוור והסטלעפסאן שעוד אינו הולך סדרינתינו למדינתכם.

ד"כ ע"ץ נוסע כעת הרב הגאון הגדיק בנש"ק הספורסים וכו' וכו' כק"ה
ר' יראל מייער-מייטלברים שלים"א האבדק"ק האצדק"ק קירה'האצא כעת דונא בק"ק סאסווסארע יצ"ו
בשליחות הרבנים האבנה. ולשכה המרכזית הארסה. נשיא הרבנים הארסה מדינתינו
להו"ל לדבר. ולעורר ולבקש מאתכם שתבוא לעזרתינו כדי שנוכל לעזור על נפשינו שנלתי זאת הסכנה גדולה למאוד בכל הענינים כמו שיאמר פא"פ.
ע"כ באנר בזה להודיע שהוא מדבר בשמינר ריש לו הכרה הרשאה לדבר בשם הלשכה המרכזית של יהדר ההרידים וב"י רב"ה יותר מחמשים רבנים גאוני ארץ הי"ר ועשרים מר"ץ הי"ר ע"ירית הפליסה מגדולי עולם וקרני למאה קהלות יראים ארסה; וכל מה שהוא מדבר או עשה הכל הרא בשמינר עשיתר כעשיתיבר.

וחזבעה"ח קלוזש.יצ"ו

נס' ועד הפועל   נסיא ההנהלה

ישיבה "אהבת תורה" טימישארא יצ"ו
JEŞIVA "AHVAS TORA" TIMIŞOARA II.

RABIN
U. J. WEINBERGER

בעזרת השם יתברך

תחת הנהלת הרב ור"ם
אשר יונה וויינבערגער

Timişoara den 21. August 1947

Hwlgb. Frau

S T E R N B U C H

B U C U R E S T

Bei Abschluss des Jahres soll bei קס"ו Ihr
gedacht werden für גלת כתבה ואל הרבה
פ. ישראל בצוקה וצלה

    Anlässlich Ihres Hierweilens geriet es mir zur Ehre und machte es mir Freude, dass Sie die Güte hatten, meine Jeschiva und meine Familie zu besuchen.
    Gemäss unserer damaligen Unterredung sicherten Sie meiner Jeschiva 30 Plätze für Bachurim und 10 Plätze für Jsolmois und erlaube mir Ihnen den Überbringer Gegenwärtiges als den Delegierten der Jeschiva vorzustellen, welcher mit sich die Liste der Jeschiva und die Fotografien mitführt, um dieselben der kompetenten Stelle zu übergeben.
    Haben Sie die Güte, den Überbringer dieses die nötigen Anweisungen zu geben, an wen er sich zwecks Überreichung wenden soll, wofür ich Ihnen bestens danke. Besonderen Dank spreche ich Ihnen auch auf diesem Wege für die Hochherzigkeit die Sie mir und meiner Jeschiva an den Tag gelegt haben, aus und die Vergeltung wird nicht säumen.
    Wenn Sie, sehr geehrte gnädige Frau, mit einem tiefen Eindruck über all das, was Sie gesehen haben, von den echten jüdischen Gesichtsausdrücken überrascht waren, da wir doch hier ein kleines Nest in ganz Europa geblieben sind in unveränderter Form, aus meiner Jeschiva gingen, um so mehr wird es Ihnen zu Ihrer vollständigen seelischen Zufriedenheit gereichen, wenn Sie meine Bachurim in ihren Handlungen beobachten werden, dass sie den Funken unserer heiligen Toire hinaustragen und ihn entfachen werden in den Herzen unseres jüdischen Volkes.
    Eine kleine Bitte habe ich an Sie und zwar meldeten sich bei mir noch einige Bachurim, cca. 10 an der Zahl, die mitkommen möchten, ebenfalls sehr würdige Kinder, dass Sie in der Jeschiva noch einige Plätze zubilligen mögen, im Falle wenn Ihnen dies möglich ist. Ich hoffe sie ebenfalls zu gut und würdigen Menschen zu erziehen, die ihrerseits weiter die Erziehungsarbeit fortsetzen werden.
    Ich schliesse mein Schreiben mit meinen besten Dank und wünsche Ihnen, dass Ihnen der Allmächtige Ihre Handlung und Taten vergelten soll Ihren Verdiensten entsprechend, die Sie sich um die Rettung unseres Volkes erworben haben.

                           Hochachtungsvoll

אשר יונה בן אאמו"ר שלי"ט ווינברגר

*Letter from Yeshivah in Roumania to Mrs. Sternbuch
regarding the rescue of its students.*

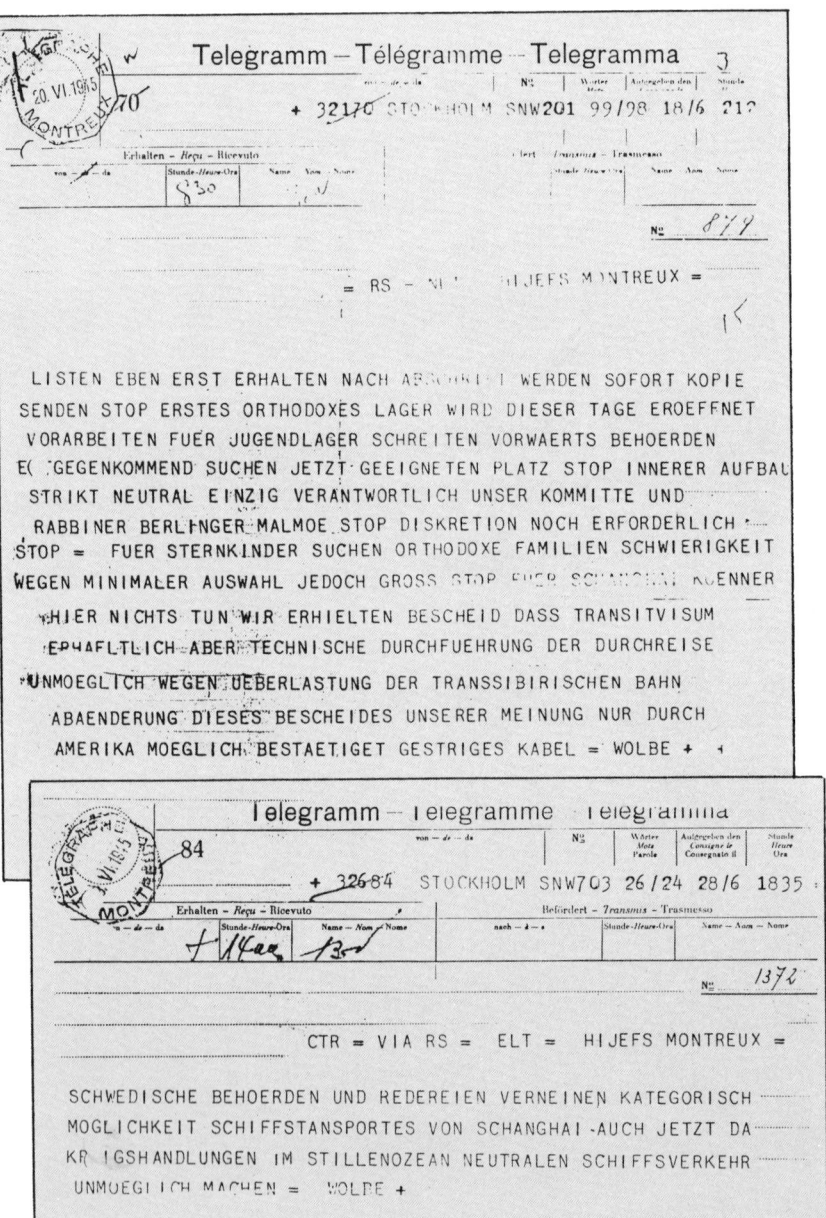

In the spring of 1945 the Sternbuchs undertook desperate efforts to evacuate the Torah scholars stranded in Shanghai when that city underwent heavy bombardment. Exchanges between the Sternbuchs and Rabbi Wolbe in Sweden describe this project and discuss the many Jewish youngsters who were saved from the concentration camps and brought to Sweden.

THE FOREIGN SERVICE
OF THE
UNITED STATES OF AMERICA

Zurich, den 9. Juli 1945

Sehr geehrter Herr Sternbuch,

Empfangen Sie meinen herzlichsten Dank für Ihre lieben Zeilen vom 6. Juli und den wunderbaren Fruchtkorb mit den Liqueur Beigaben, die Sie die grosse Freundlichkeit hatten, mir zukommen zu lassen.

Es hat mich sehr gefreut zu vernehmen, dass Sie in Paris einen guten Erfolg zur Rettung von Kindern erzielt haben, und es wird mich sehr interessieren, Näheres darüber zu erfahren, wenn Sie nach Zurich kommen werden. Da ich diese Woche für einige Zeit verreisen muss, wäre es ratsam, wenn Sie mich vorher über Ihre Ankunft telephonisch verständigen würden.

Mit nochmaligem Dank und freundlichem Gruss

Ihr
Sam E. Woods
Amerikanischer Generalkonsul

Herrn J. Sternbuch,
Montreux,
Ct. Vaud.

Letter from the U.S. General Consul in Zurich, Switzerland, congratulating the Sternbuchs for the successful conclusion of the agreement to save Jewish war orphans for Judaism.

Index

INDEX

AGUDAS HARABONIM UMACHZIKEI TORAH
192

AGUDATH ISRAEL
Moetzes Gedolei HaTorah 23, 188; Bnos 25; HIJEFS 53, 150, 225; Zeirei Agudath Israel 83; in America 81, 94, 98-99, 101, 129; Sekulener Rebbe 238; World Agudath Israel 57, 87, 88-89, 109, 220, 230, 231, 243; Poalei Agudath Israel 163,. 169, 246; Sekulener Rebbe 238
postwar work in: Germany 157, 159; Poland 163; Austria 182-183; Roumanian 189,191

AIX-LES-BAINS
see FRANCE

ALIYAH BET
31, 42

ALIYAT HANOAR
see JEWISH AGENCY

ALTESTENRAT (Ger.)
Nazi-appointed Jewish elders council, sometimes called *Judenrat*

AMERICA
see UNITED STATES

AMERICAN JEWISH COMMITTEE
96, 98

AMERICAN JEWISH CONGRESS
94, 96, 98; see also WISE, DR. STEPHEN S.

AMERICAN JEWISH JOINT DISTRIBUTION COMMITTEE (JDC)
33-34, 36, 47, 79-80, 83, 127-128, 131-132, 139, 159-160, 182, 192, 231, 239, 241

AMERICAN ZIONIST EMERGENCY COMMITTEE
95

ANTWERP
see BELGIUM

ASHKENAZI, RABBI MEIR
78-79, 83

AUFRUF (Yid.)
special *aliyah* (call to recite a blessing during the public Torah reading) for a groom on the Sabbath before his wedding

AUSCHWITZ
(Oswiencim) 23, 139, 141, 155; deportation to 73, 105, 118; death camp 106-107; plea to bomb 108-109; Birkenau (Brzezinka) 50, 141; Auschwitz Protocols 106-108, 129

AUSTRIA
Hitler's annexation of 19, 29-30; rescue from 29-30, 100; postwar work in 145, 178-184

BARUCH, RABBI NAFTALI
158

BECHER, KURT
114, 126, 131, 134

BELGIUM
internment camp 19; Antwerp 23-25; Marraburg 210; HIJEFS in 52; rescue in 100, 102; Kuhl-Sternbuch mission to 116-123; emigration to 191-194; orphaned children in 209-210

BEN-AMI, YITSHAK
98

BERGEN-BELSEN
56, 102, 105, 114, 115, 136, 143, 153

BERGSON, PETER
(Hillel Kook) 98

BERNARDINI, PHILLIPPE (Papal Nuncio)
22, 54, 57, 68-76, 104, 125; letter of recommendation from 122, 184, 198

BETH JACOB
schools, 84, 189, 204, 216; movement 234-236

BIDAULT, GEORGE AND MADAME
74

BIKUR CHAULIM
45-46

BINDER, SHMAYAHU
60-61

BIRKENAU
see AUSCHWITZ

BLACHER, RABBI DAVID AND BUNA
222

B'NAI BRITH
96

BOBOVER REBBE
220, 221

BOLOMEY, MRS.
71, 125

BOTCHKO, RABBI ELIYAHU
21, 56, 151, 181
BOTCHKO, MOSHE
150
BRAND, JOEL
111-112
BRICHA
161-162, 164, 169, 173, 181, 186, 188, 192
BRODIE, RABBI ISRAEL
230-231
BRUNNER, ZALMAN
178
BRUNSCHVIG, DR. GEORGE
65, 67, 69
BUCHENWALD
136, 141, 143, 145, 153, 201
BUNIM, IRVING
82, 132
BURCKHARDT, CARL J.
143
CENTRAL COUNCIL OF ROUMANIA
188
CHAIKIN, RABBI
202
CHAILLET, MSGR. PIERRE
73, 198-199
CHIEF RABBIS COUNCIL OF GREAT BRITAIN
151
CHILDREN
154, 253-254; HIJEFS 52; in France 56, 196-206; Bernardini's help 73-75; Kuhl-Sternbuch mission 122-123; in Poland 163, 168-172; in Italy, 184; in Switzerland 208-209; in Belgium 209-210; in Sweden 215-216; Sekulener Rebbe, in Roumania 237-242, 247
CHUPA (Heb.)
wedding ceremony
COHN, ISRAEL YITZCHOK
245-249
CONCENTRATION CAMPS
see individual camps by name
COSOR
(Comite des Oeuvres de la Resistance) 198-200
CRACOW
ghetto 45, 155
CYWIAK, RABBI LEIB
223-224

CZECHOSLOVAKIA
72, 168; HIJEFS 50, 52-53, 56; postwar work in 145, 174-178
DACHAU
31, 201, 245
DENMARK
212
DOMB, J.
90-92
DONATI, ANGELO
56, 184
DONNENBAUM, HUGO
56, 150, 185
DRANCY
73, 104-105
EICHMANN, ADOLF
110-112, 114-115
EISENHOWER, GEN. DWIGHT D.
134, 142
EISENZWEIG, SARA
248, 251
EISS, CHAIM YISROEL
66, 101
ELBERG, RABBI SIMCHA
233-234
ENGLAND
54, 57
ERETZ YISRAEL
see PALESTINE
EREV PESACH (Heb.)
Passover eve
ERLANGER, WOLF AND JACOB
56
FELDAFING
154, 156, 222
FELDMAN, FAIGA
178
FERNWALD
154, 157
FLEISCHMANN, GISI
110
FOX, JOHN P.
98
FRANCE
HIJEFS 52; rescue work in 100, 102; Kuhl-Sternbuch mission 116-121; children 170, 196-206; St. Germain 172; Aix-Les-Bains 154, 197-204, 228
FRANKEL, RABBI SHABSI
104

INDEX / *313*

FREUDIGER, PHILIP
    110-111, 113-114
GAUTING
    155
GERMANY
    and Austria 29; and Switzerland 30, 32, 38; HIJEFS 50, 52-53; emigration from 31, 100; internment camp in 102; invasion of Hungary 107; postwar work in 142-143, 145; D.P. camps in 153-159
GOLDMANN, NAHUM
    88, 95
GOODMAN, HARRY
    243
GRANATSTEIN, YECHIEL
    163-164, 247
GRIFFEL, DR. JACOB
    108, 151-152, 154, 182, 185, 192, 245
GRODZENSKY, RABBI CHAIM OZER
    24, 27, 81
GRUNINGER, PAUL
    30, 36-37
GURS
    102, 118-119

HALBERSTAM, RABBI SHLOMO
    220-221
HAMOTZI (Heb.)
    blessing recited before eating bread
HACHALUTZ
    72, 108, 112-113
HECHT, BEN
    98
HECHT, DR. REUBEN
    54-56, 75, 129-130, 132, 145, 188
HERTZ, CHAIM
    217-218
HERTZMAN, RABBI CHUNA
    84
HERZOG, CHIEF RABBI ISAAC
    150-151, 167, 178, 211, 224, 230, 231, 233
HESS, RUDOLF
    139, 141
HIJEFS
    44-56, 75, 80, 93, 118, 120; and International Red Cross 145; postwar relief 150; in Czechoslovakia 175; in Austria 179, 181-182; and children 199, 209-210; in Sweden 212, 218; in Poland 223, 235

HIMMLER, HEINRICH
    Musy Mission 52, 125-136; 139, 141
HITLER, ADOLF
    32, 134; see also GERMANY
HOLLAND
    100, 210-211
HUNGARY
    52-53, 72, 105, 107, 145, 194-195
INTERNATIONAL RED CROSS
    50, 70, 73, 84, 136, 189, 190; and HIJEFS 44, 52, 56, 145; internment and concentration camps 102, 126, 131, 143, 154, 181
ITALY
    31, 50, 184-185, 194
JACOBSON, RABBI ABRAHAM ISRAEL
    213
JACOBSON, RABBI WOLF
    213-217
JDC
    see AMERICAN JEWISH JOINT DISTRIBUTION COMMITTEE
JEWISH AGENCY
    68, 95, 108, 111; *ALIYAT HANOAR* 162, 169, 239-241
JOINT COMMITTEE FOR EUROPEAN JEWISH AFFAIRS
    98
JEWISH COUNCIL OF BUDAPEST
    110, 112
JEWISH LABOR COMMITTEE
    98
JOINT
    see AMERICAN JEWISH JOINT DISTRIBUTION COMMITTEE
JUS
    50
JUSTMAN, LEIB
    45
KALMANOWITZ, RABBI ABRAHAM
    82, 92-94, 104, 141, 151, 233, 241
KALTENBRUNNER, GEN. ERNST
    126, 134, 136
KASHRUS (Heb.)
    Jewish dietary laws
KASTNER, DR. RUDOLPH
    111, 113, 126, 128, 131, 134
KEHILLAH (Heb.)
    community
KIDDUSH (Heb.)
    blessing recited over a cup of wine at the inauguration of the Sabbath

KLAL YISRAEL (Heb.)
the Jewish people collectively
KLEIN, STEPHEN
151
KOOK, HILLEL
98
KOPETZKY, DR.
209
KORF, RABBI BARUCH
104
KOTLER, RABBI AARON
79-80, 82, 132
KOVNO GHETTO
227
KRISTALLNACHT (Ger.)
"Night of Broken Glass" — widespread Nazi attacks on Jews and Jewish property throughout Germany and Austria on November 9-10, 1937; 78, 229
KRUMEY
113
KUHL, DR. JULIUS
22, 55, 59-76, 83, 93, 101, 109, 116-123, 139, 140, 150
LADOS, ALEXANDER (Polish ambassador)
22, 54, 57-68, 82, 104, 117, 209
LANDAU, HEINRICH
157
LANDAU, HERMAN
54, 56, 71, 108-109, 135, 150-151, 171, 177, 214, 239
LANDSBERG
55, 155, 245
LATIN AMERICA
52, 73, 91, 100-105, 248, 251
LEBEL, RABBI MOSHE
123, 154, 197, 201-202, 245
LECLERC, MARCEL
143
LEIZEROWSKI, RABBI BARUCH
156
LEVENSTEIN, RABBI TOVIA
211
LEWIN, DR. ISAAC
83, 87, 89, 94-95, 151, 178, 182, 201-203, 205-206, 208-209, 210, 220, 243
LICHTHEIM, RICHARD
68, 95

LINK, GYULA
110, 113
LODZ
45, 50, 165, 173, 246
MANN, THOMAS
88
MANTELLO, GEORGE
102
MARRABURG
see BELGIUM
MATTHAUSEN
13, 154
MAYER, SALY
31-36, 65-66, 114, 126-128, 131, 134, 139-140
McCLELLAND, ROSWELL
93, 114, 131-132, 136
MERLIN, SAMUEL
98
MISHKOWSKY, RABBI CHIZKEYAHU
150-151, 178, 233
MITZVAH (pl. mitzvos) (Heb.)
Torah commandment
MOATZA
108
MONTREUX
see SWITZERLAND
MOETZES GEDOLEI HATORAH
23, 188
MULLER, MATHEW
101
MUNK, RABBI ELI
206
MUSSAR (Heb.)
Jewish ethics
MUSY, BENOIT
125, 134-136
MUSY, JEAN MARIE
71, 124-138
MUSY MISSION
52, 56, 124-138
NACHLIK, STANISLAW
65-66, 93
NUREMBERG TRIALS
98-99
ORENSTEIN, RABBI SAMUEL
165-168
OSWIENCIM
see AUSCHWITZ

OZE
  197
PALESTINE
  emigration to 31, 42, 148, 181, 184; HIJEFS 54; emigration to from Czechoslovakia 175-176; emigration to from Poland 177, 246; emigration to from Roumania 186, 189, 193, 216, 239, 242
PAPAL NUNCIO
  see BERNARDINI, PHILLIPE
PEARL HARBOR
  46, 79
PINKUSEWICZ, RIVKA
  155, 235
POALEI AGUDATH ISRAEL
  163, 169, 346
POGRAMANSKY, RABBI MORDECHAI
  203, 226-229
POLAND
  Katowice 23, 165, 167, 173, 193, 246; HIJEFS 50, 52-53, 102, 141; postwar work in 160-173; Polish consulate see LADOS, ALEXANDER (Polish Ambassador)
PORTUGAL, RABBI ELIEZER ZUSIA
  191-193, 237-244
RAND, CHASKEL
  54, 56, 150
RAVENSBRÜK
  136
REFOULEMENT (French)
  lit., repelling; Swiss policy of refusing admittance to refugees
REICHMAN, RENEE
  50
REINHOLD, ZECHARIA
  28, 35-36
RELICO
  101
RIEGNER, DR. GERHARDT M.
  86-88, 90, 92
ROKEACH, RABBI AARON
  60-62, 72, 220
ROOSEVELT, PRESIDENT FRANKLIN D.
  87-88, 94, 96-97
ROSENBAUM, JOSEPH
  56
ROSENBERG, RABBI ALEXANDER
  231

ROSENBERG, RABBI ISRAEL
  96
ROSENGARTEN, WOLF
  228
ROSENHEIM, JACOB
  57, 87-90, 93-94, 109, 220, 241
ROTH, FERDINAND
  (Rabbi Michael Ber Weissmandel) 114
ROTHMUND, DR. HEINRICH
  30-31, 33-34, 36, 65-66
ROTTENBERG, RABBI CHAIM YAAKOV
  24
ROTTENBERG, JOSEF
  24, 74, 210
ROTTENBERG, DR. MENACHEM
  24
ROTTENBERG, RABBI MORDECHAI
  21, 23-24, 105, 227
ROTTENBERG, RUTHIE MANDEL
  150
ROUMANIA
  72; HIJEFS 52-53, 56; postwar work in 186-193; Sekulener Rebbe 238-244
RUBINFELD, LEIBISH
  56
RUBINSTEIN, RABBI SHMUEL YAAKOV
  122, 204
SALZBERG, ISSER
  182-184
SCHACHNER, BENJAMIN
  168-169
SCHELLENBERG, GEN. WALTER
  126, 134, 136
SCHMIDT, DR. SAMUEL
  151-152
SCHWALBE, NATHAN
  72, 106, 133
SCHWARTZ, DR. JOSEPH
  33, 128
SEIDMAN, DR. HILLEL
  102
SEIL, RABBI S.
  197
SEKULENER REBBE
  191-193, 237-244
SHABBOS (Heb.)
  the Sabbath

SHALOM ALEICHEM (Heb.)
liturgical song traditionally chanted upon returning home from the synagogue Friday evening

SHANGHAI
47-49, 66, 77-85

SHEHECHAYANU (Heb.)
blessing of gratitude recited on special occasions

SHENKOLEWSKI, MEIR
94, 177

SHMULEVITZ, RABBI CHAIM
81, 83-84

SHMURAH MATZOS (Heb.)
matzah for Passover made from flour that has been carefully guarded against contact with moisture

SIG
31, 66; see also MAYER, SALY

SILBERSCHEIN, DR. ABRAHAM (ALFRED)
65, 68, 101

SILVER, RABBI ELIEZER
81, 151, 177-178, 182, 211, 233

SLOVAKIA
see CZECHOSLOVAKIA

SOIFER, MR. MAITRE
199, 201

SOLOVEITCHIK, RABBI MOSHE
233

SOROTZKIN, REBBITZEN CYLA (ORLEAN)
235

SOUTH AMERICA
see LATIN AMERICA

SOVIET UNION
162, 187, 191, 227, 230-231, 238

SPECIAL CONFERENCE ON EUROPEAN JEWISH AFFAIRS
96

ST. GALLEN
see SWITZERLAND

ST. GERMAIN
see FRANCE

ST. OTILLIEN
155

STEIF, RABBI YONASAN
113, 232

STERNBUCH, AVROHOM
21-22, 236

STERNBUCH, ELI
36, 45-46, 91, 116-123, 248-249

STERNBUCH, ESTHER
236

STERNBUCH, GUTA
248-249, 250-254

STERNBUCH, NAFTALI
25-26

STERNBUCH, NETTY
236

STERNBUCH, NOCHUM AND RENEE
249

SUKKOS (Heb.)
Festival of Booths or Tabernacles

SWEDEN
132, 208-214

SWERDLOFF, MOSHE
210

SWITZERLAND
41, 47, 100, 138, 252; emigration to 19, 20, 25, 26, 30-34, 71, 129, 130; Alien police 30, 36, 37, 42-43, 64-65; HIJEFS 51; interment camp 45, 54, 63 postwar work in: 207-209; Basel 26, 27; Montreux 20-21, 27, 44, 53, 135; St. Gallen 27, 30, 36, 38, 43, 45

TAYLOR, MYRON
95

TEFILLIN (Heb.)
phylacteries

THERESIENSTADT
HIJEFS 50, 56; Musy Mission 52, 129, 135, 136, 143-144, 220

TIMANING
102

TREBLINKA
92

TREISSER, HERMAN
210

TRESS, ELIMELECH
83, 151-152

TURKEY
52

UNGAR, RABBI SHOLOM (of Nitra)
175, 187-188

UNION OF ORTHODOX RABBIS OF GERMANY
157

UNION OF ORTHODOX RABBIS OF U.S. AND CANADA
52, 81, 93, 96, 109, 131, 141

INDEX / 317

UNITED STATES
HIJEFS 52, 54; alarming about Holocaust 86-89; Musy Mission 129, 139, 141; postwar assistance 142, 154, 159, 179; see also ROOSEVELT, PRESIDENT FRANKLIN D.; McCLELLAND, ROSWELL; WAR REFUGEE BOARD

UNRRA (United Nations Rescue and Relief Association)
44, 148, 155, 157, 160, 182

VAAD HATZALAH
66, 104, 116, 224, 239, 241; HIJEFS 52; Shanghai 47, 49, 79, 81-85; alarming U.S. of Holocaust 94, 98, 99; Musy Mission 126, 128-132
postwar work in: Germany 158, 159; Poland 161, 164-166; Czechoslovakia 175; Austria 178; Italy 185; Roumania 189-193; Hungary 184; France 206; Switzerland 208; Holland 211; Sweden 214, 218

VAADAH (Vaadat Ha'ezrah Vehahatzalah)
110, 112

VATICAN
68, 72-73, 95, 104

VILNA
47, 78, 81

VITTEL
23, 73, 102-103, 105, 118, 125

VON STEIGER
129-130

VORHAND, RABBI VICTOR
176, 178, 180, 226

WAR REFUGEE BOARD
44, 52, 93, 98, 104, 108, 109, 114, 128, 129, 131, 132

WARSAW
45-46, 50, 87, 90-92, 102, 165, 173, 193, 229

WASSERMAN, RABBI SIMCHA
151, 178

WEHRMACHT (Ger.)
German Armed Forces

WEINBERG, RABBI DR. YECHIEL
228-232

WEINGORT, DR. SHAUL
22, 56, 150, 185, 231

WEISSMANDEL, RABBI MICHAEL BER
66, 72, 106-111, 114-115, 220

QUEEN WILHELMINA
211

WOHLGELERNTER, RABBI S.P.
150-151, 171, 178, 182

WOLBE, RABBI SHLOMO
213-216

WORLD AGUDATH ISRAEL
see AGUDATH ISRAEL

WOODS, SAM
55, 92

WORLD JEWISH CONGRESS
68, 86, 93, 95, 137

WORLD ZIONIST ORGANIZATION
109

WISE, DR. STEPHEN S.
86-88, 93, 94-97

WISLICENY, DIETER
72, 110, 111, 113, 114

YESHIVAH, YESHIVOS
Aix-Les-Bains 198, 201, 204, 248; Bailly 205, 206, 227; Bais Pinchas 191; Etz Chaim in Montreux 20-21; Fernwald 157; Hungary 194; Landesberg 245; Mirrer 79, 84; Poland and Lithuania 162; Pressburg 175; Roumania 189; Shanghai 48, 77-85; Sridei Esh in Rome 185; St. Germain 172, 204-205; Sweden 216; Versailles 228; Vizhnitz 188

YUDASIN, SHIFRA
202, 203

ZEILSHEIM
155, 235

ZEIREI AGUDATH ISRAEL
83

ZEMIROS (Heb.)
songs of praise sung at Sabbath meals and other festive occasions

ZIEMBA, RABBI ABRAHAM
156, 222

ZIONIST ORGANIZATION OF HUNGARY
110

ZUBER, RABBI JACOB ISRAEL
213, 216

ZUCKER, SIMON
169-172, 247

ZYTNICKI, MANNES
179-181, 182

Acknowledgments

Many people helped significantly in the preparation of this work. We regret that space does not permit us to give adequate, individual expressions of thanks. They are: Gertrude Hirschler, Rabbi Shmuel Klein, Ruth Neuberger, Ernest Seewald, and Abraham Malowicki who translated French, German and Yiddish material and documents; the staffs of the Franklin D. Roosevelt Library at Hyde Park and the National Archives in Washington; Faige Zylberminc of the Library of Congress; Prof. Alois Chmela, Prof. Mary Nutley and her assistant, May O'Dougherty, of Queensborough Community College; Mrs. Joan Frederichs; Mrs. Simi Eichorn, a superb and gracious typist; and Murray Newman, an extraordinary microfilm expert.

We are deeply grateful to the many people, in addition to Dr. Julius Kuhl, who shared their memories of and insights into Yitzchok and Recha Sternbuch. From them all, we must single out a few:

Mr. Herman Landau was the Sternbuch's right-hand man as the executive director of HIJEFS. However, a mere title does not do justice to his heroic, dedicated, and effective work in helping turn the Sternbuch's vision into the reality of thousands of lives.

The children of Mr. and Mrs. Sternbuch — Rabbi Chaim and Mrs. Netty Segal, Rabbi Avrohom and Mrs. Chava Sternbuch, Rabbi Yehudah and Mrs. Esther Gutterman — gave inestimable help as well as access to over 50,000 documents. Mr. Eli and Mrs. Guta Sternbuch provided invaluable insights and guidance, in addition to Mrs. Sternbuch's moving Epilogue in tribute to her sister-in-law.

We express our thanks to Rabbi Moshe Sherer, the national and international Agudath Israel leader, who founded and supports the Agudath Israel Archives, along with Rabbi Moshe Kolodny, the brilliant archivist who made its wealth of material and information available at every turn.

We are grateful as well to the entire editorial and technical staff of Mesorah Publications. While the general public is well aware of the quality of their work, we have learned first hand how much conscientious effort goes into their quest for excellence.

This volume is based on primary sources, interviews with participants in the events chronicled, and original research in public and private collections, among which are the Sternbuch Papers, Kuhl Papers, Tress Papers, War Refugee Board Papers, State Department Papers and the Agudath Israel Archives.

More than sixty people graciously gave interviews. In addition to those mentioned above the more extensive interviews were provided by:

Rabbi Nathan Baruch
Mrs. Recha Bolog
Mr. Yisroel Yitzchok Cohen
Mrs. Feinroth
Mrs. Miriam Feldman
Dr. Reuven Hecht
Mr. Chaim Hertz
Mr. Leib Justman
Rabbi Moshe Lebel
Rabbi Shmuel Miller
Rabbi Jacob Nayman

Rabbi Shmuel Orenstein
Mrs. Rivka Pinkusewicz
Mr. Menachem Presser
Mr. Morris Rokowsky
Mrs. Oscar Rand
Mr. Zecharya Reinhold
Mrs. Rose Rottenberg
Mr. Benjamin Schachner
Rebbetzin Cyla Sorotzkin
Mrs. Elsie Taffel
Mrs. Shaul Weingort

Finally, we must ask the reader's indulgence on a matter of personal privilege — for our feeble attempts adequately to thank our families for their help and advice, and often superhuman patience and indulgence.

In the Friedenson family: Mrs. Gitla Friedenson and our three daughters and their husbands: Esther and Chaim Gruenstein, Chana and Rabbi Moshe Kahn, and Rosie and Rabbi Yosef Chaim Golding — and, of course, the grandchildren who are constant sources of joy and hope.

In the Kranzler family: Mrs. Judy Kranzler whose interest in the subject made her a sounding board and adviser; and our children Moshe, Shani, and Yaakov Meir, whose exposure to my Holocaust research have given them a rare appreciation of that era's unsung heroes and heroines. May I also mention my in-laws, the late Rabbi Yaakov Bein, ז״ל, who risked his life to save Jews in Budapest during the worst of times, and Mrs. Anna Bein, a living testimony to those times. Both were saved to a great extent thanks to the Sternbuchs.

Joseph Friedenson / David Kranzler
I Adar 5744 / February 1984